SOCIAL PROBLEMS AND THE FAMILY

FAMILY LIFE AND SOCIAL POLICY COURSE TEAM

Melanie Bayley, Editor

Ann Boomer, Secretary

David Boswell, Senior Lecturer in Sociology

Hilary Canneaux, Course Manager

John Clarke, Senior Lecturer in Social Policy

Allan Cochrane, Senior Lecturer in Urban Studies (Course Team Chair)

Juliette Cowan, Secretary

Rudi Dallos, Staff Tutor, Social Sciences

Harry Dodd, Print Production Controller

Peggotty Graham, Staff Tutor, Social Sciences

Pauline Harris, Staff Tutor, Social Sciences; Open University Tutor

Tom Hunter, Editor

Bernie Lake, Secretary

Mary Langan, Lecturer in Social Policy

Jack Leathem, Producer, BBC/OUPC

Vic Lockwood, Senior Producer, BBC/OUPC

Eugene McLaughlin, Lecturer in Criminology and Social Policy

Ione Mako, Production Assistant, BBC/OUPC

Dorothy Miell, Lecturer in Psychology

John Muncie, Senior Lecturer in Criminology and Social Policy

Roger Sapsford, Senior Lecturer in Research Methods

Esther Saraga, Staff Tutor, Social Sciences

Jane Sheppard, Designer

Richard Skellington, Project Officer, Social Sciences

Paul Smith, Social Sciences Liaison Librarian

Margaret Wetherell, Senior Lecturer in Psychology

Fiona Williams, Senior Lecturer in the School of Health, Welfare and Community Education

Michael Wilson, Senior Lecturer in Research Methods

David Wilson, Editor

Consultant authors

John Baldock, Senior Lecturer in Social Policy, University of Kent

Elizabeth Barrett, Training Officer, Ford Motor Company Ltd., Basildon, Essex

Rosaleen Croghan, Research Assistant; Open University Tutor

Sally Foreman, Research Psychologist; Open University Tutor

Norman Ginsburg, Principal Lecturer in Social Policy, South Bank University, London

Hilary Land, Professor of Social Policy, Royal Holloway and Bedford New College, University of London

Lynne Segal, Principal Lecturer, School of Psychology, Middlesex University

George Taylor, Senior Lecturer in Social Work, De Montfort University, Leicester

External assessors

Hilary Graham, Professor of Applied Social Studies, University of Warwick (Course Assessor)

Kum Kum Bhavnani, Lecturer in Applied Social Studies, University of Bradford

Caroline McKinlay, Publications Officer, Women's Aid Federation, England

Raymond Taylor, Prinicpal Training Officer in Social Work, Central Regional Council, Stirling

Tutor panel

Rosemary Collins, Open University Tutor

Helen Cowie, Senior Lecturer in Social Studies, Bretton Hall, University of Leeds; Open University Tutor.

SOCIAL PROBLEMS AND THE FAMILY

EDITED BY
RUDI DALLOS AND EUGENE McLAUGHLIN

SAGE Publications
LONDON • NEWBURY PARK • NEW DELHI

PUBLISHED IN ASSOCIATION WITH

The Open
University

The Open University, Walton Hall, Milton Keynes, MK7 6AA.

First published 1993

SAGE Publications Ltd
6 Bonhill Street
London EC2A 4PU

SAGE Publications Inc
2455 Teller Road
Newbury Park, California 91320

SAGE Publications India Pvt Ltd
32, M-Block Market
Greater Kailash–1
New Delhi 110 048

British Library Cataloguing in Publication Data

Social Problems and the Family.

I. Dallos, Rudi II. McLaughlin, Eugene

ISBN 0–8039–8836–2

ISBN 0–8039–8837–0 Pbk

306.85

Library of Congress catalog card number 92-051074

Edited, Designed and Typeset by the Open University.

Printed in the United Kingdom by Butler and Tanner Ltd, Frome and London.

This text forms part of an Open University Third Level Course. If you would like a copy of *Studying with the Open University*, please write to the Central Enquiry Service, PO Box 200, The Open University, Walton Hall, Milton Keynes, MK7 6YZ.

CONTENTS

CHAPTER 1
DOMESTIC VIOLENCE

SALLY FOREMAN AND RUDI DALLOS

CHAPTER 2
THE ABUSE OF CHILDREN

ESTHER SARAGA

CHAPTER 3
MENTAL HEALTH

RUDI DALLOS AND DAVID BOSWELL

CHAPTER 4
OLD AGE

JOHN BALDOCK

CHAPTER 5
JUVENILE DELINQUENCY

EUGENE McLAUGHLIN AND JOHN MUNCIE

CHAPTER 6
THE PROBLEM OF POVERTY

ALLAN COCHRANE

CHAPTER 7
HOMELESSNESS

RICHARD SKELLINGTON

PREFACE

Social Problems and the Family examines, through a series of interdisciplinary case studies, how 'the family' is constituted both in explanations of social problems and modes of state intervention. Given that the well being of society is equated with the well being of 'the family' it is not surprising that there is periodic concern that this fundamental social institution is failing in its duties. This book illustrates how public anxieties about the state of the family and aspects of family life reveal the normally implicit and taken for granted assumptions about the relationship between this institution and wider society. Inevitably, accompanying discussions about the social problems supposedly generated by the family are calls for the state to intervene in order to regulate and reconstitute both 'defective' families and 'malfunctioning' family relationships. By considering how notions of 'the normal healthy family' and 'the failed family' are framed in explanations and interventions the book documents just how pervasive and complex state regulation of family life actually is.

This book is one of a series published by Sage which are concerned with the relationships between families and the development and practice of social policy. The other two books in the series are *A Crisis in Care? Challenges to Social Work* (edited by John Clarke) and *Comparing Welfare States: Britain in International Context* (edited by Allan Cochrane and John Clarke). Each of the books in the series looks at the ways in which professional and state sponsored interventions help to shape the experience of family life in different contexts. And each also considers the ways in which particular notions of the family influence the development of social policy. We believe that only by bringing these debates together is it possible to understand key aspects of the welfare regimes being constructed in the 1990s.

This series of books was initially written as part of an Open University course (D311 *Family Life and Social Policy*), which is, as its title implies, principally concerned with the complex interrelationships between the family and the state. The family is frequently understood as a private arena within which individuals are essentially free to determine how they live their own lives. The state, on the other hand is often presented as the complete antithesis, at worst seeking to interfere in matters which should be left to private decision making, at best helping to provide a wider — public — context within which individuals and families may interact.

The course questions these dichotomies and explores the greater complexities of family life in the United Kingdom at the end of the twentieth century. It uses insights from psychology, social policy and sociology to develop its arguments, starting with a focus on the internal life of families, moving through a consideration of forms of social and professional intervention towards a comparative analysis of social policy in Europe and a consideration of possible futures. At the core of the course are concerns about the relationships between the public and private spheres, about the need to acknowledge and explore diversity in the lived experience of families and about the ways in which power and inequality work themselves out within and between families. These concerns are also central to all the books in this series.

The chapters of this book have been substantially informed by debates within the course team, drawing on ideas, evidence and methods from a range of disciplines. In other words they are the products of a genuinely interdisciplinary process in which we have all learned from each other. Without these debates and regular discussion it would have been impossible to produce this book. In such a collaborative process it should be clear that important contributions have been made to all of the chapters by people who are not explicitly named as authors.

An Open University Course Team stretches far beyond the core of academics who write for it, to include consultants, tutor-testers and assessors who give invaluable advice, a course manager who somehow brings the pieces together, editors and designers who make it all look good, and secretaries who manage — against all the odds — to produce high quality manuscripts to deadlines which everybody else does their best to forget. The work of all of these people is reflected in this book as well as in other parts of the course. We thank them for it.

ACKNOWLEDGEMENTS

Grateful acknowledgement is made to the following sources for permission to reproduce material in this book:

TEXT
Chapter 1: page 29 'Help for victims of domestic violence', *Press Release: News from the Law Commission*, 8 May 1992, The Law Commission. Chapter 5: Jackson, J., Barnes, G., Chandler, J. and Mackay, D. (1989) 'Now even girls join the thugs', *Daily Mirror*, 7 September 1989, Syndication International Ltd.; Chapter 6: Holman, D. (1991) 'Heirs to years of living dangerously', *The Guardian*, 27 November 1991, © The Guardian; Chapter 7: Rayment, T. and Fowler, R. (1991), 'Norman, a tragedy that slipped through the net', *Sunday Times*, 12 March 1991, © Times Newspapers 1991; Jones, J. (1992), 'The hotels with guests who can't go home', *Independent on Sunday*, 22 March 1992.

FIGURES
Figure 2.3: Courtesy of EPOCH/APPROACH; Figure 2.9: Courtesy of ChildLine. Figure 3.1: Davison, G.C. and Neale, J.M. (1982) *Abnormal Psychology*, John Wiley and Sons Inc; Figure 3.3: Hollingshead, A.B. and Redlich, F.C.. (1985) *Social Class and Mental Illness*, John Wiley and Sons Inc, © Frederich Redlich; Figure 3.4 Gottesman, I.I. (1991) *Schizophrenia Genesis: The Origins of Madness*, W.H. Freeman & Co., © 1991 by Irving Gottesman. Figure 5.1: adapted from Allen, R. (1991) 'Out of jail: the reduction in the use of penal custody for male juveniles 1981–22', *The Howard Journal of Criminal Justice*, Vol 30, No 1, 1991, Basil Blackwell Ltd.. Figures 6.1 and 6.3: from Hills, *The State of Welfare* (1990), © Oxford

University Press 1990. Reprinted by permission of Oxford University Press; Figures 6.2 and 6.4: from Oppenheim, C. (1990) *Poverty the Facts*, CPAG Ltd. Figure 7.1(a): Central Statistical Office, *Social Trends*, reproduced with the permission of the Controller of Her Majesty's Stationery Office; Figure 7.1(c), 7.4: Courtesy of the Council of Mortage Lenders; Figure 7.2: Central Statistical Office (1992), *Social Trends 22*, reproduced with the permission of the Controller of Her Majesty's Stationery Office; Figure 7.3: Platt, S. (1989), 'The forgotten army', *New Statesman and Society*, 3 November 1989, © New Statesman and Society; Figure 7.5: Department of the Environment, *Homelessness Statistics*, reproduced with the permission of the Controller of Her Majesty's Stationery Office.

TABLES

Table 1.1: adapted from Dobash, R.E. and Dobash, R.P. (1980) *Violence Against Wives: A Case Against Patriarchy*, Open Books. Table 1.2: Homer, M., Leonard, A.E. and Taylor, M.P. (1988) *Private Violence: Public Shame*, Cleveland Refuge and Aid for Women and Children, © M. Homer, A.E. Leonard and M.P. Taylor 1988. Table 3.1: Hollingshead, A.B. and Redlich, F.C. (1958) *Social Class and Mental Illness*, John Wiley and Sons Inc, © Frederich Redlich. Tables 3.2 and 3.3: Cochrane, R. and Bal, S.S. (1989) 'Mental hospital admission rates of immigrants to England: a comparison of 1971 and 1981', *Social Psychiatry and Psychiatric Epidemiology*, Vol 24, Springer-Veralg Inc. Table 4.3: adapted from Henwood, M. and Wicks, M. (1984), *The Forgotten Army: Family Care and Elderly People*, Family Policy Studies Centre. Table 5.2: Pratt, J. (1989) 'Corporatism: the third model of juvenile justice', *British Journal of Criminology*, Vol 29, No 3, Summer 1989, by permission of Oxford University Press. Table 6.1: Taylor-Gooby, P. (1990) 'Social welfare: the unkindest cuts', in Jowell, R., Witherspoon, S., Brook, L. and Taylor, B. (eds) *British Social Attitudes, The Seventh Report*, Gower. Table 6.2: Horrell, S., Rubery, J, and Burchell, B., (1989) *Unequal Jobs, Unequal Pay, The Social Change and Economic Life Iniative*, Working Paper 6, 1989, Economic and Social Research Council (data refers to the Northampton labour market). Table 6.3: Department of Employment (1990) *Employment Gazette*, March 1990. Table 7.1: Department of the Environment, *Homelessness Statistics*, reproduced by permission of the Controller of Her Majesty's Stationery Office.

PHOTOGRAPHS

Pages 35–6: Maggie Murray/Format; page 95 Maggie Murray/Format; page 108: Joanne O'Brien/Format; page 125 (top left): Brenda Prince/Format; (top right): Raissa Page/Format; (bottom): copyright Caroline Laidler 1989; page 127: reproduced by courtesy of the Trustees, the National Gallery, London; page 158 (top): Topham; (bottom) Billie Love Historical Collection; page 167: copyright Pressens Bild AB/Photo: Stassan Almqvist ; page 198: Mike Abrahams/Network ; page 214: Neil Libbert/Network; pages 227, 228, 239, 255 and 258 David Hoffman; page 263: Maggie Murray/Format.

CARTOON/ILLUSTRATIONS

Page 7: Courtesy of the Women's Aid Federation England Ltd; page 15: Rae Sibitt; pages 106, 109, *Punch*; page 134: Colin Wheeler; page 170: Cathy Balme ; page 175: The Spectator/Garland; page 190: BRICK/Community Care; page 230: Mary Evans Picture Library; page 257: Steve Bell.

CHILDREN'S DRAWINGS

Our thanks to Anna and Rohan Walder and Kiran and Leilah Moodley for the drawings reproduced in Chapter 2.

INTRODUCTION

RUDI DALLOS AND EUGENE McLAUGHLIN

The interdisciplinary case studies assembled in this volume examine how 'the family' is constituted both in explanations of social problems and in modes of state intervention. From the outset it is necessary to recognize that there is considerable ambiguity surrounding the nature of the relationship between the family and other institutions, including the state. Many continue to view the family as the basic institution of organized social living and there is still the widespread notion that there are (and should be) clear boundaries marking off the private world of the family from the public world of the state and wider society. Some commentators would go as far as arguing that the family and the state naturally inhabit the separate spheres of the private and the public. As a consequence, concern is expressed when it is felt that other societal institutions have unnecessarily trespassed in the private world of the family. The primary function allocated to 'the family' by contemporary Western society is to carry out its reproductive, nurturing and socialization duties in an effective and efficient manner. And there are regular complaints that intrusions by other institutions, particularly in the post-war period, have damaged 'the family' as the repository of fundamental authorities and functions.

Given that the well being of society is equated with the well being of 'the family', it is not surprising that there is periodic concern that it is failing in its duties. When it is publicly asserted, usually in the form of a moral panic, that 'the family' is the source of a particular social problem it is possible to be clearer about the nature of the relationship between this supposedly most private of institutions and the public world of state intervention. Public anxieties about aspects of family life tend to reveal the normally implicit and taken for granted assumptions about the relationship between this institution and the wider society. Inevitably accompanying the discussions about the various social problems supposedly generated by 'the family' are calls for the state to intervene in order to regulate, reconstitute and if necessary punish both 'malfunctioning' family relationships and 'malfunctioning' families. The case studies in this book, by focusing on how notions of 'the healthy normal family' and 'the failed family' are framed and articulated in explanations of and interventions in social problems, show just how pervasive and complex state regulation of family life actually is.

In the first three case studies in this book, domestic violence, the abuse of children and mental health, we explore how and why these particular issues are viewed as essentially 'private troubles'. Although the family home is traditionally viewed as a harmonious haven from the pressures and strains of contemporary life, society is being increasingly forced to recognize publicly that it is also a location of routine violence against women and children. The chapters on domestic violence (Chapter 1) and the abuse of children (Chapter 2) survey the different micro-theoretical explanations and different forms of intervention that are currently utilized in relation to these particular social problems. In doing so, the authors illustrate how the manner in which a particular problem is theorized and conceptualized as either essentially a 'private trouble' or a 'public issue' tends to determine the nature of the intervention that is mobilized to deal with the problem. Because these issues tend to be viewed as being related to the interior, interpersonal and psychological world of family life, interventions tend to take place at the level of the family and are geared towards reconstituting 'failing' (or dangerous) family forms. The authors consider what the implications of such a conceptualization are in terms of understanding the problems under discussion and what are the limitations of such explanations and interventions.

There are a number of questions that can be asked of such an approach. For example, how far can the family be viewed as being both the cause of, and the solution to, the same social problem? As a consequence, the chapters include perspectives which question traditional conceptualizations. Thus, in the case of child abuse and domestic violence, for example, considerable use is made of feminist research which has fundamentally challenged the dominant perspectives by showing how these particular problems are woven into the patriarchal social relations which permeate British society. Such research has considerable implications for conventional modes of intervention because it has also forced these previously defined 'private troubles' onto the public agenda.

Chapter 3 on mental health explores the oppression that people who have been labelled as suffering from mental illness experience. The confusions and contradictions inherent in medical explanations, and in particular the very notion of psychological problems as an illness, are critically examined. Mental illness is analysed in terms of causation at the individual (biological) level, the societal (social deprivation) and the interpersonal (family dynamics). It is argued that explanations focusing on family dynamics are, on the one hand, liberating for the individual since the onus of blame and stigma is removed from her/him but, on the other hand, may serve to perpetrate blaming by pointing to the family as responsible. The chapter considers how mental illness is defined by society and is part caused by structural inequalities and imposed stresses. The shifts from institutional care to community care of the mentally ill is discussed as potentially damaging for individual 'patients' and their families if not adequately resourced. Without such resourcing, it is argued, further distress and aggravation of mental health problems in families will be the likely outcome.

The first three chapters raise important questions about the contradictory assumptions concerning causation that can confuse policies of intervention or even lead to policies which may be punishing to those already suffering in families. They consider how excessive focus on the individual or the interpersonal level has served to put further stresses on families or abandoned them as 'pathological' rather than locating the problems in terms of gender, class and racial inequalities which need to be addressed at the societal level.

On the other hand, certain other social problems — as the case studies on poverty (Chapter 6) and homelessness (Chapter 7) demonstrate — are conventionally seen to lie within the public sphere of social policy. And as the case studies show, structural factors are used in the construction of explanations of these particular problems and in the framing of interventions to resolve them. Traditionally the role of the family is not so clear within these macro explanatory frameworks. When the question is asked 'Who is to blame?' for poverty and homelessness it is not so easy to locate the blame immediately with the family. The family normally appears in terms of the impact that these social problems have upon family life and these chapters explore this important dimension. However, they also analyse how the family is being allocated an increasingly central role within certain explanations of poverty and homelessness. The poverty chapter, for example, considers the increasing popularity of theories of 'the underclass' certain of which argue that traditional social policy approaches and interventions have failed to give due consideration to the role that particular 'pathological' families play in producing and reproducing social problems. This stress on personal responsibility and free choice finds echoes in the arguments of those who argue that certain categories of the homeless, for example young people, are undeserving of state support because they have intentionally placed themselves outside of the family and society. Thus, 'the underclass' thesis has considerable implications for traditional interventions which try to solve these problems through welfare based social policies. It could be argued that this type of theorizing is effectively attempting to relocate these matters within the private world of family and individual responsibility. As a result they represent the attempted privatization of certain social problems.

The case studies concerned with old age (Chapter 4) and juvenile delinquency (Chapter 5) straddle both levels of explanation in a complex manner. Ageing is conventionally viewed as a private matter. The 'frail' elderly are expected to inhabit the private world of the home and leave the public world for the 'dynamic' young. However, because of the demographic shift to an increasingly elderly population and the resultant pressures on the welfare state, ageing is increasingly being defined as a significant social problem. The consequences for the family are enormous as it is increasingly being identified as the primary care institution and the chapter assesses the implications of such a shift. It also considers alternatives to the present family/community care policies. Juvenile delinquency has traditionally been viewed as a serious social problem because of the crime and disorder problems that seem to accompany young working class men's assertion of their masculinity. However, this public problem has considerable consequences for the family because many explanations and interventions are based upon the idea that the family is the source of private discipline and public order. It is argued that if parents looked after their children and took their socialization responsibilities seriously public order would be easier to maintain. Much of the criminal justice legislation introduced during the last decade, for example, has been premised on the notion that parents should be held responsible for the delinquent actions of their children. This chapter explores the implications of such theorizing for the families of young people who get into trouble.

CORE THEMES

In order to establish a coherent framework for analysing the explanatory and policy connections that have been made between social problems and the family, the chapters have been written around core themes. From the foregoing discussion it is obvious that the chapter authors view the *private-public* dichotomy as being one of the key organizing themes. It is this dichotomy that continues to set the parameters for understanding and analysing the problems under discussion. However, we wish to stress that none of the authors in this book view the private-public distinction in an unproblematical manner. Instead, we try to explore how the meaning and import of the distinction differs in relation to the different case studies. The case studies also illustrate how the private and the public are constantly being reconstructed and the boundaries between them remapped in a complex manner. Thus, the private-public is not a simple, natural or unproblematical dichotomy.

In addition all the chapters focus on definitional issues, questions of power and inequality and the issue of diversity.

I ISSUES OF DEFINITION

One obvious starting point is developing an adequate social scientific definition of the family. There is considerable debate and discussion about whether we should use this term given the diversity of living arrangements that can be found in contemporary Britain. However, all of the chapters illustrate how an idealized version of 'the family' manifests itself in many explanatory frameworks and regulatory practices. Thus, we would argue that 'the family' needs to be understood as *a structuring idea*; an idea which helps organize state responses to what are perceived to be pressing social problems. As a consequence, a fundamental task for social scientists interested in social problems becomes analysing the ways in which this idea is used to explain the connections between public troubles and private ills.

The book also raises questions about how social problems are defined and who does the defining. It is by no means straightforward to produce an unproblematical definition of any of the social problems under discussion in this volume. Certain private troubles seem to become fully-fledged social problems more 'easily' than others and they also remain in the public domain more readily than others. In the course of their social construction all take on a particular public stereotypical representation. Furthermore, there is a tendency in our society to 'rediscover' social problems. Many of the social problems analysed in this book seem to be rediscovered and reconstituted generationally and it is important to realize that social problems have their own often 'forgotten' definitional histories. Such definitional issues have important consequences for those attempting to ascertain the exact nature and extent of a particular social problem and for those devising appropriate levels and types of intervention.

2 POWER AND INEQUALITY

No one would deny that families and family life can produce strains, tensions and problems. It is also the case that particular problems emerge at different 'stages' of family life. Some of them, most significantly separation, divorce and death can destroy a particular family form. However, much of the discussion about the relationship between families and social problems ignores the extent to which problems result from power imbalances and inequalities embedded within conventional family structures. The inequities of wider society also find expression in the private world of family life and can be the cause of particular social problems. Problem-specific crisis intervention may in fact sustain, legitimate and reproduce these inequalities. This is the reason why the impact of the structural inequalities of gender, race and class are considered in all the case studies. Once we acknowledge these wider considerations it is possible to identify some of the limitations of locating the cause of social problems solely with 'the family' and viewing it as *the* solution to social problems. We also need to remember that inequalities of power exist between families and professional welfare agencies and professionals. As a result of a private trouble becoming defined as a public or social problem a fundamental remapping of the boundaries between the private and public may take place such that the family finds itself 'open' to public scrutiny, intervention and regulation. These intrusions through the exercising of the powers of the state have considerable implications for those families or family members defined as a problem.

3 DIVERSITY

Finally, the case studies illustrate the diverse forms of explanation and types of intervention that are actually utilized in dealing with social problems. Certain problems are traditionally defined as being more amenable to psychological interventions whereas others are recognized as 'belonging' in the sphere of social policy. Consequently, it is necessary to move away from thinking about state interventions in a monolithic manner. In addition, a diverse range of state agencies are involved, all with their own specialized bodies of professional knowledge and preferred models of explanation and intervention. Recognizing this allows us to explore the shifts that take place in conceptualizing and dealing with a particular problem. The theme of diversity also reminds us that there are different forms of family and living arrangements in contemporary Britain whereas many of the interventions operate with a particular definition of the family and family life. By operating with such a narrow conception of 'the family' many explanations and interventions fail to recognize that it is a diverse and changing institution. Dramatic changes in family structures and behaviour have taken place during the last twenty years due to increases in the numbers of people choosing cohabitation, lone parenthood, separation and divorce. The traditional family is only one of many possible family forms in Britain today. However, it is this idealized conception that the other family forms are matched against and inappropriately assumed to be inferior. This means that certain families/ living arrangements/types of household are more easily stigmatized, defined as deviant and more vulnerable to intervention and regulation because they do not conform to this supposed norm.

CONCLUSION

It seems likely that the family will continue to figure prominently in future debates about the causes of, and solutions to, social problems — particularly since the nature and meaning of welfare provision is being radically redefined in Britain. There is the distinct possibility that in the course of the 1990s we will move to a situation where it is the family not the state which will be expected to take responsibility for looking after its members 'from the cradle to the grave'. This shift has been detected in many of the chapters in this book. Throughout, we have attempted to desimplify the assumptions that different forms of explanation and intervention make about what role the family plays in relation to social problems and the resultant confusions and contradictions in social policy proposals and practices have been analysed. One of the conclusions that can be drawn from this book is that the issues arising from our discussion of the private and the public, power and inequality and diversity need to be critically addressed by those professionals involved in constructing interventions which are geared towards resolving social problems. They also need to ask themselves whether 'the family' is the appropriate institution for managing social problems in the 1990s.

CHAPTER I
DOMESTIC VIOLENCE

SALLY FOREMAN AND RUDI DALLOS

1   INTRODUCTION

The husband also might give his wife moderate correction. For as he is to answer for her misbehaviour the law thought it reasonable to entrust him with power of restraining her, by domestic chastisement in the same moderation that a man is allowed to correct his servant or children.

(Blackstone, 1765)

The feminist movement has taken the lead in bringing to light the extent of domestic violence and in raising challenges to some of the implicit assumptions about domestic violence and 'privacy' in our society (Yllo and

IN 1877, A MAN COULD BEAT HIS WIFE WITH A STICK – IF IT WAS NO THICKER THAN HIS THUMB

SO WHAT'S CHANGED?

WOMEN'S AID FEDERATION (ENGLAND) LTD
PO BOX 391, BRISTOL, BS99 7WS

Bograd, 1988). A discourse on the family as 'private' is likely to contain two linked assumptions: first, family members have the 'right' to say or do what they like within the confines of their own home without undue interference from outsiders. Second, privacy can imply that families should be able to resolve their own problems, regardless of how desperate their experiences may be, they 'should' not want to seek any outside interference.

Feminist writers have raised questions about whose rights are to be protected; the wife's, the children's or the husband's? In Blackstones' time in the eighteenth century and later in the nineteenth century a husband had almost total rights over the members of 'his' family and it was essentially *his* right to privacy that was protected and supported by the law. Husbands and wives were not supposed to be equal, but rather husbands were expected to be dominant and it was legitimate for a man to use any means to control his wife; including force and violence. Consequently there was little in the way of legal protection for wives who had been attacked.

Which members of a family are to 'sort out' the 'family's' problems? Since the nineteenth century the burden of this task has fallen increasingly on the women in families. Women came to be seen as not only responsible for the nurturance of the children but for the management of all relationships and feelings. This responsibility is predicated on the assumption or discourse of natural differences between men and women with women being regarded as naturally more nurturing, caring and sensitive (Parsons and Bales, 1956). On the one hand, women were largely responsible for providing a 'decent' home and ensuring that their husbands were satisfied and happy. This could be interpreted to mean that women were expected to 'service' their husbands domestically and sexually (Jeffreys, 1990). It could also be interpreted to mean that because of their greater 'sensitivity' women were 'better at' working out ways of resolving conflicts than men.

Feminist and other researchers have pointed out that these kinds of discourses particularly placed working class women in impossible dilemmas since poverty, squalor and drunkenness were frequently beyond their capabilities to control yet they faced the blame for running a 'poor' home. It was often assumed that a drunken, violent husband was a result of the wife's sluttish immorality. She therefore deserved the beatings she received which only symbolized her 'failure' as a woman and virtuous wife. The image of the 'ideal woman', constructed largely by the middle-classes, was a woman who kept the house clean and comfortable for her man to come home to. She was seen as non-sexual, non-aggressive and was able to control her impulses in contrast to the view of men who were seen as essentially driven by and unable to control their impulses. Within this discourse women in the nineteenth century were regarded as being morally superior to men and therefore generally better able to sort out 'family matters'.

The dichotomy of 'deserving' and 'undeserving' also related to women in their roles as wives. Women who were sexually immoral, unfaithful to their husbands, prostitutes or drunken were seen as undeserving of help or sympathy but deserving of the beatings they received or even of being raped. A prerequisite for a civilized society was seen to depend on women being able to control men's more brutish impulses; to have a 'civilizing effect' on their husbands (Moore, 1979). In Chapter 5 this theme of women controlling and civilizing men is taken up in the idea of a period of 'wild' and uncivilized adolescence which comes to a natural end when the young men marry and start families of their own — or 'settle down'. It is not clear though just how a wife is expected to exert her 'civilizing influence'. When being 'nice' and sensitive is insufficient she may be forced to resort to tactics such as 'nagging' — inducing her husband to feel guilty — manipulation and bribery — such as refusing sex — until he learns to behave himself. Yet these tactics could at the same time brand the woman as an 'inadequate' or 'cold' wife who deserved the assaults she received.

In Blackstone's time women were not expected to be equal to men; by the late nineteenth century women could achieve equality by virtue of being morally superior in terms of their self-control and civilizing effect on the family. Within modern discourse husbands and wives are supposed to be *equal but different* with women better suited to the home and domestic matters. This discourse in effect covered up the reality that they are different but unequal. The assumption of equality in the face of the reality of inequality often affects responses to violence: 'The equal status of women in society today precludes any preferential treatment for them otherwise the law would fall into disrepute' (Dobash and Dobash, 1992, p.151). Because women are presumed to be equal then it would be unfair if the law was to come down on their side.

Theoretically there is now more of a widespread consensus that husbands should neither dominate their wives, nor use violence to control them. However, as we will show in this chapter, male assumptions of superiority still prevail quite extensively and, as a result, violence is employed by some men as a form of control of women. Likewise, discourses on privacy, as well as discourses about the causes of violence itself, may operate to cover up, justify and rationalize gross abuses of power, which represent a culturally shared and agreed attempt at controlling women.

It is still rare for a woman to have as much or the same type of power as a man. Even if they did have relatively equal power, physical differences in size and strength would still unbalance the equation in the man's favour. Without some form of protection or control, whether it be external in the form of the law or internal in the form of personal beliefs against the use of violence, the *potential* for male violence is inevitably latently present. The law, by 'coming down' on the side of women, is not giving them preferential treatment but merely equalizing the balance of power. If the law does not 'come down' on the side of women then it is actually giving men preferential treatment; maintaining men's dominance and women's subordination. In fact, as will be seen in Section 4.1, in general the law is becoming more supportive of abused women. It might seem obvious that women should be protected, and yet the discourse of privacy often prevents women seeking help and protection from the police and others who are in a position to offer it. Professionals, such as some members of the police, may at times justify their inaction or *non-intervention* on the grounds of family violence as 'private', as 'being their own business', or the 'different but equal' discourse despite changes in the law which allow protective measures and sanctions to be taken. This denies the reality that women and men are not equal and that women frequently are materially dependent on men.

The aim of this chapter will be to examine the extent to which violence is, and has been for many years, a part of 'family life'. Recently, there has been a growing awareness of the extent of the suffering inflicted on some people as part of their daily experience in their families and this will also be examined. Again central to this chapter, and particularly to the nature of the interventions adopted, are moral and ethical questions such as: Should violence be construed as 'criminal' and the perpetrator 'punished' according to the laws available? or Should domestic violence have some special status and not be predominantly thought of as a criminal matter? A further, more fundamental question is: Why is it that actions which if committed between strangers in public, for example, in the street or a pub, are defined in law as grievous bodily harm or attempted murder and liable to severe prison sentences, not dealt with in this way when committed between men and women who live together? In law domestic violence is a criminal offence but has rarely been treated as such in the context of 'family life'.

Both the development of academic interest and forms of practical assistance that have emerged to assist women owe a great debt to feminism. The extent of the problem and inadequacies of earlier explanatory models was highlighted by feminist writers. Consequently this chapter is framed within a feminist perspective which is employed to offer both a critique and a framework in its own right. At the same time, an attempt is made to draw out some tensions between varieties of feminist accounts and integrations with other perspectives such as those emerging from interactionist psychology.

2   PATTERNS OF DOMESTIC VIOLENCE

2.1   DEFINITIONS

It is important and interesting to consider what would commonly be considered as 'domestic violence' in a family.

We will largely be concerned with violence by men towards women in families. In one sense there is no problem in defining what counts as violence since it is clearly defined in law. However, some behaviour such as threats, damaging property, energetic sexual behaviour or play fighting are possibly more ambiguous. It might be suggested that there is a key 'subjective' element in the definition in the extent to which a couple agree that a form of behaviour is acceptable in their relationship. Above all it could be argued that it is the meaning and context of the violence that is central, the meaning of male violence towards women is different from that of female violence towards men. In part this may be due to the likely seriousness of the harm done but it is also to do with male violence being linked to attempts by men in general to control women and keep them subordinate. Women in contrast are unlikely to use violence to control their husbands or to keep them fearful and subordinate, but are more likely to use it in self-defence.

In a vast number of cases there is little doubt that the actions constitute quite clear evidence of common assault and 'grievous bodily harm' as defined in law (see p.27). The attacks range from wives being kicked, pushed through windows, thrown down stairs, punched, thrown against walls, choked, hit with bottles and stabbed with knives. Most typically the attacks involve punches to the face and body which, not infrequently, lead to severe bruising, bleeding and fractured or broken bones.

2.2   STATISTICS

A common assumption is that domestic violence, although widespread, is relatively minor in comparison to violence in the streets, pubs and so on. Yet figures suggest, as Table 1.1 compiled from statistics gathered in Edinburgh and Glasgow illustrates, that domestic violence appears to account for nearly a third of all reported violence. These figures are based on small samples from Scotland and it would be dangerous to generalize too broadly from them. However, more recent data from other studies support these figures and further suggest that women are likely to experience violence in approximately one in four marriages (Bakowski et al., 1983). From these figures we can see that violence perpetrated by men on their partners within the family accounts for nearly a quarter of all reported violence and over 70 per cent of violence in the home. In contrast violence by wives against their husbands seems to account for only 1 per cent of reported domestic violence. It is possible that such figures distort the real level of violence; more women may be attacked than is reported and the violence reported by men to have been inflicted on them by women may largely be due to self-defence.

ACTIVITY I

Examine Table 1.1 which relates to patterns of violence in 1974 in one area of Great Britain and then answer the following questions:

1   What patterns emerge about who is more likely to commit violence in the home as opposed to be a victim of it?

2   What proportion (percentage) of all violence is domestic violence and what proportion (percentage) of all violence committed is due to violence by men against women?

Table 1.1   Offences involving violence reported to selected police departments in Edinburgh and Glasgow in 1974.

Offence	Total number of offences	Percentage of offences	Percentage of domestic offences
Violent: family			
Wife assault	776	24.14	73.8
Alleged wife assault	32	1.0	3.0
Husband assault	13	0.40	1.2
Child assault	110	3.42	10.5
Parent assault	70	2.18	6.7
Sibling assault	50	1.56	4.8
Total	(1051)	(32.70)	
Violent: non family			
Male against male	1196	37.20	
Male against Female	292	9.08	
Male against police	452	14.06	
Female against female	142	4.42	
Female against male	53	1.65	
Female against police	29	0.90	
Total	(2164)	(67.31)	
Grand total	3215	100.00	

From: Pahl, 1985, p.6.

In a study of women who attended refuges for battered wives in South East England Pahl (1985) found that the majority of the women who had been battered were in their twenties or early thirties: 52 per cent were aged between 20 and 29, and another 29 per cent were between 30 and 34. The women had generally been in long-standing relationships; 50 per cent had been with their violent partner for at least six years and only 12 per cent of the couples had been together for less than two years; 62 per cent of the women said that the violence had gone on for three years or more. Other studies show the percentage of women reporting violence to be even higher — the Women's Aid Federation found that 73 per cent of women in their sample said that the violence had persisted for at least three years (Binney et al., 1981).

The potential contribution of class and unemployment is indicated by a study conducted in Cleveland based upon women attending the Cleveland Refuge and Aid for Women and Children. Couples where violence had occurred were found to have come from all social classes but there was a preponderance of working-class couples and in particular unskilled working-class couples.

Table 1.2   Socio-economic status of husbands

Category	Number	Cleveland refuge study %	Cleveland* %	England* and Wales %
Employers, managers and professional	7	9.0	15.2	23.0
Other non-manual	2	2.6	16.5	20.1
Skilled manual	29	37.2	41.2	37.5
Semi-skilled manual	11	14.0	18.0	14.9
Unskilled manual	20	25.6	9.1	4.5
Unclassifiable	9	11.6		
TOTAL	78	100.0	100.0	100.0

Source: Cleveland Refuge and Aid for Women and Children, 1984.

* The figures for Cleveland and England and Wales indicate the proportion of men in the general population employed in the various occupational categories.

The figures do appear to offer some support for a commonly held view that violence is more likely to occur in poorer homes with unemployment and other stressful factors. However, the figures may also reflect the impoverished circumstances of the women who had no alternative to turn to other than the refuge. Likewise in Pahl's (1985) research sample over 40 per cent of the women were relying on social security for their sole source of income. She adds that a majority of the women had stayed in a violent relationship because they perceived that they had very little alternative financially, especially if they had young children whom they wished to avoid exposing to excessive material or emotional hardship. It is important to note the discourse in operation here — the welfare of the children is essentially the woman's responsibility, albeit with some limited support from the state.

3 CAUSES OF VIOLENCE

ACTIVITY 2

Read the following extract and write down briefly what you think are possible explanations for the abuse reported below:

> At first I used to think he was crazy — hitting me like that for no good reason but in the end I thought it was me — that I must be no good to anybody or anything. You know what I mean — no confidence in myself. And I just let myself go... and if I did get dressed up he would say 'You don't look any f— different, you're nothing but a great big fat ugly cow — and nobody would want you except me'. I got that for three and a half years solid. So I believed it in the end. Sometimes I used to think I was going round the bend — he used to go fishing all night sometimes and then sleep all day. And we had this great big carving knife downstairs and I used to go upstairs and stand with it and think 'If I stick it in him — will I get done for murder?' And sometimes after he threw me out I used to get three or four bottles of aspirins and go in a cafe and think 'Get meself a couple of cups of tea — take all these and the problem's solved — all this will be finished with'. But there was always Paul to consider. I used to think if I leave him with him what's he going to grow up like — twisted — like his dad.
>
> (CRAWC, 1984, p.4)

DISCUSSION

Some of the common explanations for abuse are as follows:

1   The violence arose because the couple are 'incompatible' and such conflict is frequent when there is great disagreement and animosity between them.

2   The couple are suffering from excessive stress and frustration in their lives and therefore they take it out on each other.

3   The man has learned to use violence to control his partner from watching films or television or through observation of his own family.

4   All men are naturally aggressive.

5   He is unlike other men, he is abnormal/pathological; she is masochistic or excessively awkward and provocative.

6   Men as a group have more power than women and attempt to maintain their positions of dominance by controlling women and violence is a very effective strategy for doing this.

There are many other possible 'explanations' but the above are the most common. It is important to distinguish here between (1) explanations that

Helpful and unhelpful explanations for male violence

social scientists may hold; (2) explanations that are held by the partici-pants; and (3) explanations held by those who are asked to intervene in cases of domestic violence. In this section we will attempt an appraisal of some of the explanations of domestic violence and show that they exemp-lify widely held 'discourses'. Current scientific theories derive from preva-lent discourses but at the same time have become a part of the folklore of 'common sense' which has a currency in the explanations that couples themselves give for violence. Putting this more bluntly, many men are skilled at employing a variety of theories to rationalize their actions. Those who are asked to intervene in the violence, such as policemen, may also explicitly or tacitly accept and condone such rationalizations.

3.1   DISCOURSES ON VIOLENCE

The discourses on the causes of violence can be broadly categorized in two ways:

1   Private or within the family factors — this includes models of individ-ual pathology as well as interactional models as in explanations 1, 4 and 5 above.

2   Violence as public or related to wider structural socio-economic and ideological factors determining the nature of the relationships between men and women in our society. As in explanations 3, 6 and perhaps 2 above.

PRIVATE: INSTINCTS AND PATHOLOGY

THE INSTINCTUAL DISCOURSE

This discourse suggests that 'Man is a violent creature', that there is an instinct for aggression that is 'wired' into us all in order to protect the individual and the species (Storr, 1970). This instinct is likely to result in aggressive behaviour when we are frustrated or under threat. It is argued that human behaviour is essentially similar to animal behaviour, and since in most of the higher species of animals males are habitually more aggressive than females, this is taken to suggest that gender differences are 'natural' and inevitable. This type of theory minimizes human rationality, that we can think, plan, reflect and communicate about our own and others' behaviour. The link between instinct and behaviour, especially in humans, is indirect; cognitions may intervene and shape the choice of target, severity, perceived risk to self and whether to employ violence at all. Some men after all do not behave aggressively when frustrated or under threat and some women do even when their young are not being threatened. Cognitions may also intervene in terms of perceptions as to what constitutes a threat or frustration and what form the violence takes.

Psychodynamic theorists also believe that aggression is a result of the blocking or frustration of other instincts (Fairbairn, 1952). Tension, rage and aggression is seen to result when the infant's basic needs are not satisfied by the primary caretaker, usually the mother. Rage is seen as a form of defence against underlying fears of dependency or rejection, operating to 'cover up' what in the young baby amounts to fears of its life being threatened because its basic needs are not satisfied. It has been suggested that since boys are encouraged by society to be independent of their mothers earlier they become afraid of dependency or of showing emotions other than anger (Chodorow, 1978). As we will see later a man's fear of dependency, manifested later as a fear of losing his wife, is often suggested to be a predisposing factor in domestic violence (Goldner, 1991). It is also suggested that if tension (instinctual energy) is not released, the individual will become ill; 'bottling up' and exercising self-control over one's emotions is seen to be damaging to mental and physical health. However, this view avoids any differentiation between positive and negative emotions and ignores the fact that aggression may be an ineffective and destructive way of achieving other basic unmet needs.

A widely held, and extremely destructive theory for women is that women are basically masochistic, that they enjoy pain and violence, like to be dominated, that, really, they subconsciously wish to be seized, borne off and 'violently raped' (Storr, 1970). 'I have never seen a chronically abused wife who truly objected to being abused ... wife beating can only occur with the tacit permission of its victims' (Klecker, 1978). This theory is highly problematic and damaging to women, not least because they may internalize it and therefore accept the violence inflicted upon them. The function of this kind of theory and its implications will be explored and critiqued in the section on the feminist perspective (Section 3.4).

THE PATHOLOGICAL DISCOURSE

This discourse seeks to explain why men use violence on the one hand and why women do not leave on the other. There is an assumption and a seeking out of 'evidence' that there are significant differences between men who batter and men who do not. Similarly, there is an assumption that there are significant differences between women who are battered and those who are not and women who do or who do not leave an abusive relationship. Attempts have been made to find differences between apparently 'abnormal' and apparently 'normal' individuals and these proposed differences are then suggested as the 'cause' of violence, and secondly to predispose the woman not to leave an abusing husband. Also, there is a search for pathological relationships so that the abuse is, for example, seen to emerge from an unfortunate combination of personalities. It is important to separate these two issues since whatever the causes of the violence may be many women may not leave for quite practical reasons: nowhere to go and no money.

THE MEN

Generally men who resort to violence are believed to have had 'abnormal', rejecting, insecure, depriving childhoods:

> the uncontrollable anger of a violent man emanates from unresolved conflicts with his parents resolving in a displacement of anger and aggression onto the most convenient targets in his life — his wife and girl friends... such men are described as frightened victimized bullies who experience mood swings, pain and anger... unmet needs are created in childhood and express themselves as violence in later life.
>
> (Dobash and Dobash, 1992, p.237)

One of the main 'unmet needs' are needs for attachment and dependency. It is suggested that all individuals have these needs but that men learn to fear dependency and to deny it; women on the other hand may become too dependent and unable to become independent and separate (Goldner et al., 1990). Psychodynamic theory also assumes that individuals will always be trying by covert and convoluted means to get their basic needs satisfied:

> One thing I notice that I go through every time I hit her is my intense need for her... When things get to the point that I need her a lot and I can't get her, I *want* her. I want her, that's it. I want her love, I want her attention, and I'll get it. I'll get it no matter what.
>
> (Goldner et al., 1990, p.361)

It has been argued that wives and girlfriends are not merely 'convenient targets' but that men's rage is specifically directed at women. Men are seen to be angry with and fearful of their mother's power to deprive them of their needs and this rage becomes directed at their wives (Dinnerstein, 1976). It is also proposed that violent men were victims or witnesses of violence in their families of origin; that is they have learnt 'abnormal' behaviour patterns or that 'violence breeds violence'. This is often known as the 'cycle of deprivation' or the intergenerational hypothesis. A study by Walker (1984) compared the childhood experiences of men who had battered their wives as opposed to those who had not; see Table 1.3.

Table 1.3   Childhood experiences of men who had battered their wives versus those who had not.

	Batterers	Non-batterers
Battered by mother	44%	24%
Battered by father	61%	13%
Witnessed father battering mother	63%	27%

A methodological shortcoming of the study was that it was based on uncorroborated accounts from wives about their husbands' childhoods rather than from what their husbands said. On the one hand, the figures suggest that experiencing violence, both in terms of seeing his father batter his mother and being battered himself, may be significant in determining whether a man will eventually batter his partner. On the other hand, there is not a simple relationship since some men who had experienced violence in childhood did not batter their wives and some who had not experienced it did. Unfortunately, such data is often employed as a form of exoneration taking responsibility away from the men towards family factors which are offered as justifiable 'mitigating circumstances' (Edwards, 1989).

It is suggested (Dobash and Dobash, 1992) that women who batter or kill their husbands are actually held responsible and to blame. Women who have killed their violent husbands in what often amounts to self-defence after years of abuse have generally not been able to use the defence of the mitigating circumstances of 'loss of control' (Edwards, 1989). Instead, their actions are likely to have been seen as deliberate and premeditated and therefore to be classed as murder rather than manslaughter. Men are still seen, as they were in the last century, as less able to control their 'impulses' than women. This, on the one hand, allows them to maintain their power and to avoid having to change their domineering behaviour. On the other hand, it might be argued that it is very insulting to men to be presented in this way which suggests that it is impossible for them to 'play an active role in transforming their own behaviour' (Dobash and Dobash, 1992).

THE WOMEN

The main question raised here is: Why do some women 'put up' with abusive behaviour and stay with or return to violent husbands? Again, most of the explanations are based on the idea of 'faulty' (abnormal) childhoods. This is believed to lead to their having difficulties in leaving; difficulties in stopping their husbands being violent; and, even more detrimentally, personality defects that make them provocative and therefore justify their husbands' responses of violence. Battered women have been described as suffering from 'learned helplessness', in that they seem unable or unwilling to leave the relationships or to stop themselves being battered, unable to seek help from others and come to perceive the batterers as all powerful (Edwards, 1989). It may be valid to see battered women as feeling helpless and powerless but often this is seen as the *cause* not the *result* of their experiences. Evidence suggests that in fact many women do not just 'give up' but actually actively look for help and do not feel generally helpless in all aspects of their lives (Dobash and Dobash, 1980).

Dobash and Dobash (1992) list thirty 'traits' that have been generated by various theorists to supposedly differentiate between battered and non-battered women ranging from inability to cope, a tendency to withdraw, introspection, shyness, manipulativeness, masochism to 'dissatisfaction with current status'. Included as possibly irksome are a woman's dowdiness, inability to manage the family and home, intelligence, sullen silence, nagging, depression, frigidity and incapacity for deep emotional warmth (Gayford, 1978). What is particularly interesting is that personality traits that might be associated with both 'nagging' and on the other hand 'silence' have been equally postulated as provocations by different theorists: if she talks too much she gets hit, if she does not talk enough she gets hit. The cause or 'blame' is seen to reside in the victim: there is something abnormal about her that makes her stay, prevents her controlling her husband so he does not use violence, and/or makes her provoke him to violence. The alternative explanation is that it is not something about her behaviour that is at fault but rather that she is likely to be hit whatever she does. Personal accounts from battered women suggest that in fact anything (or nothing) may cause the violence and hence the search for specific factors is misguided. A major problem is that women's accounts are frequently ignored or minimized (Edwards, 1989). The feminist perspective offers explanations both for the kind of information or research methods adopted and for the failure to treat women's accounts seriously (see Section 3.4).

PRIVATE: INTERACTIONAL AND FAMILY MODELS

Part of the discourse of domestic violence as private is the idea that somehow both partners are contributing to the violence or that they 'deserve each other'. This is a view of marriage as a partnership of equals who just happen to rub each other up the wrong way. Couples who have 'poor communication' skills are seen to resort to violence because they are incapable of discussing and negotiating issues through clear and 'mature' forms of communication (Pizzey and Shapiro, 1982; Madanes, 1981). Also it has been argued that some couples make unfortunately incompatible and explosive combinations. Examples are a couple who are both strong-willed, who both find it unacceptable to back down from confrontations, a couple in which the man is alternately sullen, uncommunicative and overreactive, a couple in which the woman goads the man excessively, perhaps calling him weak or invoking jealousy. It was suggested that either partner could also use forms of 'passive provocation', sabotage, such as deliberately making a mess of a job, prevarication or excessive fussiness, all of which could contribute to an increase in tension and frustration. The combination of the couple's characteristics, it was suggested, could lead to a volatile relationship in which there could be an escalation of frustration leading to violence. Violence within this framework came to be seen as in some sense mutual and as due to these unfortunate and potentially frustrating combinations of personalities or forms of communication.

However, as we saw in the example on pp.9–10, the man is also likely to goad or attack the woman's 'weak spots'. A problem is that although this explanation may have some validity in explaining how conflict escalates it then also serves as an explanation for the actual violence which is perpetrated almost predominantly by the man and hence serves to blame the woman for something she did not do.

Inherent in such explanations are psychodynamic ideas that couples unconsciously select each other in order to 'resolve' conflicts left over from relationships with their parents. One such idea is that a man may unconsciously choose a woman who 'reminds' him of his mother, thus giving him a chance to resolve, in interactions with his wife, the conflicts stemming from his relationship with his mother. If he has learnt to fear dependency, denies it at a conscious level, and appears to be independent, he may choose a wife who is apparently dependent thus allowing him to appear to be the independent one. This apparently dependent wife, on the other hand, who has learnt to fear independent aspects of herself, is attracted to him because she will not have to be independent. Couples are thereby seen to 'collude' in fulfilling certain needs for each other.

However, they are also seen as tending to respond and defend themselves in ways similar to when they were young. If they reacted predominantly with rage and anger as opposed to sadness when mother was not available or needed to engage in some independent activity they are likely to react in the same way to their partners' attempts to establish some independence. In short the marriages, since they are based upon a selection of people who remind them of aspects of their parents, are seen as likely to powerfully re-evoke the same defences as were used in childhood. Most importantly, if they have learned to feel rejected as children they may 'project' or imagine their partners as similarly rejecting them. This may arouse the same kind of hurt, angry feelings they experienced as children; but now, being adult, they can vent their anger and, especially in the case of men, inflict considerable damage on their puzzled and frightened partners.

Such explanations though do not explain why men typically react with anger and violence and women do not. One explanation is that boys and girls are socialized differently in families. Boys may be rewarded for displaying aggressive traits and furthermore they may be presented with these as a model by their fathers (Bandura, 1977). Girls, on the other hand, are likely to be rewarded for showing passive non-aggressive behaviours. Young men in general are rewarded for being assertive, independent, standing up for themselves, avoiding 'effeminate' behaviour such as crying or admitting their fears. Within this view boys and girls are simply socialized into different and unequal roles rather than as a result of unconscious processes of collusion.

Interactional models of family therapy deriving from systems theory further pointed out that once established the patterns of violence could become self-maintaining (Dobash and Dobash, 1992). One example of this is the cyclical model of violence: a man might initiate violence following some argument with his wife but after the violence would show contrition, perhaps buying her some flowers and chocolates and being especially 'nice'. This could lead to a brief return to a honeymoon period, romance, passionate contact and possibly sexual intimacy. It was also argued that the power relations in the couple would at least temporarily alter, with the woman often adopting a forgiving motherly role and the man becoming childlike in asking for forgiveness. In this pattern both of them could be seen to have some of their needs met and so the cycle could be said to be mutually maintained. In violent relationships the man could be seen as both powerful and also powerless in that he has to resort to violence against the woman. The woman, on the other hand, is less powerful physically but more powerful in terms of being morally in the right. This depends in turn on cultural norms so that she may or may not be regarded as less powerful if the culture or sub-culture condones violence. Though offering some explanation of how couples with a mild level of violence might function this model can scarcely explain situations in which the violence is extreme and the periods of contrition have ceased.

One of the weaknesses with all the models discussed in this section so far, including the family/interactional theories, is that there is little attention paid to the inherent inequalities of power that exists between the genders. We will now turn to this.

3.2 SOCIO-CULTURAL MODELS — FEMINIST PERSPECTIVES

MARRIAGE, INTIMACY AND GENDER

As we suggested in the introduction to this chapter, the discourse that men and women are different but equal leads to the expectation that men and women will have different duties and expectations, and that failure to fulfil these constitutes legitimate and justified grievances. Studies of violence reveal that the reasons why their men engaged in violence cited by women in order of frequency were: drink, minor argument, sexual jealousy and money. Accounts of violent episodes, excluding the factor of drink, suggest that perceived failure to carry out their duties were regarded by the men as legitimate grounds for accusations or violence. Failure to carry out sexual duties or unfaithfulness appears to have been widely accepted, e.g. in the courts as a form of justification, or at least understandable explanation for men's violence. The fact that it was not until 1991 that marital rape became a criminal offence in the United Kingdom supports the argument that the fulfilling of sexual duties in marriage was part of the marriage contract.

3.3   THE FEMINIST DISCOURSE

[T]he feminist critique of wife beating is, at heart, a critique of patriarchy. The central argument is that the brutalization of an individual wife by an individual husband is not an individual or 'family' problem. It is simply one manifestation of male domination which has existed historically and cross-culturally.
(Yllo, 1983, p.277)

Many wives are materially dependent on their husbands, or a dwindling welfare system, for the 'basic necessities of life' such as money and housing (Dobash and Dobash, 1992). Violence is seen as a way of controlling women and keeping them subordinate; their material dependency may keep them in a violent relationship, not because they enjoy pain, or collude at some level, nor because they are abnormal or pathological but because they have very little choice. Many women also feel they have no choice because they do not wish to uproot and upset the children. Women may attempt to conceal the evidence 'for the children's sake'. Consistent with this, women are likely to say that what *did* provoke them finally to leave was the fear that witnessing the abuse would damage the children or even that the violence or abuse might be inflicted on the children as well (WAFE, 1989).

Men do not simply have material power, however, they also have 'ideological power'; their beliefs, opinions, perceptions, explanations have been and still are more influential than women's. As Spender (1980) comments, women have not been listened to, their accounts, explanations and experiences, not only of violence but also of other issues have been largely ignored. Many battered women, for instance, say that 'anything' can lead to their being violently abused; they also say that the main reason for their not leaving the relationships is that they have nowhere to go. Nevertheless the search for pathology on the part of individual women continues. If women's accounts and experiences had been taken seriously then it follows, at least theoretically, that research, explanations, and interventions would also have taken a different direction. The fact that women are beginning to be listened to and taken seriously on the issue of wife abuse is due to the influence of feminism as it begins to offer an effective challenge to men's material and ideological dominance.

ACTIVITY 3

Pause for a few moments to note down any problems you can think of with theories which make the following assumptions:

1 Women unconsciously wish to be dominated, are masochistic or are provocative.

2 Men are naturally aggressive.

3 Wife-abusing men are pathological.

DISCUSSION

From a feminist perspective most of the explanations in Sections 3.1 and 3.2 serve the function of maintaining men's position of dominance within a patriarchal system. Believing, for instance, that men are naturally aggressive also implies that there is very little that can be done about it, that women will just have to put up with it or try to control men's 'brutish' impulses. Similarly, believing that wife abusers are pathological exonerates them and makes them unaccountable for their behaviour: since abusers are abnormal there is no need to look at what 'normal' men do. It therefore follows that there is no point in challenging the dominant behaviour of the abusers because they cannot help it, and also that there is no need to question the dominant behaviour of 'normal' men because they are not violent anyway, therefore the power of both 'abnormal' men and 'normal' men remains unquestioned. Believing that women are masochistic, like to be dominated, and especially that they subconsciously wish to be dominated, enjoy pain or enjoy being provocative overtly maintains men's position of dominance. The problem is not simply that men's views are more dominant but that women themselves may internalize these beliefs. In the extract at the beginning of Section 3 the abused woman says that she came to believe that she was 'no good to anybody or anything'; her husband has managed to persuade her that there was something wrong with her even though she states that at first she thought he was the crazy one. Many discourses or explanations regarding the causation of violence can be seen from a feminist perspective as essentially male discourses which serve the purpose of maintaining men's position of dominance. Women are not listened to because they are thought of as intellectually inferior, hysterical, unreliable and so on. The fact of their relative powerlessness means that it is difficult for them to get to a position where they will be heard.

Feminist accounts have also pointed out how the dynamics of relationships are shaped by a patriarchal discourse which enforces the idea that men should control women. Although men generally have a greater variety of resources available with which to control women, for example money, and housing — physical violence, or the threat of it, serves as one of the most influential: 'although there are many ways that men as a group maintain women in oppressed social positions, violence is the most overt and effective means of social control' (Yllo and Bograd, 1988). An individual man abuses an individual woman; however in the context of a society that fails to sanction effectively against it, the behaviour is his but a patriarchal society condones it.

Some social psychologists have suggested that couples evolve their own rules about power and that decisions are made by a process of negotiation coloured by these gender-based power differences (Howard et al., 1986). A feminist account here emphasizes that though this may in part be true the threat of violence, and society's tacit acceptance of it, inevitably distorts male–female relationships. There is insufficient space to develop the differences between varieties of feminist thinking here except to note that 'radical feminists' see this essentially in terms of patriarchy whereas 'socialist feminism' also views violence as emerging as a result of class-related factors of poverty, stress and deprivation.

Any couple may generate rules about what each is going to accept as a legitimate way of trying to influence the other. They may generate a rule that violence should not be used to influence, though there is evidence that conflicts arising from the process of trying to establish a rule that violence should not be used can paradoxically lead to violence (Goldner et al., 1990). These rules may be idiosyncratic or they may be similar to rules shared by the wider culture or subculture. There may also be different sets of rules for each partner concerning freedom, spending money, showing anger and so on. There can also be personal or moral rules such as that men should never use violence against women.

As already suggested, violence may only be one type of control in a whole range of controlling behaviours adopted by individual men. Women in the Cleveland refuge study (CRAWC, 1984) frequently reported that their husbands kept them short of money, even taking away their own earnings or child benefit, kept them isolated from family and friends as well as from state agencies. One woman's account of trying to get help from the Samaritans was: 'I could hardly talk because I was frightened he would hear me... and in the end I put the phone down, I thought what if they send me a letter and he finds out.'

Edwards (1989) quotes another woman as saying:

> he makes me get out of bed and stand naked for hours on end, I'm actually freezing, but I can't get back into bed, if I tried to get back into bed he'd probably kill me, he is totally overpowering... he won't let me go out to socialize, take driving lessons, go to keep fit lessons, he won't let me do anything.

Some studies, however, suggest that women are likely to be battered even if they do objectively have some material power. Some of the women in a study of black couples by Mama (1989) could support themselves financially and often the accommodation was in their name and not their husbands' or partners'. The fact that these women were fairly independent seemed to anger their men who appeared to feel that the only way they could assert themselves was to use their physical superiority. Women may be caught either way, being 'too' dependent or independent can lead to anger, frustration and resentment and attempts by the men to 'redress the balance in their favour' by whatever means possible. In general women who are not materially dependent are less likely to be abused both because they have a better chance of escape and a realization of this might make a man think twice about the 'costs' of using violence (Straus and Gelles, 1990).

3.4   A FEMINIST INTERACTIONAL APPROACH: GENDER PREMISES, POWER AND RELATIONSHIPS

One approach that attempts to integrate feminist and interactional perspectives is illustrated in the work of Goldner and her colleagues. They argue that historically there have been various assumptions made about the natural position of dominance of men in marriage: the 'henpecked' husband was seen as a joke, a figure of derision. Likewise, women were expected to be subordinate in public and to be subordinate in private aspects of the marriage such as passivity and subordination in sex. Within this perspective violence can be seen as: exemplifying *in extremis* the stereotypical gender arrangements that structure intimacy between men and women generally' (Goldner et al., 1990, p.344).

Goldner et al. have worked in a therapeutic context with couples where there has been serious and repeated occurrence of violence. They maintain that relationships in families are guided by a set of premises which are absorbed from the discourses inherent in any given society. Within violent relationships they suggest that the premises regarding gender are 'rigidly prescribed and exaggerated'. They are transmitted to children, through families, explicitly and implicitly in terms of the continuing drama of family life, interactions, arguments and seeing their parents becoming stuck in repetitive patterns of conflict. They argue that in a sense families present not just ideological assumptions to the children but paradoxes or double-blinds (i.e. situations in which whatever action is chosen receives some form of punishment) regarding gender so that the children later in their adult relationships may become similarly stuck. It is not that such families have 'got it wrong' but that they are simply demonstrating, in an extreme form, the inherent contradictions embedded in our society's discourses about gender. They give some examples (distillations of what people in violent families have said) of how the paradoxes operate and are transmitted:

Woman talking about her parents:

'Mom doesn't stand up to dad and she seems always silently angry and depressed. But, whenever I get argumentative she says that I'm "too masculine" and no man will want me.'

From a father to his son:

'You must never be a wimp or feel afraid, but watch out for women. They can do you in. For every Sampson there is a Delilah with scissors.'

From a father to his daughter:

'The reason I have to beat your mother is that "she makes me do it". If only I were married to someone understanding (like you) we could have a happy home.'

(Goldner et al., 1990)

Violent couples, they argue, are caught up in playing out in an extreme form the contradictions inherent in gender premises. They argue strongly that there are inherent inequalities of power between the genders but that this does not totally explain the violence: 'Gendered premises about masculinity are rigidly adhered to in the families of the men we have been seeing who are violent toward women'. These premises, for example, that men must be stronger than women, and that they must not be sad or afraid, are in direct conflict with psychological reality. Men, like women and children, often feel dependent, scared, sad, and in need of protection. Since the prohibitions against such 'feminized' feelings include the man's private sense of himself, and not only his public persona, the psychological task of denial is constant. This is why intimacy can be so dangerous. When the man's terror of not being different enough from 'his' woman overtakes him, violence becomes one means of reasserting gender differences and male power.

Goldner's analysis of the woman's position appears to puncture some common assumptions, especially that women are likely to be passive, weak and dependent personalities: 'They were victims, but they were, in nearly every case, women of substance who had strong opinions and conveyed a sense of personal power'.

The women in many of the cases wanted to understand why they stayed in violent relationships. One strong element that emerged was that the women were strongly influenced by the discourse that a woman's identity and worth depended on her ability to build and maintain relationships. Often the women felt they had 'failed' in some way because they were unable to help their men to overcome their violent outbursts. They were trapped into a sense of feeling sorry for and at the same time frightened by them. Even to walk out on the man was in a sense felt, by many of the women, as guilt at the betrayal of her natural role as a woman, that she was putting herself first rather than taking care of the 'sick child' that her partner really was. Furthermore, many of the women had grown up in families where there were strong sanctions against a woman putting herself first.

Goldner's analysis offers an indication of how socially shared assumptions about gender roles, including assumptions about differences in what are appropriate ways of thinking and feeling for men and women, set the stage for violence. This analysis though should not simply be taken to imply another version of the analysis which sees women and men mutually responsible for the violence. Evidence suggests that violent men are often violent again in their new relationships whereas abused women are not so likely to enter into other violent relationships (Pahl, 1985). It is more likely that most women will feel bound by loyalty to their feminine roles to abnegate themselves, which leads them to 'put up with' violence.

4   MODELS OF INTERVENTION

Our intention in this section is to illustrate how the discourses underlying various models of domestic violence form the basis for different approaches to interventions. Since domestic violence is predominantly by men against women we will be focusing specifically on interventions aimed at dealing with violence by men against women. Models of intervention broadly fall into two main categories: first, attempts to protect the victims of violence through the law, police, housing and accommodation. Second, therapy and counselling of various sorts directed at altering the behaviour of the perpetrators, helping the victim to leave the relationship if appropriate or to 'recover' from the abuse and become more effective in her life. A broader form of intervention, based on a feminist perspective, encompassing these, is the attempt to alter culturally shared premises about gender roles, relationships, the legitimacy of violence and the patriarchal system itself.

4.1   THE LAW

The law does not discriminate between assaults by a husband and other assaults. Any assault constitutes a criminal offence (Dobash and Dobash, 1992). The differences between common assault, aggravated assault and grievous bodily harm (gbh), all criminal offences, lie largely in the extent of damage inflicted and intent to cause harm, with gbh usually being the most extreme. It is also possible to arrest someone if he/she attacks a police officer who has been called in to intervene or for a breach of the peace and an attacker could also be arrested for damaging property.

Theoretically it is possible for a violent man to be arrested and charged under a range of acts; however criminal remedies are very rarely used. There are several reasons why this should be so. First, it is the victim of the assault who has to lay a complaint and press charges, not the police, and women may be reluctant to do this for various reasons, Second, many women do not appear to be aware of the law, a reflection of their relatively powerless position. Third, it is possible that the proviso of 'intent' may allow a loophole, that the defence may argue a lack of intent, and that discourses about male impulsivity and temporary lack of control could be used as evidence of non-intentionality. Lastly, there is a tendency for law enforcers to 'decrime' domestic violence (Edwards, 1989) and prefer to use civil remedies instead.

Civil remedies available under the Domestic Violence Act (DVA) include the abilities of the county courts to make various orders restraining the violent partner from molesting the other, excluding the partner from the home or parts of the home. These tend to be used as a last resort, are hard to enforce and usually have a time limit which means the violence may recur, now fuelled further by resentment at the order having been made. In addition to these, the magistrates' courts can grant personal protection orders with powers of arrest.

One of the major problems is that the power of arrest is usually only used in exceptional cases: 'bruised, bloody and damned near dead'. In a comprehensive evaluation of the effectiveness of legal protection for women and children which has been employed by the law commission the following conclusion was drawn: 'whatever legal reforms may be made, and whatever changes may be made to court procedures, without effective enforcement by police officers and by courts, injunctions and protection orders will continue to be "not worth the paper they are written on"' (Barron, 1990, p.30).

Powerful criticisms of the working of the laws on domestic violence are being advocated by the Law Commission to the effect that the laws need to be simpler, more robust and workable, as can be seen from the statement from the Law Commission on page 29.

4.2   THE POLICE

As the previous section on the law shows, domestic violence is a crime under the 1961 Domestic Violence Act; however, *the police until recently have rarely treated it as such* though of course some police officers and police departments made attempts to do so. Edwards (1989) quotes this extract from a police training manual: 'the officer's role is to preserve the peace...in domestic disputes the power of arrest should only be exercised as a last resort...the officer should never create a police problem when there is only a family problem existing', yet surely any crime is a police problem.

By the mid 1970s the women's aid and refuge movement had succeeded in calling the public's attention to the plight of battered women and pressure was put on the government to do more about it and to change existing policies and legislation. Many of the complaints by women seeking aid were about the inadequacy of the police response, a response best described as non-intervention or under-enforcement. The inadequacies of the police response have been well documented. Farragher (1978) carried out a participant/observer study of police responses to domestic 'incidents'

NEWS FROM THE LAW COMMISSION

Conquest House, 37/38 John Street, Theobalds Road, London WC1N 2BQ
8 May 1992

HELP FOR VICTIMS OF DOMESTIC VIOLENCE

Victims of domestic violence need more help from the law. Reforms to improve the remedies dealing with violence and occupation of the family home are proposed today by the Law Commission. The Commission's Report[1] deals with the ways in which family courts should be able to help.

Victims of domestic violence and abuse need the protection of the civil courts, as well as the police and criminal law. The civil law can act speedily when circumstances demand. It can grant injunctions to stop violence and other molestation, and it can decide who may live in the family home. Breach of these orders can sometimes lead to the arrest of the offender.

But the present law can fall down on the job. The Law Commission believes that it is too complicated, it discriminates between different types of victims, and it fails to offer all the protection which victims and their children need.

The main reforms which the Law Commission proposes are —

1   A single, clear set of remedies available in all courts dealing with family cases — the High Court, county courts and magistrates' family proceedings courts.

2   Protection orders against violence and molestation available to anyone with a 'family' connection. This would include couples who once lived together, engaged couples, those formerly engaged, couples in a sexual relationship, close relatives, people sharing a household (not on a commercial basis) and people sharing responsibility for a child.

3   Protection for any child involved in family proceedings, whether the case concerns the child's own future or the relationship between the adults.

4   A single, flexible power to grant orders regulating the occupation of the family home, covering orders that one person be allowed to stay or be allowed back, or that one should leave. The court could also deal with the use of furniture and the payment of rent and other expenses. In some cases they could transfer tenancy from one to another.

5   Giving a power of arrest for a breach of an order made against someone who has already used or threatened violence against the victim, unless that is unnecessary to protect the victim.

6   Empowering the police, when called to an incident of domestic violence, to apply for civil remedies on the victim's behalf.

Professor Brenda Hoggett, Law Commissioner in charge of this project, said 'the close and continuing nature of family relationships, using that term in its broadest sense, can bring out the worst as well as the best in human nature. The victims may not want or need a system of punishment or compensation, but they do need protection from harm and a way of sorting out a more peaceful and stable future for everyone'.

When a court is faced with the possibility of making an order about the occupation of the family home, the Law Commission considers that it should always do so if the order is needed to protect the applicant or a child from significant harm. The court should always look at the housing need and resources of both parties, their financial resources and the effect on them and their children of making or not making an order.

---

[1]   *Domestic Violence and Occupation of the Family Home*, Law Com, No. 207, HMSO.

in Staffordshire in which he observed the police at a police station and accompanied them to the 'scene'. He found that the police very rarely arrested the batterer; often did not know if the woman had an injunction; asked the woman over and over, often in front of the man, whether she *really* wanted to press charges; sometimes persuaded the woman out of pressing charges; or would delay doing anything about it by giving her time 'to think it over' — assuming that an 'unemotional' decision the next day would be more 'realistic'. Farragher describes the way the police handled one domestic 'incident' as follows:

> the injured party had two black eyes...she had been severely beaten about the face, with bruising also on the bridge of the nose, her lip and mouth were cut, bruised and swollen, her hands were also cut...the man and woman were taken into different rooms, the wpc spoke to the husband. She asked whether there was likely to be any repetition of the assault that night. He turned and said 'I don't think so'...she asked him to clarify. Eventually he said it was highly unlikely...the woman re-entered the room. The pc said to the woman that if she still wanted to make a complaint she should come into the police station the next day. The woman asked what protection did she have that night; what if there was a repetition? The wpc replied that it was up to her to make sure that there was not a repetition.
>
> (Farragher, 1978, p.114)

Here was a case of an obvious assault under the 1961 Act, yet there was no arrest; the husband was merely warned and the woman was left with no protection. The responsibility for her protection and for 'sorting things out' was overtly put onto the wife by the wpc. Edwards (1989) suggests that if the police are called in but the man is not charged it is in fact likely to aggravate the violence.

The main problem is that the police are allowed to use their *discretion* in dealing with domestic violence in terms of how the incident is recorded and dealt with. In practice, the attitudes of a police officer are likely to influence what he/she decides to do in domestic violence cases. Their beliefs are likely to reflect widely held attitudes and prejudices, and — since the police are 90 per cent male — male prejudices. On one hand, they are likely to share the private/public dichotomy believing that they should not intervene in 'domestics', that 'domestics' are not real police work because they are not really crimes but personal matters. On the other hand, they have been given more powers in the public sphere in the 1980s: they are able to arrest without a warrant or enter 'private' homes if they have 'suspicions about stolen goods or drugs'.

One police officer summarizes his attitude:

> I feel that it is just a private matter and I have no right being there. I know I have my own problems with my wife and I settle them myself. I wouldn't want anyone else to butt in: even if I threaten my

wife, which I don't usually do ... I would not consider that sufficient reason for somebody to butt in; because I wouldn't really do my wife any harm and I think that true of nearly all these husbands. They are really no different from me or anyone else.

(Edwards, 1989, p.99)

The above suggests that many police officers do regard it as excusable for men to use violence against their wives and this may colour their responses. A study of police attitudes in the USA found that the more they thought the violence to be acceptable the more likely they were to respond negatively (Edwards, 1989).

The main reason the police give for not arresting the husband is that they believe that the woman is highly likely to withdraw her complaint; essential because under most laws it is the victim who has to press charges. Though evidence is not conclusive, this appears to be more of an assumption than a reality. In the study by Farragher (1978) only one in ten withdrew, in the Cleveland study only three out of eighteen. Even if she does withdraw her complaint, there are many reasons for doing this, the woman may be afraid of retaliation, for example, especially if she thinks that the police or the courts will not actually keep the man away. In the Cleveland study, for instance, and despite arrest, the sentences given by the court did not serve to actually keep the man away from home for any length of time. Out of fifteen arrests, two men were sent to prison, the longest for six months, three men received conditional discharges, three were given suspended sentences, six were fined, and one put on probation. Fining the man must surely be one of the most inappropriate things to do, especially if the family is on a low income; some women complain that they themselves had to pay the fines as the men refused to do so. The police themselves may be disillusioned with what happens when they actually get the man to court if the case is dismissed or an inappropriate sentence is passed.

Women may withdraw complaints because they are materially dependent on men and are aware that they are going to have problems with finances and accommodation, especially if they know that they are not going to be easily rehoused. They may be worried about the children, materially or emotionally, if their fathers are taken away. They may also withdraw their complaints because they have had experience of being, or believe that they are going to be, treated negatively, or because they think others will see them as failures, or provokers, or inadequate because they cannot control the men themselves. Men may persuade them to withdraw either by more threats or by temporary abject apology. The police therefore assume that the women will withdraw, but tend to assume different reasons for the withdrawal from those the women themselves offer, tending to see women as 'capricious' and 'fickle'.

Women of Afro-Caribbean or Asian origins may have even more problems when calling in the police (Mama, 1989). The experience of many Afro-Caribbean groups, is that the police are racist and oppressive, so therefore to call them in is to open up the possibility of racist treatment for the woman or the man. The build-up of frustrations stemming from racist oppression and discrimination is often seen by these communities to be a cause of black male violence towards black females and calling in the police may be seen as disloyal to the black community. Perhaps the worst element in the relationship between the police and ethnic minority women is seen when the police themselves are punitive towards the victim; negative reactions may intensify, a 'triple' negative response because she is from an ethnic minority, because she is female and because she is poor. Mama (1989) describes the following shockingly punitive response by the police towards a Nigerian woman:

> ... when the police arrived the husband, who had a better command of the Queen's English than her, told the police that she had been damaging property in his flat and instructed them to arrest her, the police ridiculed the pair of them 'eenie meenie minie mo catch a nigger by the toe' while they decided who to arrest. They opted for Patience and dragged her off in a half-clothed state: when they arrived at the station she was roughed up and then kicked down the stairs into the cells where she was locked up all night shivering with cold. She was ridiculed and racially humiliated.
>
> (p.181)

This summary of police response paints a bleak picture but it is unfair to suggest that all policemen are misogynist or racist. Some police forces, for example the Metropolitan, have been commended for initiatives towards domestic violence. Suggestions for improving the police response have included: mandatory arrest; more training for the police force in dealing with domestic violence; improved communication systems, recording and classification procedures; an easily accessible data base at the station to which the police can refer to check whether there is already an injunction in operation; more awareness of other agencies the woman could be referred to; more cooperation between the police and other agencies such as refuges/housing (Farragher, 1978; Edwards, 1989). Some of these recommendations, also made forcefully by the Women's Aid Federation (WAFE), such as the setting up by the police of 'domestic violence units' and improved recording of incidents, were incorporated in a Home Office circular to Chief Constables (Home Office Circular No. 60, 1990). Such units are becoming increasingly common in large cities and the police response, though still patchy, has improved considerably.

ACTIVITY 4

Read the following description of a study on mandatory arrest and consider the reasons why this might or might not be an effective approach. In particular consider the implications it has for how domestic violence is commonly regarded.

MANDATORY ARREST — A RESEARCH STUDY

Mandatory arrest for domestic violence has been tried in some police forces. A research study in Minnesota (USA) explored the effects of different police responses on re-offending; one-third of the police used mandatory arresting and detaining, one-third used advising the couple; one-third tried removing the man for 'cooling off'. Six months later follow-up interviews revealed whether the men had re-offended.

Table 1.4   Results

	Re-offending %
Mandatory arrest and detaining	19%
Advising the couple	37%
Removing man for 'cooling off'	34%

From: Dobash and Dobash, 1992

It is not quite clear as to why mandatory arrest should work, whether it is the arrest itself, having to go to court, or the shock and unpleasantness of imprisonment. One strong possibility is that mandatory arrest is effective in part because a clear message is given to the man that his behaviour is unacceptable (and unacceptable by other *men* who largely constitute the justice system). It is argued that if the police establish an alliance with the victim so that she is confident that she could threaten the offender more credibly in the future with a call to the police, the man may think twice about using violence in the future.

Mandatory arrest makes the use of discretion more difficult, it also appears to lessen the possibility of racial discrimination. In the study above, before mandatory arrest had been introduced, 32 per cent of the arrests were of men from ethnic minorities, a proportion which declined to only 8 per cent after mandatory arrest had been brought in (Dobash and Dobash, 1992). A mandatory approach also has positive implications for women's testimony. Within the 1984 Police and Criminal Evidence Act a woman can be compelled to give evidence against her violent husband; the advantage to this may be that it is less easy for the man to blame her for 'going against him': since she is forced to give evidence it is not really her 'fault'. However, compulsion to give evidence may still lead to recrimination from some men and therefore can be dangerous if a woman is offered no further protection.

4.3   PROTECTION OF VICTIMS

The feminist movement has made a most significant contribution to the increase in awareness of gender inequalities, abuse and violence in families. This has, to some extent, filtered through to policies of intervention and also to the popular consciousness. Talk between men which might a few years ago have included remarks about beating troublesome wives may no longer be condoned so readily. Children are more likely to be aware of gender discrimination at school and grow up expecting greater equality. Paradoxically it could be argued that professional agencies have been some of the slowest to change their policies. The police and courts as we saw earlier have been remarkably slow in changing their policy and carrying out the law.

Prevention can be seen to involve a general consciousness raising through education, television, newspapers and the arts. However, use of custodial sentences, greater commitment to action by the police and therapeutic approaches do not appear to be expanding. For example, there is little commitment by government, despite rhetoric about the disintegration of the family to support counselling services for couples and families who are having problems of various sorts. Even more basically there is little real commitment to relieving some of the stresses, financial, occupational, and/or housing, that families experience and which can contribute to violence. Likewise, encouragement and opportunities for women to escape from violent relationships are lacking. Instead, most women are still likely to feel the situations would have to be very dire before they would choose to escape.

HOUSING AND REFUGES

One of the main reasons women give for staying with or returning to violent partners is that they have nowhere to go. Friends and relatives may put them up temporarily but often cannot offer more permanent accommodation if they do not have enough space. Some battered women fear that their partners will come round and 'cause trouble' in their friends'/relatives' homes and they do not wish to create problems for others. Having somewhere to go would protect the victim — she could escape from her violent partner — and providing alternative accommodation can be seen as a direct challenge to a patriarchal system that renders women dependent on men. This dependency is seen by Women's Aid Federation (WAFE) as an essential part of women's subordination to men (Dobash and Dobash, 1992). Perhaps even the knowledge that a woman could go if she wanted, that there was somewhere for her to go, might make a man think twice about using violence, and/or force him to get some kind of therapeutic help for his behaviour. It is often at the point where a woman goes or threatens to go that the man finally realizes that he needs to change.

In 1977, partly owing to the pressure of WAFE, the Housing (Homeless) Persons Act was passed. However, as is documented in Chapter 7 of this book, in the following decade the Conservative government cut local authority budgets; many local authority houses were sold to become part of the private housing market and therefore went out of their control. Very little was done to replace accommodation that had been lost in this way. In the years 1989 to 1990 over 30,000 women and children stayed in refuges in England and two-thirds of that refuge population were children. Adding

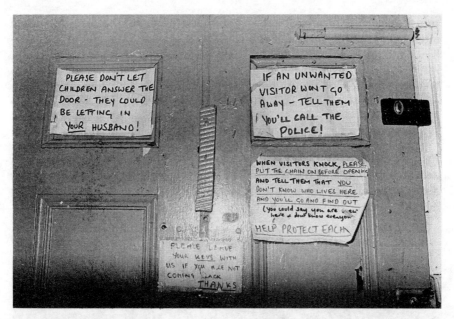

Leaving violent men

the number of women who contacted Women's Aid groups for advice and information produces a figure of 75,000 (WAFE, 1992).

Some local authorities may therefore have genuine difficulties in housing and rehousing simply because they do not have enough available housing and what they do have may be substandard, in run-down and even dangerous areas, hardly suitable for already fearful women who often have young children. Even if they do have available accommodation this does not necessarily mean they will allocate it appropriately. As we briefly suggested in Section 4.1, whether they allocate and what kind of accommodation is allocated often depend on the general attitude of the particular housing authority or its individual officers.

REFUGES

The first refuge was founded in 1972 in Chiswick and this inspired the opening of more in other parts of the country. Although refuges may vary in their ideologies (Dobash and Dobash, 1992) they have several common aims: to allow the victims of violence and their children to escape and to provide a safe place and temporary accommodation for them; to support, offer advice, information and practical help to the women; to attempt to liaise with other agencies, for instance social security, housing and the police, and more generally to draw the public's attention to the plight of battered women.

The realization that many other women have had similar experiences can help to mitigate feelings of being to blame and failure: 'At first I asked, did I do the right thing. Is it me? Now I say I don't have to put up with this any more, we're all in this together' (Dobash and Dobash, 1992). Most of the women have been very controlled in their relationships with others in the refuge because their freedom and confidence in making decisions have often been severely eroded. Feelings of increased autonomy and the capability to run their own lives can help women to cope after they leave a refuge. Lastly, a refuge can give women information about their rights to housing, to social security and to the law, information they often would not have had previously. A refuge may also liaise with other agencies, for instance in some local authorities women are rehoused quicker if they are in a refuge.

Refuges do have problems: overcrowding, underfunding, substandard accommodation, for example, and interactional problems stemming from suddenly having to live with and get on with many other women and their

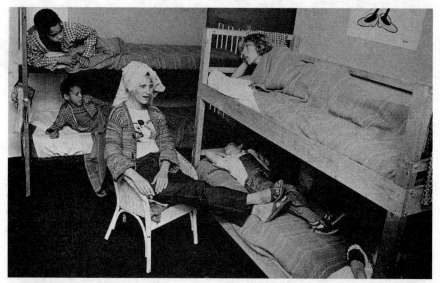

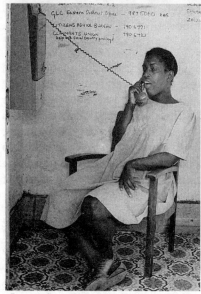

Conditions in existing refuges

children, and in some cases having to deal with racism. Nevertheless, most women have found their experiences of refuges very positive. Refuges generally try not to place time limits on how long women can stay, but obviously the eventual aim is to find them suitable permanent housing. Bottlenecks can occur with the result that refuges become extremely crowded and eventually some of the women are likely to be thrown back into the local authority housing system or, where available, to seeking provision from Housing Associations. Having attended a refuge can help some women to obtain houses but relations between refuges and local authorities vary. However, Scottish Women's Aid has suggested that being rehoused on their own is not necessarily the best solution for many women, partly because they may still not be safe from their husbands or boyfriends and also because they need companionship and practical and emotional assistance. In 1982 the first permanent communal house in Scotland opened in Edinburgh and a second opened in 1988 in Falkirk. Despite the clear need for refuges for women in 1992 there were only 270 refuges throughout the United Kingdom. This is only a third of the provision recommended in 1975 when the Government Select Committee on violence and marriage recommended one family place per 10,000 of the population (WAFE, 1992).

BLACK AND ASIAN WOMEN AND HOUSING

Mama (1989) suggests that black women experienced far less helpful responses from housing department refuges than did white women. In many cases the accommodation offered can be appalling. The responses of agencies can be seen to embody a wide range of patriarchal and racially discriminatory values which are made all the more stark by the plight of women who have been forced, not just to leave homes jointly owned or rented, but actually out of their own homes. Mama describes a number of cases with a similar scenario: typically, a black woman is living in accommodation which is in her own name; she allows her boyfriend to move in with her and he becomes violent. Even if she has children, she could be made homeless because the boyfriend has some right to the accommodation. Worse still, the housing department could prove less than helpful because technically the woman has her own accommodation.

Although the experiences of black women, as described by Mama, are shared by many white women there is a difference, as we have seen, in the degree of difficulty black women face coupled with racial prejudice. A triple level of discrimination can be seen to exist: for being a woman, for being black and for being poor. It is salutary to note, however, that Mama suggests that even the refuge movement and women's aid movements can display signs of racial discrimination, in terms of less assistance for black women with housing, welfare and the courts. Some refuges have been set up by black women to deal with the different needs of ethnic minority women and to protect them against racism by only taking ethnic minority women.

4.4   SOCIAL WORK

Social workers have no statutory responsibilities for dealing with domestic violence; they may, however, become involved as part of their duties, such as child protection or advisory roles, or because of requests by women or others to provide some assistance. One of the consequences here is that although social workers may make the first contact with cases of domestic violence they often lack support and the resources to intervene.

In 1985 Maynard analysed the case files of over a hundred social workers. These files contained details and impressions of the social workers' clients and their circumstances, and records of what advice and action had been taken; then were compiled to help keep the social workers and their colleagues and managers aware of the details of each case. Maynard commented that they may not be an exact record of what happened, in part because they were written to 'give the right impression' to others. From the study it appeared that the social workers tended to emphasize neutrality and that they aimed to keep families together, mainly for the sake of the children for whom they have a statutory responsibility:

> I had to explain my position to Mrs X. I said that I had to be seen to be neutral. I was there to help all of the members of the family. This I would be unable to do if the impression was given that I sided with any member of the family.
>
> (Maynard, 1985, p.130)

Explanations in the files as to the causes of violence appeared to 'collude' with the men's explanations rather than question these beliefs or accept the woman's explanations. There appeared to be tacit acceptance that 'a man's natural need for satisfactory domestic and sexual arrangements can equally naturally lead to drinking and violence when he does not have these so called needs satisfied'. This, even if not actually condoning the discourse of men as having uncontrollable impulses, does at least accept it as a partial explanation for the violence. The violence could be explained to the women in these terms, in effect encouraging the women to accept the men's explanations. The idea that the women provoked their husbands' violence is explicitly stated on the files: 'It seems her nagging is the trigger for his violence …and …I feel that she could be provoking his violence towards her' (Maynard, 1985, p.135).

In effect and despite believing in 'neutrality' some social workers appeared to be implicitly supporting the men by accepting their explanations rather than the women's, by trying to keep the families united at the women's cost, by pathologizing women, and by encouraging the women rather than the men to change their behaviour.

Obviously not all social workers or social work agencies share these biases: women from the Cleveland refuge reported that they had found some of the social workers helpful; several had been referred to the refuge by them, others had found that just having someone to talk to helped, and the knowledge that the social workers would be there to help them if they got desperate or wanted to leave made them feel less isolated.

4.5 THERAPY

Therapy for individuals and couples tends to assume that the violence is either an individual or relational problem. However, feminist approaches also involve interventions at the 'private' level in terms of helping to rebuild women's confidence, encouraging expression of emotional reactions. They also include interventions at the social level such as helping to equip women with information and directing them to networks of support in the community. In short the experience can help to overcome the sense of helplessness that women may have suffered.

THERAPY WITH THE MEN

An important question is: Why do men not usually seek help for their own violent behaviour? Many therapists who have worked with violent men perceive that men do not feel good about using violence (Goldner et al., 1990), although it could be argued that this is because only the men who do not feel good about it come into therapy. It may be because they do not see their behaviour as problematic or because they fear negative reactions by others if they do try to talk about the violence. Men's socialization may make it difficult for them to talk about such things or it may make them fear the exposure of their vulnerabilities.

Though not necessarily separate from custodial interventions, therapy and counselling have been employed in some cases as a way of reducing violence. Usually therapeutic approaches require, as a prerequisite, that a man agrees to stop being violent before treatment commences and acknowledges and takes responsibility for his violent behaviour. Frequently men attempt to deflect responsibility onto the women or the situation and deny the consequences of their own acts; they 'blame the victim, justify the violence, distort and minimize (only a little slap), omit and lie'. Men may be asked to reconstruct their violence, to provide accounts of what they did and said and describe their partners' reactions accepting that the violence was not simply carried out in a 'blind rage' when they were not aware of what they were doing.

In group therapy sessions men are encouraged to talk with other men about their actions, why they resorted to violence, their feelings at the time, their identities as men and so on. They may be asked to identify the 'critical moment', the point at which they could have acted differently and chosen a non-violent alternative. Violence is reconstructed as an intentional act chosen by men as a tactic to control and dominate women.

Often such groups have as an objective consciousness raising about masculinity and gendered premises about relationships and male and female roles. They also discuss alternative ways of dealing with conflicts, frustrations, felt betrayals, and so on in their relationships. Basic notions of masculinity may be challenged in such groups so that men are encouraged to express their feelings in other ways than through anger. This can be no small task for many men whose entire identity is bound up with being 'hard', not showing feelings, not 'running away' from a fight and not taking any 'crap' from anyone.

A related technique which may be a part of individual counselling or therapy is anger management: men are encouraged to examine in detail their feelings of anger, what triggers it, how they respond, how they feel afterwards and so on. The theory is that some men have not learned appropriate techniques of control in their childhood or have imitated unfortunate role models, usually their fathers, who had resorted to violence to deal with experiences of frustration or distress. These men are taught to be more aware of their inner states such as arousal levels, feelings of tension and violent thoughts and to develop preventative strategies. Consistent with the discourse that aggression can be bottled up and needs a release may be a discussion about alternative and less harmful ways of dissipating violent feelings.

4.6   THERAPY WITH COUPLES

The work of Virginia Goldner and her colleagues (also described in **Wetherell and Dallos**, 1992, *Chapter 4) attempts to combine a feminist and interpersonal approach. During therapy sessions they see couples together who have agreed to attend voluntarily for treatment, usually following advice from a doctor or social worker. Her sample includes couples from a variety of social, racial and economic backgrounds who have all stated an intention to attempt to stay together and stop the violence. This may mark them out as an unusual sample since, in many cases, the men refuse to attend for any such assistance even when their wives threaten them with divorce. Goldner is careful to point out that she does not view seeing a couple in therapy as implying mutual causation and responsibility for the violence. One of the initial demands she makes is that the man, in the presence of his partner, accepts responsibility for the violence and agrees to end it unconditionally.

The couples are asked to explore the nature of their assumptions about gender-relationships, their explanations of the violence and their expectations about their relationships. The aim of the therapy broadly is to encourage the men to explore their assumptions about gender and their presumed right to resort to violence and in turn the women's assumptions, especially that they should put up with the violence and stay in the relationships. The exploration includes an analysis of each of the couple's own family background, which has often been violent and how this has led them to see violence as acceptable. Goldner has found that very often the women are bound by the belief that they should be able to help their men

*The use of bold type here and elsewhere in this book indicates a cross reference to the Open University course D311 *Family Life and Social Policy*.

to overcome the violence and that they have failed if they retreat from nurturing and looking after the men even when they repeatedly attack them. This pattern of violence and caring is echoed in the accounts offered by other researchers:

> I think I more or less pitied him. He'd got nowhere else; his family doesn't really want him; his mum's not in a position to offer him a home — she's living with another of her sons whose marriage has broken down, and I suppose I felt really sorry for him. You've got to have shelter somewhere and being as I knew what it's like to be without, I think this is why I took him back. But we're not really settled; I don't think we ever will be to be honest.
>
> (Pahl, 1985, p.58)
>
> He comes in all sort of miserable and weepy and all this. You see, and you've got to switch yourself off, and you've got to sit down and think, 'Don't give in and don't feel sorry; just think of what you went through'. That's what I have to do, otherwise I would just be as soft as sugar and sit there and say, 'Oh, well, yes, you might as well come back'.
>
> (Pahl, 1985, p.61)

An important element of Goldner's approach is to assist the women to realize that their beliefs about gender roles lead them to respond with nurturing even when they have suffered acute attacks. Couples are encouraged to contemplate splitting up if necessary in order to break out of this cycle of attack–remorse–forgiveness and in particular the women are encouraged to make it very clear to the men that they will not tolerate further violence. In some cases her couples decide to separate permanently, in others they resume a relationship on new terms. She argues though that it is helpful for both the men and the women to reappraise some of their assumptions and change their habitual ways of feeling and responding in order to be able to improve their relationships or embark on new ones with less risk of repeating the same patterns.

5   DISCUSSION AND CONCLUSION

As we have seen in this chapter, home is anything but a haven for many women and children. Domestic violence appears to be widespread and violence against women by their male partners appeared to account for over 70 per cent of violence in the home and one in four of all violent crimes. In some early studies it does seem clear that this form of violence has held a status different from other forms: it has largely been regarded as 'private' and as a family matter. Privacy in terms of family life is two-edged: on the one hand people's rights to privacy in their own homes might appear to be a justified and worthwhile principle to uphold. On the other hand, the principle of family privacy appears to operate to countenance a range of oppressive actions against women.

In our survey of explanations of domestic violence we have focused on feminist theories which consider domestic violence as '*in extremis*' a version of the wider inequalities between men and women. It has been argued that men expect to be dominant in their families and society allows them to use violence in order to control and subjugate women. At the same time we need to be cautious for a number of reasons of accepting this as a sufficient explanation. Many men, perhaps the majority, do not resort to violence to control their partners, or at least not to the extreme extent of some of our case examples. Even accepting a feminist position we need to try to take account of the 'diversity' of family life. Differences between families alert us to the danger of making simple generalizations. The discourses regarding gender expectations prevalent in society appear to be absorbed in different ways in different families. Another line of argument is that diversity in the use and severity of violence is linked to the presence of a 'significant' challenge by a woman of a man's authority. In order to identify what counts as significant we need to look at the particular family — the private dynamics. There is some support for this in the work of Goldner et al. (1990), which showed that initially at least the women could be strong and challenging. The great danger here, however, is that women may simply be pathologized or blamed for being awkward, provocative or prone to violence. A related argument is that families pass on such patterns through the generations and again this explains some violence but not all of it, since not all violent men appear to have witnessed violence in their own families and not all men who have violent fathers become violent towards women.

The slippage from the public to the private is particularly difficult for domestic violence and other forms of abuse in families. As soon as we focus on private, individual or interactional properties of family life, there is the danger that we start to blame families, which in turn largely punishes women. What seems to have bedevilled attempts at intervention has been this continual slippage between private and public explanations. The law has not been used effectively because it was felt that at least some cases of violence were to do with personal, private problems. At the same time, therapy was thwarted by the fact that couples operate under confusing premises about whether violence is legitimate or not. We feel that some of Goldner et al.'s therapeutic work here is illuminating. For many men violence appears to be an attempt to extort respect, obedience and love (love, honour and obey — as the marriage vows have it) from their partners as society seems to lead them to expect. Once violence has been employed their chances of securing these things are progressively reduced and a desperate cycle is set up in which this failed solution is repeatedly attempted only to produce increasingly terrified, bitter, resentful wives incapable of showing any feelings except fear and anger. Such systems-based therapies attempt to intervene directly in problematic interactional cycles, but so does mandatory arrest. By framing his actions as criminal rather than pathological the man may instead come to see himself as 'criminal' rather than 'sick' and therefore as accountable and responsible for his actions and potentially able to act and react differently. Part of the change must be to challenge the age-old discourse of male impulsivity, which exonerates men from all kinds of appalling behaviours, not only domestic violence but also rape, wife murder and child abuse.

There are also questions about whether, and to what extent, explanations of domestic violence come to constitute 'excuses' which can be employed by the perpetrators and by agencies involved in dealing with the families, such as the police and social services. To think no further than punishment does little to help the development of our understanding of domestic violence and in consequence how we might be able to formulate better policies of prevention and treatment, but likewise, to ignore the need for punishment and protection and focus too heavily on therapy ignores the need for the victims, predominantly women, to be protected. The clear application of the law also gives an unambiguous message that violence is not to be sanctioned and permitted in our society. Quite obviously this message has not been, and is still not, convincingly given by the courts and police. Such a clear message might also have a 'therapeutic' effect in that it clarifies what rights couples should expect and allow each other and where the line must be drawn. Such a process of clarification of rules, boundaries, rights, duties and obligations is also seen as a prerequisite in most therapeutic approaches.

The law quite clearly states that domestic violence is a crime: it could be argued, therefore, that this statement is sufficient — we do not need to explain it, understand it, nor find reasons for it, it is simply a crime and should be treated as such. The same behaviour should simply carry the same sanctions wherever it occurs, whoever does it and to whom it is done. The main question in this case would be whether this would actually prevent it occurring. The Minnesota study (which was discussed in Section 4.2) appears to suggest that mandatory arrest does work in the prevention of the reoccurrence of violence, but then presumably so do some kinds of therapeutic intervention. One important difference between arrest/imprisonment and therapy is that therapy is largely voluntary rather than compulsory. One similarity is that both insist that the violence must stop, the man is held accountable for his behaviour. Both give a clear message that the violence is unacceptable. Part of the problem appears to be that the wider society generally gives an ambiguous message, the law itself states that it is a crime and unacceptable but the actual operation of the law and other involved agencies is saturated with interpretations, biases, beliefs, perceptions about privacy, gender, equality, 'marriage' and contradictory discourses about the causation of violence, which generally add up to the likelihood of the man being exonerated in some way. As well as this, both mandatory arrest and therapy intervene in the power relations between men and women at least in so far as they intervene to prevent the abuse of physical power. Therapeutic interventions may also explore the relationship in more detail, addressing a couple's power structure and beliefs about gender and therefore theoretically being more likely to allow the couple to make permanent and more profound changes. There are competing explanations about why mandatory arrest works; the man has undergone emotional/cognitive changes about the morality of violence and male–female relationships or he simply just stops being violent because of the fear of further punishment.

A mistake can be to separate such interactional analyses from a societal one. One way to 'help' men to halt such a cycle is by the force of the law and a clear message from society that such behaviour is not acceptable. Without this there is little reason why they should not start the first circuit of such a cycle. We are not suggesting that this fully explains violence but we think it captures the line of arguments marshalled together in this chapter. Without some integrated model of domestic violence we cannot attempt to explain the diversity of family life. Both clear legal sanctions and enforcement of the law are needed not only to protect women but to help men not to embark on ultimately destructive violent careers in their families. A broader commitment is needed to change women's position through the provision of safe alternative accommodation and refuges, and indeed through a more thorough insistence on real equality, such as alternative accommodation and child care facilities. Some of the responsibility for this must rest in the hands of central government.

SOURCES OF INFORMATION

Women's Aid Federation England, PO Box 391, Bristol BS99 7WS

WAFE (1987) *You Can't Beat a Woman,* Women and Children in Refuges, WAFE.

WAFE (1989) *Breaking Through: Women Surviving Male Violence,* WAFE.

WAFE (1990) *Getting Free: A Handbook for Women in Abusive Situations,* WAFE.

WAFE (1992) *Women's Aid Federation Information Packs,* WAFE.

REFERENCES

Bakowski, M., Murch, M. and Walker, V. (1983) *Marital Violence: the Community Response,* London, Tavistock Publications.

Bandura, A. (1977) *Social Learning Theory,* London, Prentice-Hall.

Binney, V., Harkell, G. and Nixon, J. (1981) *Leaving Violent Men: a Study of Refuges and Housing for Battered Women,* London, Women's Aid Federation England.

Chodorow, N. (1978) *The Reproduction of Mothering,* Berkeley, University of California Press.

Cleveland Refuge and Aid for Women and Children (1984) *Private Violence: Public Shame,* Middlesborough, CRAWC.

Dinnerstein, N. (1976) *The Mermaid and the Minotaur: Sexual Arrangements and Human Malaise,* New York, Harper and Row.

Dobash, R. E. and Dobash, R. P. (1980) *Violence against Wives: a Case Against Patriarchy*, Shepton Mallet, Open Books.

Dobash, R. E. and Dobash, R. P. (1992) *Women, Violence and Social Change*, London, Routledge.

Edwards, S. (ed) (1989) *Policing 'Domestic' Violence*, London, Sage.

Fairbairn, W. R. D. (1952) *An Object-Relations Theory of the Personality*, New York, Barni Books.

Farragher, T. (1978) 'The police response to violence against women in the home', in Pahl, J. (ed).

Finkelhor, D., Gelles, R.J., Hotaling, T. and Straus, M. A. (eds) (1983) *The Dark Side of Families*, London, Sage.

Gayford, J. J. (1978) Battered wives: a study of the aetiology and psychological effects among one hundred women, MD thesis, University of London.

Gelles, R. J. (1979) *Family Violence*, London, Sage.

Goldner, V. (1991) 'Sex, power and gender: a feminist systemic analysis of the politics of passion', *Journal of Feminist Family Therapy,* 3, pp.63-83.

Goldner, V., Penn, P., Sheinberg, M. and Walker, G. (1990) 'Love and violence: paradoxes of volatile attachments', *Family Process*, 29, 4, pp.343–64.

Howard, J. A., Blunstein, P. and Schwartz, P. (1986) 'Sex, power and influence tactics in intimate relationships', *Journal of Personality and Social Psychology*, 51, pp.102–9.

Jeffreys, S. (1990) *Anticlimax: a Feminist Perspective on the Sexual Revolution*, London, The Women's Press.

Klecker, J. (1978) 'Wife beaters and beaten wives: co-conspirators', *Crimes of Violence,* 15(1), pp.54–6.

Madanes, C. (1981) *Strategic Family Therapy*, San Francisco, Jossey Books.

Mama, A. (1989) *The Hidden Struggle*, LRHRU.

Maynard, M. (1985) 'The reponses of social workers to domestic violence', in Pahl, J. (ed).

Moore, D. N. (1979) *Battered Wives*, London, Sage.

Pahl, J. (ed) (1985) *Private Violence and Public Policy*, London, Routledge & Kegan Paul.

Parsons, T. and Bales, R. F. (1956) *Family: Socialisation and Interactional Process*, London, Routledge & Kegan Paul.

Pizzey, E. and Shapiro, J. (1982) *Prone to Violence*, Feltham, Hamlyn.

Spender, D. (1980) *Man Made Language*, London, Routledge & Kegan Paul.

Storr, A. (1970) *Human Aggression*, Harmondsworth, Penguin Books.

Straus, M. A. and Gelles, R. J. (1990) *Physical Violence in American Families*, New Brunswick, NJ, Transantra.

Walker, L. E. A. (1984) *The Battered Woman Syndrome*, New York, Springer.

Walter, J. D. (1981) 'Police in the middle: a study of small city police intervention in domestic disputes', *Journal of Police Science and Administration,* a(3), pp.243-60.

Wetherell, M., and Dallos, R. (eds) (1992) *Interactions and Identities*, Milton Keynes, The Open University.

Yllo, K. (1983) 'Using a feminist approach in quantative research', in Finkelhor et al. (eds) *The Dark Side of Families*.

Yllo, K. and Bograd, M. (eds) (1988) *Feminist Perspectives on Wife Abuse*, London, Sage.

CHAPTER 2
THE ABUSE OF CHILDREN

ESTHER SARAGA

1   INTRODUCTION

During the last twenty years, violence in the family has been put back on the agenda, and the abuse of children, particularly sexual abuse, has been constructed as one of the major social problems of our time. Violence against children reached a new peak in the late 1980s/early 1990s when a seemingly never-ending series of 'secret horrors' were 'uncovered' and reported by the media. These included reports of children being killed, 'tortured' or sexually abused by members of their own families. And there were stories of 'ritual/satanic' abuse; of abuse within children's homes, and of bullying at school. These reports sparked off a call for new legislation, but failed to generate any real debate about why the violence occurred.

Ill-treatment of children is of course not new. It has a long history documented by writers such as Gordon (1989). But the present discourses surrounding it *are* new, and for the first time there is a demand to hear 'the voices of the children'. This demand has come from adult women survivors of child abuse, and from organizations like the National Association of Young People in Care (NAYPIC). The importance of listening to children has also been recognized in professional responses to abuse. For example, in the Report which followed the Cleveland Inquiry — an inquiry set up to investigate the circumstances in which a large number of children had been taken into care over a short time span as a result of suspected sexual abuse in the Cleveland area — it is argued that '…the children themselves may be overlooked. The child is a person and not an object of concern' (Butler-Sloss, 1988, p.245). As a response to increasing reports of child abuse the first counselling service for children, ChildLine, was set up in 1986 and is inundated daily with calls. The Children Act 1989 enshrines in law the recognition that children have the right to be heard and to have their wishes and feelings taken into account in judicial proceedings.

Discussions about the abuse of children can never be purely academic. The pain and suffering are real, even though the meanings attached to their hurt will vary with the historical and political context, and with the social and personal circumstances of each child. Thinking about child abuse can provoke powerful feelings. It touches us all in personal ways, whatever our own relationship to the issue. Sometimes these feelings block thinking and action, because they are too distressing, or because how we feel is in conflict with what we think. Acknowledging and analysing our feelings not only helps us to be able to think about the issues, but also to make sense of the common responses to child abuse, and this may in turn assist the development of theory and explanation.

While children are hurt in a wide variety of ways — many totally unconnected with family relations — current discourses focus mainly on abuse within the family. The abuse of children by their parents violates fundamental beliefs that most of us hold about the nature of family life, which is seen as the cornerstone of society. A common response to this dilemma is denial: 'child abuse doesn't really happen', or 'child abuse is being exaggerated by over zealous or fanatical social workers/feminists/ evangelical Christians'. When outright denial becomes impossible we may distance ourselves, or seek someone to blame, for example by assuming that abuse only occurs in problem families, in overcrowding or in rural or isolated areas, anywhere but in our *own* homes or families. We may persuade ourselves that the abusers must be 'sick', mentally ill or 'monsters'. We can all get angry with children, but no normal person, it is assumed, could ever harm a child, particularly their own child. So abuse is seen as something that occurs *within* families, rather than outside them, and within *other* families, never our own, and to be *exceptional* rather than the norm.

At a political level there is also concern to keep child abuse 'within the family', or more specifically within a set of 'dangerous' or 'inadequate' families, so that the 'normal' family as a valued social institution, and the cornerstone of society, need not be questioned. Thus, following publicity about a case of abuse, the press and public ask 'What went wrong?'. But they are not seeking an explanation for the abuse, rather assuming that there has been a failure of intervention. By focusing on intervention, much more difficult questions about family life, and about the ways that children are abused or neglected through lack of social provision, through poverty, or by racism, are avoided.

More generally, there has been a serious failure to ask *why* abuse occurs. Instead, we frequently find an implicit assumption that the abuse of children will always be with us, so that our concern should be focused on *protecting* children. Consider for example the following statement about child sexual abuse: 'Imagine a society which cared enough about its children to protect them from sexual abuse ... The elements of a child protective society ... include awareness of the problem, provision of help for abusers or potential abusers...' (Cashman and Lambelle-Armstrong, 1991, p.120). It is worth thinking about why it did not seem possible for the authors to write : 'Imagine a society in which children are not abused'.

In this chapter we shall examine the ways in which the physical and sexual abuse of children have been 'rediscovered' since the 1960s, and discuss issues raised by attempts to define and discover the 'facts' about abuse. We shall argue that the way in which the abuse of children has been constructed as a social problem and the way in which it has been theorized have had an enormous impact on intervention. While all accounts are contested, a major theme of this chapter will be the contri-

Figure 2.1

bution made by feminist perspectives. Feminist perspectives are important in defining the problem of child abuse because many of them start
from the *lived experiences* of women and children survivors. Feminists
have also made a major contribution to the development of theory (why do
people abuse their children?), to the opening up of debate, to challenging
what were considered to be 'accepted' ideas and practices and therefore to
helping children and their families.

2 THE 'REDISCOVERY' OF CHILD ABUSE

The abuse of children can be said to have been 'discovered' at the end of
the nineteenth century by social reformers and at the time it became a
matter for great concern in both the USA and Britain. It also led to the
setting up of Societies for the Prevention of Cruelty to Children in both
countries. These societies had a major impact on state intervention, the
goal of which was to reform or improve parenting. In the early part of the
twentieth century, the problem seemed to disappear, while in the period
immediately after the Second World War, the major concern in relation to
child welfare was with 'neglect', and with the relationship between 'maternal deprivation' and 'juvenile delinquency'. Individual cases of cruelty
were recognized, but abuse of children was not seen as a major social
problem. Physical abuse of children was 'rediscovered' in the 1960s, and
sexual abuse in the late 1970s. The way that these are constructed today
as social problems is, in part at least, a result of the different ways in
which they came to the attention of both professionals and the public. We
shall now briefly trace the history of how this all came about.

2.1 PHYSICAL ABUSE

In the 1960s, some doctors, mainly paediatricians, 'discovered' that a number of their young patients had received injuries that could not be explained in terms of either disease or accident. They described this problem in medical journals as the 'battered child syndrome', a choice of label which was very significant because 'it played down the legal and socially deviant aspects and defined it as an illness — a syndrome...' (Parton, 1985, p.51). Later research reported in the medical press identified a whole range of mistreatments of children variously labelled as 'failure to thrive', 'non-accidental injury', 'child abuse' and 'neglect'.

Having 'discovered' abuse, the medical profession were also influential in providing explanations for it, and in early government policy developments. Doctors saw their major concern as *preventing* abuse by *predicting* which children were 'at risk'. They had two major goals: to identify abuse at an early stage, and to intervene, in a therapeutic way, with the parents. Abuse was associated with 'family breakdown', and with parents who had particular psychological characteristics such as 'immaturity', and 'poorly controlled aggression', resulting from their own 'emotionally deprived' childhoods. Research thus focused on identifying these 'risk factors', so that social workers could be provided with 'check lists' against which they could try to 'measure' families. Since 'family breakdown' was usually judged in relation to the white, middle class 'normal' family, these ideas were likely to reinforce racist and class stereotypes about black and working class families. As we shall see in Section 5, this desire to 'predict' which children are 'at risk', and the conceptualization of abuse as a 'symptom' of family breakdown have remained very influential amongst health and welfare professionals.

It was not until Maria Colwell was killed by her stepfather in 1973, that child abuse was finally seen as a major *social* problem. The public inquiry into this case received wide publicity in the media, and had an enormous influence on public attitudes to social work, as well as on policies and procedures for state intervention. Since then, further child deaths, particularly that of Jasmine Beckford, have also had a major impact on child protection practice.

In line with the 'disease' model, it was also argued that child physical abuse occurred equally within all sections of society, even though intervention was directed largely at poor families, who were more likely to come to the attention of the 'authorities'. However this dominant view came to be challenged by other writers who suggested that physical abuse of children was predominantly, though not exclusively, a 'crime of poverty', which required amelioration of the conditions of peoples' lives rather than 'treatment of families'. More generally these writers criticized the focus on abuse within the family, which ignored the wider impact of material conditions and inequality on children's development (Parton, 1985).

2.2 SEXUAL ABUSE

As I mentioned earlier, sexual abuse was 'discovered' in the late 1970s, but like physical abuse, this was '...only a rediscovery of a problem well known to social workers in the nineteenth century' (Gordon, 1989, p.7). In the years between, there was very little awareness of children being sexually abused within their families. Instead the problem was understood in terms of 'perverted strangers' and 'sexually delinquent' girls. This lack of awareness of sexual abuse was strengthened by the influence of psychoanalysis on all casework and therapeutic practice, since Freud had denied the existence of actual abuse, arguing that children fantasize about sexual experiences with their parents. The 'rediscovery' of child sexual abuse has generated a fierce controversy about psychoanalytic theory and practice on sexual abuse, in particular among feminists and psychoanalysts (see e.g. Scott, 1988).

Gordon argues that it is only during periods in which there is a strong women's movement that violence against both women and children is put on to the public agenda. Important elements in the 'rediscovery' of child sexual abuse have therefore been the 1970s feminist campaigns on rape and domestic violence, and the 'speaking out' literature of novels and autobiographies in which women wrote about childhood experiences of sexual abuse (see for example Morrison, 1981; Angelou, 1984; Walker, 1983). These feminist campaigns and literature focused on violence from men, and highlighted the secrecy, denial and disbelief that surrounded sexual abuse. During the 1980s incest survivors set up self-help groups, and feminists produced theoretical accounts which made links between the abuse of women and children within and outside the family, and which described sexual abuse as an 'abuse of male power'.

Professionals too began to recognize the existence of child sexual abuse, but their focus was on abuse within the family, particularly father–daughter incest. They did not acknowledge gender as central to understanding why abuse occurs. Instead, most professionals fitted sexual abuse into their existing analysis of 'dangerous families'. We saw in relation to physical abuse that the terminology itself can convey important meanings, and this is also true of the terms 'incest' and 'child sexual abuse', which are often used synonymously. Feminists suggest that the professional focus on 'incest', while calling it 'child sexual abuse', perpetuates the idea that sexual abuse occurs only or mainly within the immediate family, an idea that is challenged by research evidence (see Section 4.)

The role that adult survivors themselves played in putting child sexual abuse on to the public agenda, has had an enormous impact on the discourses surrounding it, in particular the way in which the need to listen to children is emphasized by professionals from all theoretical perspectives. The disbelief and denial associated with psychoanalysis were replaced by an emphasis on helping children to 'disclose' the abuse, and on believing what they say.

Figure 2.2

However it was the 'Cleveland Crisis' of 1987, and the subsequent Inquiry report, which brought child sexual abuse fully on to the public agenda, just as the Maria Colwell Inquiry had done earlier in relation to physical abuse and neglect. But there was an important difference. Whereas Maria's death was seen as a 'failure' of the social and welfare services, in the Cleveland case medical and social work professionals were accused of 'gross overreaction' when a large number of children were removed from their homes over a short period of time, on suspicion of sexual abuse. The events in Cleveland have subsequently been extensively documented and argued over (see e.g. Campbell, 1988; *Feminist Review*, 1988; Richardson and Bacon, 1991), but one immediate effect of Cleveland was to strengthen again public and professional reactions of denial and disbelief, and to make professional workers more cautious. As with the Inquiries into child deaths, this Report led to further government tightening up of policies, procedures and training.

Since Cleveland there have been further 'scandals' and inquiries reported in the media, some involving allegations of organized or 'ritual abuse' and also evidence of sexual and physical abuse of children in foster and residential care. While this has led to some recognition that abuse does not occur only within the family, nevertheless as we shall see the dominant discourses still focus on the family.

We have seen from this brief historical review that the 'mistreatment' of children has not always been described as 'abuse', and that there are widely differing perspectives on how the abuse of children is explained. Before exploring these perspectives further (in Section 5), we need to take a step back, and ask ourselves some questions about definitions, and about what we can learn from research about the nature of abuse.

3   WHAT IS CHILD ABUSE? — ISSUES OF DEFINITION

In the discussion so far I have effectively taken it for granted that we all know and agree on what is meant by the term 'child abuse'. But such agreement is not reflected in most discussions in the literature on the topic. This is both frustrating: How can we begin to understand the issues when the 'experts' cannot agree among themselves what they are talking about? and worrying: How can we know how widespread the problem is when we don't even know what is being measured? 'If something is to be identified and quantified, it needs unambiguous definition ...the term is unduly vague' (Birchall, 1989, p.3). Practitioners also express concern about the 'absence of a uniformly accepted operational definition' (Richardson and Bacon, 1991, p.18). On the other hand, a Department of Health guide, 'Protecting Children', recognizes that definitions of child abuse will always involve making judgements, and that 'judgement as to what constitutes abuse is therefore in part a matter of degree, opinion and values' (Department of Health, 1988, p.7).

It might be useful to think about how you would define child abuse yourself, and thus see how opinions and values can enter into the argument. Is it possible to have an unambiguous definition?

ACTIVITY I

What does the term 'child abuse' mean to you? It's a good idea to 'brainstorm' — i.e. write down on a piece of paper all the things you can think of that can be done to children, and which you consider to be abusive. The list may become very long, so try to group the items under headings. For example, you might like to use the standard categories used by government departments for headings:

  neglect
  physical abuse
  sexual abuse
  emotional abuse

Did these categories help you to group the items in your list? Are there some items that don't fit into any of these categories? What is missing?

Finally, from your experience with this exercise, do you think it is possible to come up with a satisfactory definition? Pause for a moment and think about some of the difficulties you had trying to produce your own definition.

You may have found, as you were doing this exercise, that you thought of more and more ways that children can be harmed or mistreated or neglected. This has happened in the child abuse literature too. Dingwall suggests that 'the original concerns have been transformed to include virtually any problem which may have an adverse impact on a child and can possibly be attributed to some act of commission or omission by an adult' (Dingwall, 1989, p.29). You may also have recognized the fact that children are harmed not only within their families, or by individuals outside the family, but also by the lack of opportunity to develop, perhaps through poverty, inadequate health or education services, because of racism, sexism, heterosexism or attitudes to disability.

Some writers have acknowledged this wider perspective on child abuse. For example, Gil includes in his definition 'any act of commission or omission by individuals, institutions, or society as a whole, and any conditions resulting from such actions which deprive children of equal rights and liberties, and/or interfere with their optimal development ...' (Gil, 1970, p.16).

BOUNDARIES BETWEEN 'GOOD CARE' AND 'ABUSE'

Defining abuse involves our making judgements about what is 'normal' or 'acceptable'. Some of these judgements may seem quite straightforward, so that in doing Activity 1, you may have decided that some adult behaviour is clearly abusive. But there may be other behaviour about which you felt much less certain. If, at its most general, abuse is defined as anything that deviates markedly from 'good child care', then one way of further developing ideas about definitions is to think about the *boundaries* between 'good care' and 'abuse' in a variety of situations. The following two Activities give you an opportunity to do this in relation to both physical and sexual abuse.

ACTIVITY 2

Think about different ways that parents discipline children. In particular, it might be useful to consider two questions that Newson and Newson asked mothers of young children in a long term survey of child-rearing practices: 'How do you feel about smacking? Do you think it is necessary to smack children?' (Newson and Newson, 1970, p.446).

Whatever your view of smacking, where would you draw the line between legitimate punishment and abuse? Try to give reasons for your answers. Consider to what extent your beliefs are affected by your own experiences as a child or as a parent, and whether you feel comfortable about judging other people's child-rearing methods, or about having your own practices judged.

DISCUSSION

Opinions on smacking differ widely, and people frequently hold their views very strongly. Some people consider that it is always wrong and inexcusable; others oppose smacking but can understand that children can be very 'difficult', and that parents may sometimes lose control; others see it as an appropriate and effective way of teaching children how to behave. Whatever their view, most people would draw a line somewhere. Did you find that your judgement was affected by, for example, the age or gender of the child, the reason for the smack, how hard the child was smacked, whether the child was used to being smacked, and/or whether or not it produced a physical injury?

The Newsons' study, which was started in the late 1950s, is still considered to be the most comprehensive account of attitudes and practices in relation to parental discipline, though you may have noted that in fact it was mothers who were interviewed. The Newsons found during their study that smacking children was very common. For example, 62 per cent of mothers interviewed were willing to smack their one-year-old babies, and 97 per cent of mothers smacked their four-year-old children, 7 per cent of them more than once a day. Although smacking became less common as children got older, boys were smacked much more often than girls. In a more recent study, the Newsons found that despite greater public awareness about physical abuse, 'there has been no decrease in the proportion of mothers willing to smack a one year old baby: 63 per cent of mothers...said they smacked their one year old' (Newson and Newson, 1989, p.1).

Thus the meaning of smacking has to be considered within a wider context of what is considered 'normal' or 'acceptable'. It is clear that in Britain, such behaviour towards children at home is very common. Although five European countries have banned parental physical punishment, in Britain it is not illegal. However, at the time of writing, in early 1992, the Scottish Law Commission is considering whether, and to what extent, parental 'smacking' should become illegal.

ACTIVITY 3

Let us now consider the boundaries between 'normal' affection or touching between adults and children, and sexual abuse.

Consider the following argument from Kempe and Kempe about the boundary between 'what is normal behaviour and what is harmful to the child and the family':

> Most parents have by instinct a good feeling of what is 'right' as they judge it from their own upbringing, from their expectation of normal sexual modesty developing in childhood, and from an understanding that what is appropriate for a small child may be highly inappropriate for an older one. For example, most fathers do enjoy having their baby of either sex with them in the bath and having them safely experience playing in warm water in a happy and asexual setting. This would not be true if the daughter were to bathe with her father at age 3, to say nothing of age 8.
>
> (Kempe and Kempe, 1984, p.48).

What do you think of their example? Would you also be concerned about a 3-year-old girl bathing with her father? Or did you find yourself thinking,

The no smacking

guide to good behaviour

PENELOPE LEACH

Figure 2.3

'Well it depends on the circumstances'?. Were you influenced in your judgement by the norms in your own family? Were there any other norms you found yourself thinking were relevant?

DISCUSSION

For me whether or not the activity was acceptable would depend upon a range of circumstances: for example whether the child wanted to share a bath, or was 'made to'; what the norms were in the family, e.g. how nakedness was handled and whether they usually shared baths. I might wonder whether there was a particular reason for sharing the bath; for example, did the child have a disability requiring physical help, or was there a shortage of hot water? In other words, in order to judge the event, I have to try to understand its *meaning*. Did you note in this example too, how Kempe and Kempe switched from talking about a baby of either sex, to concern for a daughter? Why do you think they did this? Would you make a different judgement about a boy bathing with his father? What about either child bathing with their mother, how would this affect your judgement? And how would these judgements change with the age of the child?

From these examples of smacking and bathing, we can see that, although it is difficult to define physical or sexual abuse *per se*, we can identify some of the factors that affect our judgements of where the boundary lies between 'good care' and 'abuse'.

ACTIVITY 4

Before reading on see if you can make a note of some of the factors which occur to you. Are they different for physical abuse and sexual abuse?

DISCUSSION

Thinking about Kempe and Kempe's example, my own list included: the activity itself (some are clearly abusive under all circumstances); the context and meaning of the behaviour; the intentions of the adult; the child's wishes; the relationship between child and adult; family and cultural norms; the age of the child; the gender of the child and of the adult. I also thought that there were similarities and differences between physical and sexual abuse. In both cases my judgements would vary with the meaning and context of the behaviour, the age of the child and the relationship between the child and adult. However, there were two important differences. Firstly, the gender of the child and the adult seemed to affect the meaning of the behaviour much more for sexual abuse than for physical abuse. Secondly, although the wishes of the child were very significant when judging 'bathing together', they were not relevant to my judgement of smacking.

This last point raises the important issue of 'consent', which is often used as a defence against accusations of sexual assault. On the one hand, it seems to me that the child's consent is relevant when judging activities, such as kissing or hugging, which are 'normal' and 'acceptable' if the child wants them, but which could be considered abusive if 'forced' on the child. On the other hand, there are many acts that I would judge as abusive whatever the wishes of the child. Thinking about 'consent' is important because many children who have been sexually abused feel guilty because they love their abusers, and because they may even have said 'yes'. But if we believe that a child could never understand the full meaning and consequences of sexual activity with an adult, then saying 'yes' is not the same as 'consent'. This issue of consent does not arise with physical abuse of children, since it is never assumed that they consent to being hit, even though they are sometimes said to have 'asked for it', when the adult justifies using physical violence by saying 'I warned her/him that if they did that again, I'd beat them ...' In the previous chapter, we saw that the idea that women like a 'good beating' is often used as an excuse for domestic violence.

We have also suggested that judgements of 'good care' and 'abuse' may depend upon family or cultural norms, and in Activity 2 you were asked to consider whether you felt comfortable about judging other people's child rearing methods, or about having your own practices judged. It is clear that there are no absolute standards of 'good care', and in their study the Newsons certainly found class differences in child rearing practices, including the use of smacking. So how do we make judgements of practices which are different from our own? On the one hand, it is important not to use what is done in our own family as a 'norm' against which to judge other people. On the other hand, if we see all practices as equally valid, interpreting any differences as 'culture', then abusive behaviour may be ignored by explaining it away as 'normal' for that particular family or community. Judgements about child abuse can be difficult to make about groups identified in terms of class, 'culture' 'race' or 'ethnicity', because the child care practices found in white middle class families are too often taken as a norm against which other groups are judged. This means that such judgements must be analysed particularly carefully as they may easily be expressions of racism or class prejudice.

If labelling particular behaviours as 'abuse' will always remain, in the end, a matter of opinion and values, rather than one of definitional accuracy, then we also need to consider who has the power to define abuse. As Dingwall says, 'the struggle to change definitions or to replace one set by another is a conflict which is fundamentally linked to the core values of the society and their implications for the way members should behave towards each other. The outcome of that struggle reflects the distribution of...power...child maltreatment is always a political question' (Dingwall, 1989, p.43).

In this section we have suggested that it is more useful to consider the issues raised when trying to define child abuse than to come to some consensus. However, the lack of simple agreed definitions can cause problems for people who are engaged professionally in the protection of children. To them discussions and debates can seem like a luxury, when they are expected to make decisions and to act. For this reason, all relevant agencies produce guidelines on what constitutes abuse, and the government has provided definitions to be used as a guide for those making decisions about whether to place a child on the Child Protection Register (i.e. the list maintained by social services departments of children felt to be at risk of abuse).

ACTIVITY 5

Think about the following guidelines in the light of the earlier discussion about definitions.

They are taken from *Working Together under the Children Act 1989*, a

Figure 2.4

guide to arrangements for inter-agency cooperation for the protection of children from abuse in England and Wales.

CATEGORIES OF ABUSE FOR REGISTRATION

The following categories should be used for the register and for statistical purposes. They are intended to provide definitions as a guide for those using the register ...

Neglect: The persistent or severe neglect of a child, or the failure to protect, a child from exposure to any kind of danger, including cold or starvation, or extreme failure to carry out important aspects of care, resulting in the significant impairment of a child's health or development, including non-organic failure to thrive.

Physical injury: Actual or likely physical injury to a child or failure to prevent physical injury (or suffering) to a child including deliberate poisoning, suffocation ...

Sexual Abuse: Actual or likely sexual exploitation of a child or adolescent. The child may be dependent and/or developmentally immature.

Emotional Abuse: Actual or likely severe adverse effect on the emotional and behavioural development of a child caused by persistent or severe emotional ill-treatment or rejection. All abuse involves some emotional ill-treatment. This category should be used where it is the main or sole form of abuse.

(Home Office et al, 1991, p.48)

How useful do you think they would be for deciding whether or not a child is 'suffering from or likely to suffer significant harm'. Do any of the categories seem more problematic than others?

4   CAN WE KNOW THE 'FACTS' ABOUT ABUSE? — THE PROBLEMS OF RESEARCH

When dramatic cases of child abuse 'hit the headlines', public anxiety is raised about the scale of the 'problem'. People want to know: How common is the abuse of children? In addition, there is a desire by the public and professionals alike to be able to 'spot' or identify actual or potential abusers. In this section we shall examine the research in this field, to see what is 'known' about child abuse, and to consider whether these questions can be answered.

Most research on child abuse has been based on 'cases' from one of the health or welfare agencies, for example analysing data from the child abuse registers, or studying a sample of families receiving 'treatment' at a hospital. Unfortunately these samples are likely to be highly selective. Firstly, they only provide information about abuse that came to the attention of an agency, and this is likely to be a very small proportion of the abuse that actually occurs. Secondly, we have to consider how these particular cases came to the agency's attention. Were they, for example, the more serious incidents or were class and 'race' biases operating? In her historical research Gordon demonstrates the way that such biases can operate not only in terms of *who* is on file, but also in the way that they are described. She points out that most of the cases she looked at involved immigrants to the USA, and that 'the records abound with derogatory references, even when made with kind intent. One girl making an incest allegation against her father in 1910, and being accused of lying, was called "a romancer but no more so than the average foreign born child." ... White immigrants came in for similar abuse ... The characterization of clients was also saturated with class arrogance' (Gordon, 1989, p.14).

An alternative approach to research is to survey large populations of people. Research on physical abuse has usually surveyed parents, asking them about their attitudes towards, and actual practices in, disciplining their children, as for example in the study by Newson and Newson discussed in the previous section. In contrast to this focus on parents, 'population' research into sexual abuse attempts to study 'victims' by asking a random sample of adults about their childhood experiences. It is interesting to consider why these different approaches have been adopted, in particular why it seems feasible to ask parents about their disciplining of children, but not about their 'sexual' behaviour towards them. The research on sexual abuse is more recent, and has been influenced by the feminist emphasis on learning from the survivors of sexual abuse.

These population studies are likely to yield much richer information, and to avoid the problem of selective samples. They are also the only way of trying to obtain accurate figures on the scale of the problem. The data collected may be presented as *incidence* figures, that is the *number* of children abused each year, or more commonly as *prevalence* figures, that is the *frequency* of abuse within a given population. From the discussion in Section 3, it will be clear that all research findings will depend upon how abuse is defined. A study by Kelly et al. (1991) demonstrates very clearly both the way that the definition used can affect prevalence figures for sexual abuse, and also how assumptions about the meaning and impact of abuse can be implicit in the definition.

In this research, Further Education students were asked an open-ended question about 'unwanted sexual experiences' before the age of 18. The prevalence figures obtained varied from 50 per cent to 5 per cent for women, and from 27 per cent to 2 per cent for men, depending upon which reported experiences the researchers decided to include as 'sexual abuse'. The higher figures included a wide range of experiences, such as 'flashing' and unwanted touching, generally considered 'less serious' abuse, whereas the lower figures included only those experiences involving 'some form of penetration or coerced/forced masturbation' which 'in law, and public perception, would be defined as *serious* abuse'. However this restricted definition excluded 'several on-going abuse experiences where the abuser is a family member' (Kelly et al., 1991, p.21).

It is also interesting to consider 'who' is studied. We have seen that most research has studied 'victims'. Where 'parents' are studied, research in practice focuses mainly on mothers. This was true of the Newson and Newson study, and also of many 'case studies' which include interviews with the mothers, whether or not they are suspected of the actual abuse. While this may be explained in part by the fact that the mother is more likely to be available, it also reflects a view that whoever actually hurt the child, the mother bears some responsibility for failing to protect her or him. Large scale surveys of abusers have not been carried out because they are unlikely to volunteer to take part in research, so information on them has been derived from individual case studies, and is therefore limited in the ways that we described earlier. Nevertheless, attempts to list the psychological characteristics of abusing parents, and to group them into 'typologies', have continued since the 1960s, despite the fact that no consistent patterns have been found. Reviewing some of the early research Gelles found 'profiles of my students, my neighbours, my wife, myself and my son' (Gelles, 1973, p.615). Similarly, working with sexual abusers, Snowdon found that he 'couldn't stop being amazed that they were all regular guys, ordinary working men and average pillars of the community' (Snowdon, 1980, p.56).

Abuse is difficult to talk about, and much of it has been hidden for a long time. Research findings therefore will depend also upon how questions

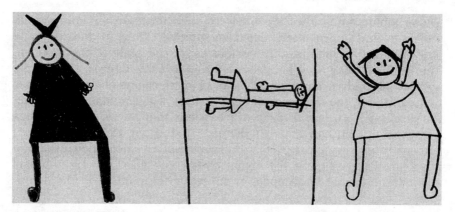

Figure 2.5

are asked, and who is asking them, since this may affect the willingness of parents to admit to certain forms of behaviour, or of adult survivors of abuse to describe their experiences.

While taking account of the difficulties of research discussed here, it may be useful to summarize some of what we do 'know' about physical and sexual abuse, and to draw out some of the important differences between these two forms of abuse.

4.1   SEXUAL ABUSE

Retrospective studies show that sexual abuse occurs both within and outside the family. Apart from 'flashing', which is usually perpetrated by strangers, most abusers are heterosexual adult males who are known personally to the child, and in a position of trust and authority. Children also experience a significant amount of abuse from other children. While both girls and boys are sexually abused, such abuse is more frequent for girls. Girls are more likely to be abused by a family member, boys by a stranger. All research, however conducted, shows that the vast majority of sexual abuse is perpetrated by men. While in the early 1990s some writers were claiming that sexual abuse by women is still waiting to be 'discovered', others point out that despite strenuous efforts to find them, they remain a small minority of cases. Population surveys consistently find that sexual abuse occurs equally in all groups and communities within society; it is not linked in terms of incidence to class, 'race', culture, religion, or area of the country. Case studies of abusers show that it is not possible to identify 'types of men' who abuse, or 'social circumstances' associated with abuse, and that men who abuse within their own family are likely also to abuse children outside the family. There is no strong research evidence of links between sexual abuse of children and domestic violence, although many survivors describe their fathers being beaten by their mothers.

4.2 PHYSICAL ABUSE

Physical abuse of children occurs mainly within the family, and its incidence is linked to class factors, particularly poverty. While research is much more dependent upon 'files' than for sexual abuse, it is argued that this link is not just an artefact of the way in which cases come to the attention of 'the authorities', since even within lower social classes, incidence is related to levels of poverty. No independent link to 'race' or 'culture' has been found. Statistics derived from child abuse registers suggest that women abuse more often than men, but 'if the data is analysed by who the child is living with at the time, then natural mothers were implicated in 36 per cent and natural fathers in 61 per cent of the injury cases when the child was living with them' (Creighton and Noyes, 1989, p.21). Cases of serious injury and death are fortunately rare; the most common form of injury to the children is bruising, which may nevertheless be a cause for serious concern. Research in the USA shows a clear link between physical abuse of children and domestic violence (Finkelhor, 1983, p.22).

Although it is difficult to draw detailed conclusions from the research, nevertheless we can see that some clear patterns have emerged, and that there are some differences between physical and sexual abuse. In the next section we shall be examining the different theoretical perspectives on why abuse occurs, and it will be important to see how well these perspectives can account for the research findings.

5 HOW CAN WE EXPLAIN? — DIFFERENT PERSPECTIVES ON CHILD ABUSE

We want to turn now to the more fundamental question: '*Why* does abuse occur?'. This is not a simple question to ask, let alone answer. It can be asked at different levels, seeking different kinds of answers. For example, we can ask how it is possible for adults *ever* to abuse children, or why particular individuals abuse children, in particular ways. We may try to understand the different gender patterns of abuse, and the differences between physical and sexual abuse. We can ask questions about why abuse is allowed to continue, about what are the ideologies and institutions that sanction, legitimate and even encourage abuse, and about what are the links between violence perpetrated at the level of the individual, and other forms of violence within society.

Spelling out this range of questions helps us to recognize that writers adopting different theoretical perspectives often address different issues, making them sometimes hard to compare. When you come to analyse and evaluate the various perspectives it is important that you consider how the questions are asked as well as how they are answered. Before doing that, you may find it useful to think about all the possible explanations. This may include explanations already referred to in this chapter or the previous chapter, or others that you have thought of, read about, or heard other people put forward.

ACTIVITY 6

Make a list of all the possible explanations for physical abuse and sexual abuse you can think of. Try to 'brainstorm', so as not to restrict yourself to explanations that you find convincing. You may find it easier to focus first on one form of abuse, say physical abuse, and then to consider whether the same set of explanations also apply to sexual abuse. When you have done this, see if you can group your explanations into the following broad headings:

1 Explanations that focus on the individual and his/her psychological characteristics, or childhood experiences.

2 Explanations that describe abuse as a family problem.

3 Explanations that focus on social structural issues — the social circumstances in which people live, or the organization and patterns of inequality within society.

Note that these categories are neither exhaustive nor mutually exclusive. But they help us to characterize the main theoretical perspectives to be found in the literature on child abuse. They are also, of course, similar to the broad categories that you considered in the previous chapter in relation to domestic violence.

Now that you have grouped your explanations into these categories, let us consider them in more detail, and in relation to the research evidence discussed in the previous section. We shall draw out similarities and differences between physical and sexual abuse where appropriate.

5.1 INDIVIDUAL/PSYCHOLOGICAL EXPLANATIONS

One of the apparently most straightforward 'common sense' explanations of child abuse, is that there is 'something wrong' with the perpetrator. S/he may be 'sick' or 'abnormal' or 'criminal'. However, we saw in Section 4 that there is no evidence that abusers can be characterized as certain 'types' of people. Professional discourses have therefore moved away from 'typologies' to consideration of the life experiences of abusers, arguing in particular that adults become abusers because they were themselves abused in childhood. This idea, which is described as the 'cycle' or 'intergenerational transmission' of abuse is so widely accepted, that it has acquired the status of 'truth', and is rarely subjected to critical examination.

When we examine the evidence we find that, although some abusers were themselves abused in childhood, many were not, and many abused children do not grow up to become abusers. Unfortunately most researchers only study abusers, with no control group of non-abusing adults. An exception to this is a study by Herrenkohl et al. on parental discipline, which concluded that the 'intergenerational transmission' of abuse is 'by no means ... an unvarying pattern, (Herrenkohl et al., 1983, p.306).

That the 'cycle' of abuse does not operate in a simple way is apparent if we consider sexual abuse, since the majority of victims are girls yet very little sexual abuse is perpetrated by adult women. Some researchers have tried to deal with this gender discrepancy by considering also the childhood experiences of the child's mother, arguing that women who were sexually abused in childhood are likely in adulthood to seek violent men as partners, and/or to be unable to protect their own children. Other writers have interpreted 'abuse in childhood' more broadly to include a wide range of adverse childhood experiences. But even so, the evidence does not suggest that such experiences will do more than 'significantly increase the risk that a parent will mistreat his or her own children' (Herrenkohl et al., 1983, p.315). It may well be the case that for some individuals their response to experiences in childhood, including experiences of abuse, may be *part* of the psychological processes that lead to their abusing. But research into the 'cycle of abuse' does not help us to understand these processes since it only provides correlations. Attempts to theorize the link between childhood experiences and abusive adult behaviour have made use of several psychological perspectives. For example, it has been suggested, in line with a social learning model of psychological development, that '...victimization at an early age can lead a person to batter his or her own children: battery becomes the model for discipline' (Cole, 1985, p.24). Alternatively, using psychoanalytic concepts, it is argued that '...identification with the aggressor ... can lead to enactment of abusive sexual behaviour towards younger children, either in a homosexual or heterosexual way' (Bentovim and Boston, 1988, p.29). It has also been suggested that women who were not adequately 'mothered' themselves will not be able to provide adequate mothering for their own children, or more generally that 'parents who have been emotionally deprived as children are often consumed with their own needs, turn to their children to fulfil these needs, and become abusive when frustrated in these excessive expectations' (Herrenkohl et al., 1983, p.306).

Thus there are a variety of ways in which abusive adult behaviour is explained in terms of characteristics of the individual, most often in terms of their childhood experiences. However, while experiences in childhood may be formative, they do not *cause* women or men to abuse, nor women to seek abusive partners. All sorts of factors intervene to affect how we deal with childhood experiences. Moreover, the psychological explanations discussed here all fail to consider the social, material and ideological context in which a person's development takes place. Thus it is possible that some women feel disappointed and frustrated with 'motherhood', not only because of their personal experiences of being mothered, but also because of the gap between the ideology of motherhood and the 'real thing'. Similarly some men who were sexually abused may deal with the impact of this by 'acting out' the abuse done to them, by abusing a child, because they have internalized ideologies of masculinity, and learned that sexual behaviour and violence are ways of dealing with anger and powerlessness.

5.2 FAMILY EXPLANATIONS

Perspectives that focus on the family, shift attention away from the behaviour of individual members and suggest instead that abuse is a *family problem*, resulting from events within the family, rather than the actions of individuals. There are different versions of this perspective, but typically a family is viewed as a system, to be understood in terms of both the patterns of interaction and communication within the family, and the 'roles' that individual members adopt. In one particular version, commonly applied to child abuse, it is argued that the needs of individuals are met when all parts of the system are 'functioning' properly. Abuse therefore occurs in, and is a 'symptom' of, 'dysfunctional' families.

A crucial concept in this approach is the notion of 'circular causality': the idea that 'behaviour occurring within a ... family is ... the product of all the members rather than of any one individual ... that one person's behaviour is affected, influenced and maintained by the behaviour of the rest' (Triseliotis, 1987, p.7). Thus, although the child is described as a 'victim' of and 'not responsible' for the abuse, the child is nevertheless part of the circular pattern of interactions. 'He can himself trigger off or provoke some of the responses that subsequently lead to what can be severe physical abuse or other forms of abuse' (Bentovim, 1987, p.60). Similarly the non-abusing partner plays a central role. Thus Dale argues that all the reports of cases of child death support the view that ' ... incidents of serious child abuse invariably involve a triangular relationship between the perpetrator, the victim, and the partner who adopts the role of "failure to protect" the child ...' He describes ' ... the deep pathology within the partner who chooses not to act on warning signs, or who actively supports an escalating process of child cruelty ...' (Dale et al., 1986, p.32).

While this approach has been applied to all forms of abuse within families, it has been particularly influential, and controversial, in relation to child sexual abuse, arguing that it occurs in dysfunctional families in which gender and generational boundaries have broken down. Abuse is thought to serve the function of restoring some kind of equilibrium, and professionals have distinguished different 'types' of 'incestuous families':'conflict avoiding families' in which 'the abuse seems to serve the purpose of avoiding open conflict between the parents' and 'conflict regulating families' in which the 'child is "sacrificed" to regulate ... conflict and to avoid family breakdown' (Porter, 1984, p.11). However, the characteristics of the 'non-abusing' partner, in these cases invariably the mother, is often seen as crucial. Such mothers are described either as having 'withdrawn' from the family or as having failed to fulfil their expected roles, emotionally and sexually. In contrast abusing 'fathers' are described as very dependent and likely, if their needs are not met, to turn to a dependent child for satisfaction of both emotional and sexual needs. So, according to this view, mothers are expected to satisfy the needs of all

Figure 2.6

other members of the family, while men are seen as unable to control their own sexuality, if not 'satisfied' by their wives. Women are also said to 'collude' in the abuse, that is to actively encourage it, or at least not to prevent it, because it serves their own purposes, perhaps, for example, by lessening the chances of domestic violence.

It is this discourse on gender relations and sexuality, and in particular the 'mother blaming' which has produced the most hostility towards the family approach, particularly from feminists (MacLeod and Saraga, 1988), and these criticisms have been accepted by many writers not otherwise sympathetic to a feminist position. More generally critics of the 'family approach' argue that the concept of the 'functional family' supports the ideology of the traditional patriarchal family, with rigidly defined gender roles. It fails to analyse power relations within the family and to see how these are a reflection of the broader societal context. Specifically they argue that it cannot account for (1) gender differences in patterns of abuse, (2) sexual abuse perpetrated by adult men known to the child who are outside the family, and (3) the evidence that men who abuse within their family are very likely also to abuse outside the family.

We saw in the previous chapter that some family therapists have attempted to combine a feminist and family systems approach, arguing that a 'family systems approach is useful if it does not ignore the social structure and societal context' (Masson and O'Byrne, 1990, p.173). Even so, they often fail to consider the meanings conveyed by the concepts and language that they use. For example, Masson and O'Byrne continue to use expressions such as 'abusive families' or 'sexually abusive situations' to describe the families of children who have been abused, as if the 'family' or 'situation' is abusive, not the abuser. Family therapists working from a constructivist position have paid much greater attention to the process of labelling, construction of meanings and the implications of using language which appears to support a view of the family as responsible rather than the individual abuser (Dallos, 1991; Goldner et al., 1990). Some therapists in fact insist as a starting point that the abusing adult fully accepts responsibility. More generally though, the concept of 'circular causality' has been criticized by feminists for offering a meaning which to some extent shares responsibility for the abuse among all family members, including the child.

5.3   SOCIAL CIRCUMSTANCES, SOCIAL STRUCTURES AND CHILD ABUSE

Neither of the approaches considered so far addresses questions posed at the more social level. To examine these, we have to turn to perspectives which analyse the material, social and ideological context of people's lives, and in particular the impact of power inequalities. If you look again at the summaries of research evidence, you will see that the major aspect of social structural inequality linked to the incidence of abuse is different for physical and sexual abuse. Whereas physical abuse has been described as a 'crime of *poverty*', sexual abuse has been described as an 'abuse of *male power*'.

POVERTY AND PHYSICAL ABUSE

In considering the association between poverty and abuse, we need again to move beyond a simple correlation. Poverty does not *cause* abuse; not all children who grow up in poor circumstances are abused, and it is clear that physical abuse also occurs in affluent and middle class families. So how do we make sense of this link?

Most commonly it is argued that the economic, social and psychological 'stress' experienced by people living in poverty, causes individuals to 'hit out' against their children, particularly when they feel 'at the end of their tether'. This kind of explanation fits with 'common sense': most of us have experienced feelings of anger and aggression in the face of frustration, and the desire to be physically violent, whether or not we have acted upon the desire. It is further argued that although people living in poverty are likely to experience *more* stressful situations, explaining the link between incidence of abuse and degrees of poverty, not all poor people will abuse their children, as individuals respond to stressful circumstances in very different ways. Because stress can also be triggered by frustrations that are unrelated to material conditions, abuse will also occur within more affluent families.

There are several problems with this account. Firstly, the meaning of 'stress' needs to be examined carefully, or there is a danger of simply using 'stress' as a label to describe any circumstances in which abuse has occurred. Secondly, it does not explain why, even though women bear the major responsibility for child care, if time and opportunity are taken into account, men are more likely to abuse. Thirdly, it does not account for some of the more 'dramatic' and horrifying cases of abuse, that have involved systematic abuse over long periods of time. Finally, and most

Figure 2.7

importantly, whatever the level of violence, or gender of the abuser, it does not explain why *children* are the target of that abuse. We may feel at the 'end of our tether' in many different situations, most of which do not result in violence. Children are a possible target for aggression and anger, simply because they are weak, and powerless to retaliate. But there are also many ways in which violence towards children is socially legitimated. For example, children are viewed as the property of their parents, who may justify physical abuse in terms of legitimate punishment, or because children fail to live up to parental expectations. So, while the link between poverty and physical abuse must be taken very seriously, in order to explain it we need to consider it within a much broader social context.

5.4   FEMINIST EXPLANATIONS FOR THE ABUSE OF CHILDREN

Feminist perspectives on child sexual abuse developed out of the experiences of adult women survivors of 'domestic violence', rape or sexual assault. They consequently start from the lived experience of women and children, and see power inequalities based on gender as central to any explanation. While many feminists have focused on sexual abuse *within* the family, seeing this as a particularly appalling abuse of power, they make links between all forms of male violence, against women and children, sexual and physical, within and outside families. As with the other approaches discussed, there are different versions of the feminist perspective, but they have in common the description of child sexual abuse as an act of *violence*, and an abuse of *male power*, thus taking the debate away from families, and laying the responsibility for the abuse squarely on the shoulders of the abuser.

Although sexual abuse is indeed an appalling abuse of (usually) male power, to describe it as such is not to *explain* it. All adults have the power to abuse children, simply because of their greater physical strength. Parents also have the emotional power to confuse and control children, as well as the opportunity to abuse in privacy. But recognizing this does not explain why only some adults abuse children, nor does it explain the gendered pattern of sexual abuse. For an *explanation*, we need to examine why power is abused, and why the abuse takes the particular form that it does.

In order to do this feminists analyse the nature of the power inequalities between men, women and children in society, and focus in particular on the construction of male sexuality. Dominant discourses of masculinity describe male sexuality in terms of power, domination and control. At the same time it is seen as 'driven' and 'out of control'. In contrast female sexuality is seen as passive, to be aroused by men. Yet women are also seen as provocative, and as having to take responsibility for controlling men's urges. Boys' experiences of their sexuality develop within this context, so that they learn to objectify women and girls, and to view their sexuality as something powerful that can be used to dominate, to compensate for feelings of powerlessness, or to express anger. Boys have to make sense of their sexuality within the context of ideologies of childhood, femininity and masculinity which legitimate and encourage these feelings. Crucially, feminists argue that these characteristics of sexuality are not peculiar to abusers, but part of 'normal' male sexuality. One reason why feminist accounts are often treated as dangerous and subversive is because, in contrast to the 'individual approach' discussed earlier, they refuse to link abuse to the 'abnormal', sick, or 'deprived', but see it as intimately connected with *normal* relations between men, women and children within society.

Feminists have also criticized the 'mother blaming' that typifies the family approach to explanation, showing how an analysis of the position of women as mothers can help both to explain the extent of 'mother blaming', and also why *some* mothers do not suspect that their children are being sexually abused, or react with disbelief and anger against their child on hearing the news. Firstly, they argue that mothers are seen as 'responsible' for everything that happens to their children: 'good mothers' should, after all, know what is happening to their children, and protect them from all harm. These aspects of the ideology of motherhood are internalized by women themselves, as well as by their children and by professionals. So we can begin to understand the common feelings about 'mothers' and to see why they often come in for even more opprobrium than the men who have carried out the abuse. Secondly, feminists argue that women do not choose to live with, and have children by, men they believe capable of abusing their children. So any suspicions they may have are likely to be reinterpreted in more acceptable ways. Finally, reactions of shock, disbelief, and anger on learning about the abuse are common reactions to bad news, well understood in relation, for example, to bereavement. Subsequently, with hindsight, many women believe that they can 'see' the signs that they missed, and this may add to their sense of self-blame and guilt.

For a long while feminist accounts were ignored, or there was a token acknowledgement of the contribution that feminists made in bringing the issue to light, and of the valuable work that they do in relation to adult 'victims' of rape or domestic violence. However, the growth of a feminist literature which challenged approaches to professional practice, and put forward an alternative feminist practice, meant that these ideas became hard to ignore. While some of the feminist criticisms of 'mother blaming' have been taken on board, feminist accounts have in turn been criticized for denying abuse by women, for applying a model of sexual abuse to an understanding of physical abuse, and for equating the needs and interests of women and children.

Feminists do acknowledge that some women sexually abuse, and that women can be extremely violent and cruel to children. However, the fact remains that they rarely *sexually* abuse, and feminists argue that we will not begin to understand sexual abuse if we ignore gender. Moreover, as many feminist insights into sexual abuse have been more widely recognized, feminist analyses of physical abuse of children have also developed. The focus again is on the power relations between women, men and children, and the recognition that the social bases of femininity and masculinity create different structures of opportunity for women and men, and different patterns of behaviour. Thus women and men, in general, take very different responsibilities for children, and spend very different amounts of time with them. These differences are not only likely to influence their levels of stress, but also the meanings that children have for them. For many women, although motherhood is a central part of their identity, their experience of childcare is very isolating and unrewarding, and it seems likely that children will be the focus of their anger and frustration. For men, physical abuse, like sexual abuse, is seen as an expression of masculinity, of men's 'need' to be powerful and dominant in relation to women and children. So attention is drawn to the evidence, described in Section 4, that, if time and opportunity are taken into account, then fathers are *more* likely than mothers to physically abuse children, and also to the links between domestic violence and physical abuse by fathers.

We can see that for feminist analyses of both physical and sexual abuse 'gender' is central, and that individual behaviour is understood in terms of the ideologies and social conditions of femininity and masculinity, and of motherhood and fatherhood. They recognize differences between physical abuse and sexual abuse, and acknowledge the power that women have in relation to children. While recognizing that the needs of women and children are not identical, they continue to argue that, whether or not women are 'good mothers', the welfare of children is inextricably linked to the welfare of women. However, this perspective also needs to take account of wider social structural factors. And on its own it cannot explain why some individuals abuse, while others do not.

5.5   SUMMARY OF THREE CATEGORIES OF EXPLANATION

At the beginning of this section we suggested that theoretical questions and debate are avoided in most of the literature. It may also be important to consider why some theoretical accounts have been more widely accepted than others. In particular ideas of 'the dysfunctional family' and 'the cycle of abuse' have gained the status of an 'orthodoxy' which cannot be challenged even though, as we have seen, they only address a limited set of questions, and cannot account for many aspects of the research evidence. Such explanations may be popular precisely because they are 'simple'. They suggest that it may be possible to 'predict' who is likely to abuse and to 'treat' individuals or families. At the same time, they can make us feel comfortable, distance 'us' from 'them', take away blame, and explain feelings of powerlessness to prevent abuse. If we do want to try to prevent abuse or 'treat' abusers, then we need to analyse some of the processes that lead particular individuals to become abusers, and to examine the impact and meaning of personal experiences within a much broader social context.

Explanations in terms of social structural factors cannot answer questions about individual abusers, but they attempt to address much broader questions about why abuse occurs, and why it is allowed to continue. We have argued here that there is a particular reluctance to take seriously feminist analyses of gender. One reason for this may be because they raise difficult and painful questions about the relationships between women, men and children and about the nature of families.

We shall see in the final section that how we explain has a crucial impact on how we intervene. It is therefore crucial that all explanations are subjected to critical scrutiny.

6   HOW CAN WE HELP?: THE IMPLICATIONS OF THEORY FOR INTERVENTION

In the final section of this chapter, we shall consider, in general terms, the implications for intervention of the issues that we have discussed. In particular, we shall examine how intervention itself is understood, and the impact on intervention, of the way in which the problem of child abuse has been constructed, defined, and explained.

The most striking development in approaches to intervention since the 1960s is that they have become increasingly bureaucratic, emphasizing the importance of 'multi-agency' cooperation, and applying specialist 'skills', within the correct framework of law and policy. In the 1990s work in this area is described as 'child protection', and there is an emphasis in government guidelines, and in the 1989 Children Act, on the need to work 'in partnership with parents', and to take account of the child's wishes and feelings, and the culture and background of the child and family. (See also **Cochrane, 1993**, for a discussion of the implications of 'partnership'.)

The intense public and professional concern about child abuse has meant that 'social work with families has come to be almost exclusively child protection work ... any sign of a family not coping is almost routinely treated as a case of possible child abuse' (Mellon and Clapton, 1991, p.22). So more general concerns about child care and the welfare of families have been supplanted by 'child protection' issues. Concern that a child may have been abused results in an 'investigation' or 'assessment' to determine the 'facts' — whether or not abuse has occurred, and who is responsible. Prosecutions and care proceedings are, in fact, rare but the focus of such investigations is on the need to obtain *evidence* that can be used in criminal or civil court proceedings, rather than to help children, in a therapeutic sense, to tell their story in their own way. Social workers have argued that the protection and future welfare of the child are being defined in terms of the needs of the police and the law'. '... [T]he investigation ... is often all the local authority help a family receives, in what are often desperate circumstances of poverty and stress ...' (Mellon and Clapton, 1991, p.22). There are virtually no resources in the state sector, and only a few in the voluntary sector, offering long term help or support for either non-abusing parents or for children who have been abused. Yet the need for such services is shown by the fact that ChildLine, operating as a charity, is the only mental health service for children to use. At the time of writing (1992) it receives 10,000 attempted calls a day, of which about 2,000 can be responded to.

How should we understand these developments in state intervention? Firstly, the recognition that children are so consistently abused within their own families can be seen as creating a crisis about the family. There is a need to contain the problem within the realm of the 'abnormal', so that the ideology of the family as the best place for children to be reared can be maintained. It is assumed that 'normal' families cannot only be left to get on with rearing their own children, but also that they can cope without any state intervention, in terms of resources. The state only intervenes into families that fail. Thus '... the child abuse issue helps to define the "good" family and the boundary of state intervention into families' (Frost and Stein, 1989, p.48).

Secondly, 'child protection' work is extremely difficult both because of the feelings that it arouses, and because of the public scrutiny of the work. Not surprisingly therefore there is a huge professional desire for 'certainty' about the nature of abuse, about who does it, why they do it, and what to do to prevent it and to 'treat' abusers. It is important for workers and for agencies to believe that there is a way of 'getting it right', so long as procedures are correctly applied. If things 'go wrong', then the subsequent inquiries also focus on the 'technicalities', examining where the individual workers or procedures 'failed'. 'It becomes almost as if child abuse is *caused* by lack of communication, missing memos or whatever other problems an inquiry has uncovered', and social workers are 'blamed for child deaths as if they were *personally* responsible for them' (Frost and Stein, 1989, p.49).

Figure 2.8

This development of technical solutions can be seen as a way of avoiding theory and debate, which are seen as unhelpful to practitioners struggling to carry out such a difficult task. But this view is based on a misconception that actions, policies and procedures can be theoretically neutral. We have seen how even the terminology and definitions used convey meanings that reflect the perspective of the writers. And apparently 'neutral' discussions of abuse also contain implicit theoretical assumptions. For example, consider the frequent references in the literature on child abuse to 'parents', rather than to 'mothers' and 'fathers'. Treating 'parents' as a unit fails to recognize that mothers and fathers have an unequal relationship, and that they have different relationships both to children and to abuse and it therefore limits the options for helping. When such assumptions are implicit they are much harder to challenge and debate.

The 'technical' approach offers little scope for examining the causes of abuse, for considering resources, or for helping abused children to understand the meaning of their experience and to recover from it. Theoretical debate is vital if we are to offer the best possible help to children, as theory underpins even the smallest actions. This is put very well by Nelson in relation to child sexual abuse:

> ... decisions on how you deal with each family member depend crucially on how you theorize about them. Is he/she mad, bad, sick or

Figure 2.9

inadequate; blameless, collusive or responsible for the whole thing? Are we looking at a family pathology, a Freudian spider's web, a legacy of patriarchy? Theory decides whether you believe a runaway girl's story ... It shapes what you tell the tearful mother ... It determines the policy you design for the offender ... It decides whether or not you intervene at all ...

(Nelson, 1987, p.97)

If actions are always influenced by how we explain, then we need to examine the way in which the dominant explanations have shaped state intervention into families. We have already seen that the accepted 'orthodoxies' are those which preserve the ideology of the 'normal' family, since they locate the abuse of children firmly within the realm of the 'abnormal'. In contrast to this the perspectives which define and explain abuse in terms of social structural inequalities criticize state intervention for preserving the traditional family and gender inequalities, and also for avoiding issues of material inequality and cutbacks in welfare. We have also seen that we may require different explanations for physical and sexual abuse, so it is important to consider them separately when discussing intervention.

ACTIVITY 7

Pause for a moment, and consider for yourself, in general terms, the implications for intervention of some of the approaches discussed in the previous section. In particular, it would be useful to contrast:

1   the 'individual' and 'structural' approaches in relation to physical abuse; and

2   the 'family' and 'feminist' approaches in relation to sexual abuse.

6.1   PHYSICAL ABUSE — 'INDIVIDUAL' AND 'STRUCTURAL' APPROACHES

The 'individual' perspective is associated with the development of 'check lists' of predisposing factors, which help to *predict* in which families abuse is likely to occur. Although there is no evidence that such predictions are possible, check lists can seem very reassuring to workers, and they continue to be sought. The implication of this approach for intervention is that scarce professional resources should be 'targeted' on these families, to monitor them, and to support them in 'better parenting'.

In contrast to this, the 'structural model' explains abuse in terms of the material conditions under which people live, and therefore emphasizes both the provision of resources and political change. It has therefore often been interpreted as an argument for non-intervention — a position which, as its proponents acknowledge, ignores the needs of individual children — and is of little practical use to practitioners. Feminist theory and research have also shown that although state intervention has become increasingly authoritarian it should not be seen purely in terms of 'social control'. Many women seek support from the state for themselves and their children, in relation to violent men, even when this involves the risk of losing their children (Gordon, 1989).

6.2   SEXUAL ABUSE — 'FAMILY' AND 'FEMINIST' MODELS

If abuse is seen as a symptom of something wrong in the family, then decisions about 'protection' of the child focus on whether or not the family is or can be helped to become a safe place, or whether the child should be removed from home. In practice, much of the discussion focuses on the mother's role in the family, in particular asking whether she 'knew' about the abuse, whether she 'colluded', and whether she 'failed to protect' her child. By conveying a meaning that she *should* have known, the intervention may serve to strengthen her denial. In contrast, a practice influenced by a feminist perspective emphasizes the responsibility of the individual abuser, and therefore aims to remove him rather than the child from the home, so that the child can remain in the 'non-abusing' part of the family. It also recognizes that the mother has herself suffered a loss and betrayal, that she may need help in her own right to accept what has happened in order to be able to make decisions, and to support her child.

From these brief descriptions it is clear that different perspectives lead to very different approaches to practice. However there is reluctance among professionals to acknowledge this. A further consequence of the 'technical' approach to intervention is that the meaning and impact of abuse for individual children is ignored. We want to conclude this section by illustrating this in relation to (1) the impact of 'race' and racism on child protection work, and (2) the process of 'survival'.

6.3   'RACE' AND RACISM

Although we have seen, from the research, that there is no relationship between 'race' and the incidence of physical or sexual abuse, nevertheless any form of abuse may occur as a direct or indirect expression of racism. 'Race' and racism can have a profound impact on the *recognition* of abuse, on the *meaning* for abusers and 'victims', and on the *options* available to children and to families. We shall illustrate this in relation to sexual abuse.

Firstly, whether abuse is *recognized* may depend upon a range of myths and stereotypes about particular groups. For example, black women have written about the way that racism and the cultural stereotypes associated with it, have contributed to a silence about the sexual abuse of black children,

> ... sexual abuse ... has for a long time been portrayed and dealt with as a 'white' problem. Books ... have ignored and excluded any experiences of what it means to be a Black survivor ... Incest has been seen and believed to be the norm within the Black culture and way of life. This is not true.
>
> (Bogle, 1988, p.134).

Secondly, racism has an impact on the *meaning* that children may take for what has happened to them. 'What ... it means to have been abused is different for each incest survivor, depending on their other experiences. Black women survivors have the experience of racism as a factor in the meaning for them' (Bogle, 1988, p.134). This point is graphically illustrated by the personal account of a Jewish woman sexually abused by her father:

> I didn't know who I could tell. I didn't really want other people to find out. The children at school already taunted me with being a 'dirty jew'. There was a lot of anti-Semitic feeling then. They would get in a circle and chant 'yid, yid, dirty yid', so I thought they would see what my father was doing as part of being a dirty jew.
>
> (Driver and Droisen, 1989, p.74).

Thirdly, this last example also illustrates the way *options* for children to tell may be even further limited by racism. 'I didn't tell anyone at school about it...I didn't want to hurt my family, and I certainly didn't want to be seen to be doing so. I was Black and my teachers were white. I didn't want to be taken away to a white children's home' (Driver and Droisen, 1989, p.81). So, for children who are part of a community that is a target of racism, 'disclosure' may seem like an even greater betrayal. It can also result in greater losses, loss of community and culture, as well as of family, if the child is removed from home.

And because of racism, state intervention has a very different meaning for black families.

> Black women, in trying to protect their own children, face racism from the police which can compound the abuse already suffered by the children... They find themselves in a cleft stick wondering whether to go for police involvement or not. Social Services are often not sympathetic to the quandary that mothers and children feel on this question.
>
> (Bogle, 1988, p.134)

6.4   THE PROCESS OF SURVIVAL

Finding an explanation is also a crucial part of the process of *personal* survival for those who have been abused. 'Why did he do it?' and 'Why me?' are part of the agony experienced by child and adult survivors, who often find it hard to move away from blaming themselves. Different theoretical perspectives again have different implications for understanding survival, and therefore also for helping. Traditionally, children are seen as showing 'symptoms of abuse' leading to 'long term effects' or 'consequences', requiring medical or psychiatric treatment. For example, child sexual abuse is said to be likely to lead to prostitution, to becoming an abuser (for men), or to becoming a 'victim' of abuse, or a 'colluding mother' (for women).

In contrast, feminists see abuse not as a 'symptom of a disease', but as an experience which can be survived. The term 'survivor' itself came from incest survivors who rejected the use of the term 'victim' because it implied passivity. As a result most of the discussion of survival has focused on sexual abuse. 'Survival' is seen as an active process, as a journey to recovery, and it is recognized that even young children may resist what is being done to them, even though they may be powerless to stop it. 'Symptoms' such as 'cutting off their feelings', technically described in the medical discourse as 'disassociation', can be reinterpreted as acts of resistance. This approach also recognizes that there may be different routes to the same outcome. For example, some sexually abused girls may have been directly taught prostitution, while others may enter into it as a way of 'getting at' men, and some as an expression of self-hatred. Or there may be no direct connection; young women who protect themselves by running away from home, may find that prostitution is the only way that they can earn money to live.

Theorizing about survival in this way is important because it allows survivors to tell their own story in a way that can take account of both personal circumstances and experiences such as racism, disability, or sexual preference. Although the abuse can never be forgotten, it can become less painful and cease to dominate a survivor's life. Other insights from theory and research may be relevant too. Thus, many survivors of sexual abuse have described the importance for them of being believed and supported by their mothers, and the pain and distress that can continue into adulthood if this has not happened. So feminist practices at earlier stages of intervention, that focus on trying to support the relationship between a woman and her child, can be seen to be contributing also to long term survival.

Figure 2.10

Discussions of child abuse can leave us feeling helpless and powerless, and there is a danger that we respond to that with disbelief and denial. It can be helpful to remember that human beings do often survive the most horrific experiences, including child abuse. To stress this is not to deny the nature of many of their experiences, nor to deny that some children may be completely crushed by them. But it is important to learn about the process of survival in order to help others to survive, and it is important for survivors that they are not viewed, and do not see themselves, purely in terms of their experience of abuse. Accounts of individuals surviving a range of traumatic experiences, have demonstrated that struggling to find a meaning is a key part of the process of recovery, a meaning that the survivor can live with and which removes self-blame (Levi, 1989). It follows that the meaning that professional workers convey through the language that they use, the way that they explain and how they intervene, will have an enormous influence on the survivor's own construction of the meaning of the abuse.

REFERENCES

Angelou, M (1984) *I Know Why the Caged Bird Sings*, London, Virago.

Bentovim, A. (1987) 'Breakdown of parenting function in abusing families: how can professionals think about these issues and be helpful?' in Maher, P. (ed) *Child Abuse – The Educational Perspective*, Oxford, Blackwell.

Bentovim, A. and Boston, P. (1988) 'Sexual abuse — basic issues — characteristics of children and families' in Bentovim, A., Elton, A., Hildebrand, J., Tranter, M. and Vizard, E. (eds) *Child Sexual Abuse within the Family: Assessment and Treatment*, London, Wright.

Birchall, E. (1989) 'The frequency of child abuse — what do we really know?' in Stevenson, O. (ed) *Child Abuse*, London, Harvester Wheatsheaf.

Bogle, M.T. (1988) 'Brixton Black Women's Centre: organizing on child sexual abuse', *Feminist Review*, 28, pp.132–5.

Butler-Sloss, E. (1988) *Report of the Inquiry into Child Abuse in Cleveland 1987*, Cmnd 412, London, HMSO.

Campbell, B. (1988) *Unofficial Secrets*, London, Virago.

Cashman, H. and Lambelle-Armstrong, A. (1991) 'The unwanted message: child protection through community awareness' in Richardson, S. and Bacon, H. (eds).

Cochrane, A. (1993) 'Challenges from the Centre' in Clarke, J. (ed) *A Crisis in Care? Challenges to Social Work*, London, Sage.

Cole, S. (1985) 'Child battery' in Guberman, C. and Wolfe, M. (eds) *No Safe Place*, Toronto, The Women's Press.

Creighton, S. J. and Noyes, P. (1989) *Child Abuse Trends in England and Wales 1983–1987*, London, NSPCC.

Dale, P., Davies, M., Morrison, T. and Waters, J. (1986) *Dangerous Families*, London, Tavistock.

Dallos, R. (1991) *Family Belief Systems, Therapy and Change: a Constructional Approach*, Buckingham, Open University Press.

Department of Health (1988) *Protecting Children: a Guide to Social Workers Undertaking a Comprehensive Assessment*, London, HMSO.

Dingwall, R. (1989) 'Some problems about predicting child abuse and neglect' in Stevenson, O. (ed) *Child Abuse*, London, Harvester Wheatsheaf.

Driver, E. and Droisen, A. (eds) (1989) *Child Sexual Abuse*, London, Macmillan.

Feminist Review (1988) 'Family Secrets: Child Sexual Abuse', Special Issue no.28.

Finkelhor, D. (1983) 'Common features of family abuse' in Finkelhor et al. (eds).

Finkelhor, D., Gelles, R. J., Hotaling, G. T. and Straus, M. (eds) (1983) *The Dark Side of Families*, London, Sage.

Frost, N. and Stein, M. (1989) *The Politics of Child Welfare*, London, Harvester Wheatsheaf.

Gelles, R. J. (1973) 'Child abuse as psychopathology: a sociological critique and Reformulation', *American Journal of Orthopsychiatry*, no.43, pp.611–21.

Gil, D. (1970) *Violence against Children*, Cambridge Mass, Harvard University Press.

Goldner, V., Penn, P., Sheinberg, M. and Walker, G. (1990) 'Love and violence: paradoxes of volatile attachments', *Family Process*, vol. 29, no. 4, pp.343–64.

Gordon, L. (1989) *Heroes of Their Own Lives*, London, Virago.

Herrenkohl, E. C., Herrenkohl, R. C, and Toedter, L. J. (1983) 'Perspectives on the intergenerational transmission of abuse' in Finkelhor et al. (eds).

Home Office, Department of Health, Department of Education and Science, Welsh Office (1991) *Working Together under the Children Act 1989*, London, HMSO.

Kelly, L., Regan, L. and Burton, S. (1991) *An Exploratory Study of the Prevalence of Sexual Abuse in a Sample of 16–21 year olds*, London, Child Abuse Studies Unit, Polytechnic of North London.

Kempe, R. S. and Kempe, C. H. (1984) *The Common Secret*, New York, W. H. Freeman & Company.

Levi, P. (1989) *The Drowned and the Saved*, London, Sphere.

MacLeod, M. and Saraga, E. (1988) 'Challenging the orthodoxy: towards a feminist theory and practice', *Feminist Review*, 28, pp.16–55.

Masson, H. and O'Byrne, P. (1990) 'The family systems approach: a help or a hindrance?' in Violence Against Children Study Group (eds) *Taking Child Abuse Seriously*, London, Unwin Hyman.

Mellon, M. and Clapton, G. (1991) 'Who are we protecting?', *Community Care*, 7 March, pp.22–4.

Morrison, T. (1981) *The Bluest Eye*, London, Triad Grafton.

Nelson, S. (1987) *Incest: Fact and Myth*, Edinburgh, Stramullion.

Newson, J. and Newson, E. (1970) *Four Years Old in an Urban Community*, Harmondsworth, Penguin.

Newson, J. and Newson, E. (1989) *The Extent of Parental Physical Punishment in the UK*, London, APPROACH.

Parton, N. (1985) *The Politics of Child Abuse*, London, Macmillan.

Porter, R. (ed) (1984) *Child Sexual Abuse Within the Family*, London, Tavistock/CIBA Foundation.

Richardson, S. and Bacon, H. (1991) (eds) *Child Sexual Abuse: Whose Problem?*, Birmingham, Venture Press.

Scott, A. (1988) 'Feminism and the seductiveness of the "real event"', *Feminist Review*, 28, pp.88–102.

Snowdon, R. (1980) 'Working with incest offenders: excuses, excuses, excuses', *Aegis*, 29, pp.56–63.

Triseliotis, J. (1987) '"Family Therapy" or working with families', *Practice*, 1, pp.5–13.

Walker, A. (1983) *The Color Purple*, London, The Women's Press.

CHAPTER 3
MENTAL HEALTH

RUDI DALLOS AND DAVID BOSWELL

I   INTRODUCTION

This chapter develops the theme of family problems and models of intervention as divided between the private and public. Following a brief historical review we will attempt to show how traditional definitions of 'mental health' persist and continue to construct the experiences of those undergoing psychological distress as well as those treating them. A range of models and their links to the prevailing discourses will be presented followed by the implications for their treatment. In comparison with domestic violence and child abuse the mental 'illness' appears to be viewed with more compassion in our society. However, this appearance of benevolence may be illusory and instead may serve to perpetuate a distortion of mental distress as simply a 'private', personal matter — the 'myth of mental illness'. This may distract attention from 'problems of living' which arise in our society from the 'public' domain, such as racial, gender and class related stresses and inequalities that individuals and their families have to contend with.

As with the earlier chapters we want to discuss how culturally shared discourses construct the experiences of individuals and families. In the case of mental illness the discourses construct how sufferers regard themselves, and their experiences and what hope for recovery they and their families may have. Likewise, the discourses construct the development of scientific explanations and interventions that are formulated and implemented. In addition to the discourses about 'failure' that are attributed to and pervade the experiences of families where abuse and violence have occurred, a process of 'invalidation' can occur in families who experience mental illness. There is a tendency to regard mentally ill people as having a 'faulty' view of the world, as being irrational, incoherent, in short that we cannot make sense of what they are saying and doing. Yet as we will see later, personal accounts suggest that mentally ill people can be coherent and are able to reflect eloquently on what is happening or has happened to them. The discourse of psychological distress as evidence of 'mental illness' or 'madness', however, can contain the all-encompassing assumption that all of a person's actions are senseless or 'mad' (see Porter, 1987).

The widely used terms; madness, lunacy, possession, craziness are now embraced by the apparently more neutral term, 'mental ill health'. First, the term 'mental ill health' contains the assumption that disruptions in our psychological state, our emotions and thoughts are basically analogous to physical illnesses or diseases. Second, but less obviously, the term contains the assumption that we are talking about individuals, mentally

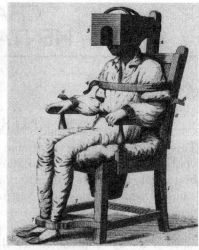

Figure 3.1   (a) The crib, an early method for restraining mental patients

(b) The 'tranquillizing chair' used by Benjamin Rush as a means of treating mental disorders

Source: Davison and Neale (1982) pp.20–2

healthy or unhealthy persons rather than a mentally unhealthy society or, as we will discuss later, mentally unhealthy groups of persons, namely families. The linking of the terms mental and health encourages us to ascribe individual responsibility for our mental health. Just as we can become ill by eating the wrong foods, not getting enough exercise, drinking and smoking too much, so it follows that we can, in a similar way, make ourselves mentally ill.

This line of reasoning may seem 'natural' and compelling yet Foucault (1967) describes how, in one form or another, the 'mad' have generally suffered in various, sometimes horrendous, ways throughout the ages, from the activities in the middle ages to exorcise demons to the dunking and burning of 'witches', women who were in some ways deviant and not infrequently mentally disordered. Even the reforms of the nineteenth and twentieth centuries, marked historically by Pinel's removal of chains from the insane in the La Bicêtre asylum in Paris, did not halt the detention of mentally disturbed people in asylums against their will and in many cases probably against their own good. Thomas Szasz, an American psychiatrist, argued passionately that 'the detention of persons in mental institutions against their will — is a form of imprisonment ... it is a crass violation of contemporary concepts of fundamental human rights' (Szasz, 1970, p.113).

In the guise of offering help and sanctuary, gross violations such as electric shock treatments, lobotomy, immersion in water, medication, being locked in various forms of restraint such as the straitjacket, the 'tranquillizing chair' and the 'crib' have been carried out (see Figures 3.1(a) and 3.1(b)).

It is salutary to note in the context of these forms of 'treatment' that most attempts at assessing the state of mental health in the general population have found that a large proportion of us display, at one time or another, symptoms no less serious and acute than some of these 'patients' had on entry to a hospital. Until relatively recently it was a fairly safe bet that a person would deteriorate in places like a Victorian lunatic asylum, and that the chronic and even some florid states that patients displayed were not the causes of their confinement but a result of years of institutionalization. In many cases they were initially no more disturbed than many ordinary citizens who do not, for a variety of reasons we will explore later, ever spend time in hospital. From this perspective we can see such treatments, albeit perhaps well-intentioned, as more akin to torture and an abuse of human rights. Some of the unfortunate effects of an abstract discussion are to distance ourselves from and depersonalize the sufferers, to treat them as if they were essentially different — less than human. This can be a very unfortunate and damaging error as the following account poignantly illustrates:

CASE STUDY 1

I know I'm a 37-year-old woman, a sculptor, a writer, a worker. I live alone. The illness has certainly stripped me of any pretence now, leaving me, instead, feeling hollow, yet hurting....There are still occasional episodes of hallucinations, delusions, terrible fears, and I have medication for these times. It relieves my mental stress, but I hate my bodily responses to it and the dulling of my healthy emotions. Therefore, I stop using the drug as soon as the storms in my mind subside. And I kept wondering why there isn't more emphasis on alternative therapies...I've searched in library books and in articles about schizophrenia hoping to find other solutions and answers to my whys, how long, what's the cure.

I'm still searching, questioning — I know all the negatives: schizophrenia is painful, and it's craziness when I hear voices, when I believe people are following me, wanting to snatch my very soul. I am frightened too when every whisper, every laugh is about me; when newspapers contain curses, four-letter words shouting at me; when sparkles of light are demon eyes. Schizophrenia is frustrating when I can't hold on to thoughts; when conversation is projected on my mind but won't come out of my mouth; when I can't write sentences but only senseless rhymes; when my eyes and ears drown in a flood of sights and sounds...

Should I let anyone know that there are moments, just moments, in schizophrenia that are 'special'? Where there's an awareness, a different sort of vision allowed me? Moments which I can't make myself believe are just symptoms of craziness and nothing more.

Source: McGrath, M. E. (1984), in Gottesman, (1991), p.41–3

2   PERCEPTIONS OF MENTAL ILLNESS AND ITS LEGAL MANAGEMENT

The notion of illness contains both 'subjective' and 'objective' aspects. A person may have a set of experiences that are likely to be felt as negative — distressing, handicapping and frightening. The experiences may range from acute disorientation, hallucinations such as hearing voices or an all encompassing sadness and sense of worthlessness; in depressive illnesses: 'I feel miserable ... I just feel hopeless ... I'm worried about everything. ... I don't see any point to living ... I loathe myself. ... I don't feel anything towards my family. I don't give a damn about them. I know this is terrible but sometimes I hate them' (Beck, 1967, extracts from pp.14–21).

Added to this experience is likely to be the culturally shared belief that, unlike physical illnesses, their condition is unpredictable, inexplicable and without a clear sense of hope for recovery. For the family of a sufferer this culturally shared pessimistic view can add to the sense of despair, anxiety and feeling of impotence regarding how to help their relative. The experiences described by people are necessarily subjective and idiosyncratic. To say that two people hear voices does not tell us what the voices are saying or what the messages mean to each of them.

One of the major concerns of psychiatry has been to place mental illness on a 'scientific' footing, moving beyond subjective definitions of problems by developing 'objective' diagnostic systems in order to distinguish between and classify various forms of mental disorders. One of the first attempts at classification of mental illness was by the Greeks in the fifth century BC when Hippocrates classified mental disorders into *mania, melancholia* and *brain fever* and suggested that they were illnesses with natural causes and hence should be treated like other common maladies such as colds and constipation. Through several revivals this ancient formulation has persisted and was refined to suggest that there were two major groups of severe mental illness; dementia praecox (madness of adolescence), now termed schizophrenia, and manic-depressive psychosis (American Psychiatric Diagnostic Standard Manual III revised, 1980).

Although the particular patterns of mental illness will be discussed in later sections, it is most important to understand that doctors' perceptions of what constitutes madness and how it may be noted in different social milieux is not an end of the matter. The legal definitions and status of mad people and the codification of the ways in which they may be treated are part and parcel of the experience of being treated as mad. In Britain the Lunacy Acts have always raised the significance of civil liberties but the legal specification of modes of treatment and places of detention have done little more than indicate the official staff duties and authorized places in which patients could be detained, i.e. admitted and treated against their will. Diagnosis has been left to the doctors of the day and the laws direct the procedures for dealing with those categories of people assessed as being liable to them.

Joan Busfield stresses the association between conceptions of treatment, i.e. asylum as an end in itself, the role of asylums in the general poor law inmate system after 1835, the lack of places in which to put such people away and the alliance of capitalist and philanthropic interests in such reform (Busfield, 1986, pp.249–50). Certification by the local magistrates, and after 1890 by a magistrate's order following medical certification, was not based on curability and medical direction was required rather than treatment. The 1913 *Mental Deficiency Act* established the ways in which those termed mentally defective should be similarly dealt with. Although the law set out to safeguard civil liberties, and hence left authority with lay magistrates, once certified a person's legal status was in general effectively changed permanently, and discharge from a certified institution required extensive procedures of its own.

The 1930 *Mental Treatment Act* and the 1959 *Mental Health Act* extended hospital treatment of 'voluntary' patients and concentrated on the legal problems of detention, extending the decision making to doctors and mental welfare officers, and left the rest to local authorities to develop if they wished. Busfield (p.141) points to changing models of care, in particular the medical model of illness based on the inner workings of the individual, with which were associated both a psychiatric professionalism, based on acute treatment rather than custodial direction, and its general mode of operation through the use of psychotropic drugs. But it was a national system of medical and social work organization, coupled with social security payments as out-relief, that made the role of residual institutional provision and policing less necessary and appropriate. This use of hospitals as places for treatment was emphasized in the 1983 *Mental Health Amendment Act*, which introduced the concept of consent to treatment and reinforced the civil liberties of potential patients. During the period between the implementation of the two Acts, 1961–1984, the percentage of compulsorily detained, rather than informally admitted, in-patients had fallen from 20.6 to 8.0 per cent.

Irrespective of the medical or general definitions and perceptions of mental illness in contemporary societies, problems presented by such people have been largely managed through processes of law and medical administration. This indicates just how much public action has been taken with reference to what may often be presented and diagnosed as individual misfortune or illness.

2.1 PRIVATE VS PUBLIC PROBLEMS: WHOSE PROBLEM IS IT?

For whom is mental illness a 'problem'? The medical definitions smuggle the assumption that it's a private and personal problem into both the subjective and objective definitions. Yet this ignores the fact that mental illness is also seen as socially deviant and the behaviour of mentally ill people is regarded as problematic and a 'nuisance' in short, socially disruptive to those who are contrasted as 'normal'. The behaviours of the mentally ill are regarded as violating important social rules and norms and thereby inducing embarrassment, anxiety, anger and fear in others, perhaps most significantly members of the person's family and friends. The relatives may feel that they are unable to 'control' the actions of the mentally ill person yet feel obliged to do so. What is acceptable varies however within our own culture according to gender, class and race but is likely to be experienced within the family, and sometimes by mental health professionals, in an undifferentiated way. Superimposed on all this is the legal and administrative framework through which problematic people are dealt with, sometimes leading to short- or longer-term detention, and a variety of health and other services may be provided. The assumption is that most people will look after their own mentally ill relatives or if not that they will perform reasonably satisfactorily in the community at large.

3   PATHWAYS TO MADNESS

Goldberg and Huxley (1980), in reviewing a series of studies which attempted to assess rates of mental disorder in the community at large, concluded that: 'it is quite clear that even in the developed countries of the world, most mentally disordered patients are not being treated by the psychiatric services' (Goldberg and Huxley, 1980, p.3). In random samples of people interviewed visiting their GPs, in Manchester in the UK and in the USA, they found that 250 out of 1,000 said they experienced distressing psychological symptoms. Of these 230 had complained to their GPs about their problems, of whom 140 were identified by the GPs as having clear psychological problems. Seventeen were referred to a psychiatrist and of these six ended up in a psychiatric hospital or residential unit. For serious forms of mental illness it has been suggested that approximately 1 per cent of the population are likely to suffer from schizophrenia in ways that lead to treatment, though the number having some symptoms is likely to be far higher. In the case of depression, Brown and Harris's (1978) study of housewives in south London found that: 'as many as seventeen per cent of the 458 women we saw in Camberwell were psychiatrically disturbed at some time in the year. ... Most of these were suffering from depression' (Brown and Harris, 1978, p.57). In addition, a further 19 per cent were described as borderline cases showing some significant signs of depression and anxiety. One in seven women and one in eight men are likely to suffer from some form of mental disturbance severe enough to lead to psychiatric treatment at some time in their lives.

Mental disorders therefore appear to be widespread in the community but only a small proportion of people experiencing problems end up on the registers of the mental health services. Goldberg and Huxley suggest that whether people end up receiving treatment depends not only on the severity of their symptoms but also on the initial responses of people with whom they are in frequent or regular contact. They suggest that the 'pathway to psychiatric care' can be seen as a series of 'filters' (see Figure 3.2).

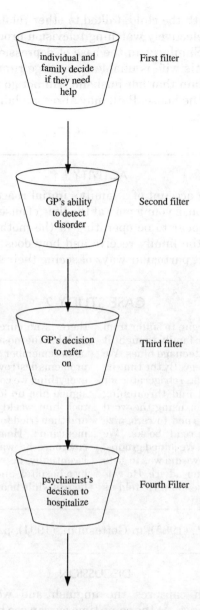

individual and
family decide
if they need
help

First filter

GP's ability
to detect
disorder

Second filter

GP's decision
to refer
on

Third filter

psychiatrist's
decision to
hospitalize

Fourth Filter

Figure 3.2

The first of these 'filters' involves the person and those closest to him or her. Progress through this filter depends upon a number of factors such as the tolerance level of their family, whether there is a tradition in the family of coping with distress in their members by calling in outside professionals, the psychological state of the other members of the family and the general tolerance of their local community (Haley, 1980; Burnham, 1980). For example, parents frequently describe how, over a period of time, they have noticed strange behaviours on their child's part and become concerned about what to do about it. They may have tried to discuss matters with the child, talked to other relatives or friends, read books or started selectively watching television programmes which deal with such issues. Similarly, in the case of depression, a man may start complaining that his wife is unable to manage running the house, or a woman may complain that her husband will not go to work or carry out his chores around the house. Both may also complain that their relationship is deteriorating.

ACTIVITY I

Read the following account of a family's initial reactions to signs of disturbance in their son, a young man at the time of onset. Make a note of the discourses that appear to be operating in the mother's accounts. What initial advice did the family receive and how does this appear to have started to construct particular ways of seeing their son?

CASE STUDY 2

When Dan first began to suffer from schizophrenia, our family thought it was just a case of teenage blues. We sent him off to college. By the time he began attacking the refrigerator for reading his mind and threatening family members for using the word 'right', we had learned to recognize his disease. We read books. We attended lectures. We joined groups. But the first thing we did was to go to our family doctor for advice. He was an honest and wise man. He told us there is no cure for schizophrenia, and that the most important thing for us to remember was not to let Dan's problems destroy the family... We did everything we could to help Dan. We signed him up for a specialist... We took him weekly to a psychiatrist, and then tried to see that he took his medicine ... He never took his medicine once he was away from us ... Eventually, he would be reaccepted by a hospital, and we sat with heavy hearts while heaving sighs of relief.

Source: Piercy, B.P., (1985), in Gottesman, (1991), p.167

DISCUSSION

This account both captures the anguish and weariness that often envelops such families. At the same time we can see how from a definition of their son's problems as 'just a case of the teenage blues' they come, through their contact with the medical professions (in the first instance their family doctor), to 'recognize' his problems as indicative of an 'illness' for which there is 'no cure' and which could, if they were not careful, 'destroy the family'. This was a very powerful framing of the problem and one with which their son, in his reluctance to take his medication, appeared, initially at least, to disagree. The discourse of the mentally ill as irrational and not capable of responsibility; this therefore implies that Dan does not know what is best for him and must therefore be persuaded or even compelled to take his medication.

Family members are the most likely to voice the initial signals of concern because such care is generally considered the family's 'responsibility' or their *'obligation'* (Finch, 1989). Friends, neighbours, and even the police may also be called in, especially in cases of the more bizarre or violent aspects of schizophrenic behaviour, to assist the family. We should note that it is precisely at this point of crisis that hidden culturally-shared assumptions about the *duties* of family members to 'care' for each other become explicit. In fact often family members attempt to shoulder the burden of responsibility for an excessively long time not just because they feel guilty but because their guilt is aggravated by others if they try to unload the burden and seek help (Terkelsen, 1983). A second example illustrates a family's sense of duty even in the face of a progressive deterioration:

CASE STUDY 3   THE MARTIN FAMILY

The Martin family consisted of Terry aged 26, and his two parents. Both parents were university graduates and involved in the teaching profession. They had been keen for Terry to pursue his education which he had attempted to do, attending various universities but dropping out of each course after a year or less. At university he was something of a 'radical' and dressed very colourfully, took some illegal drugs, generally behaved in an increasingly anarchistic manner and was reported by his parents as becoming increasingly withdrawn, disordered and rambling in his speech, generally disorganized and unable to run his life. In between university courses he occasionally worked in various jobs for a short while such as bookshops. His parents were committed socialists, critical of conventional social values in general and Terry had attended CND marches with his father and other political events. As Terry's anarchistic phase progressed he increasingly directed his criticism and anger at his parents and accused them of having 'sold out' on their political beliefs. He would come round to their house and engage in 'urban terrorism'; breaking in, leaving the house squalid and insisting they give him money. Eventually the parents sought help from their local G.P. and contacted the police to try to protect themselves (though in fact Terry never physically attacked them). Following some attempts at providing medication for Terry, which did little to halt his actions towards his parents, the GP referred him to a psychiatrist for assessment.

Terry was seen by a psychiatrist and eventually was compulsorily admitted under a mental health act section to a psychiatric hospital with suspected schizophrenic symptoms and put on a programme of medication. Terry bitterly resented the hospitalization and on release from hospital resumed the 'urban terrorism' with increased vigour. The mental health services were not sure that hospitalization was the most appropriate intervention. A psychiatric social worker was attached to Terry and his family and assistance was offered to find him housing and help him with other practical matters. The GP continued to provide a low level of medication.

A pattern became established however whereby Terry would get into debt in his accommodation and then start to make increasing demands on his parents. Eventually after several repetitions of this, with break-ins to their house, Terry received a short prison sentence.

Source: Dallos, R. (1993)

Particularly at times of distress and crisis friends and others typically step aside to 'allow' close family members to assume their expected duties. It is precisely this sense of a family 'pulling together' in the face of adversity against misfortune that helps to confirm their sense of belonging and intimacy but, conversely, it is precisely this sense of pride and confidence that can be shattered if professionals intrude or make the family feel inadequate and incompetent. In effect, there is a delicate tension between the family's wish to remain 'private' and the conflicting need to seek 'public' help and risk their boundaries being invaded.

It is also frequently the case that the person who is being seen as having a problem starts to accept this definition of events within the family. The internalization of a deviant label is therefore not an individual matter but a shared family construction (see Dallos, 1991). In effect a family such as the Martins has constructed a version of reality which contains a definition of mental health problems that is faithful to the prevalent medical models and which places the fulcrum of causation within one person. This has been described as a 'family myth' (Ferreira, 1963) and a myth shared by our culture (Hardwick, 1989). Nevertheless, it is likely to be a construction of events which is consistent with widely held views of problems and, significantly, which is likely to be validated by the family's first contact with professionals.

The process whereby people come to be diagnosed and gain entry to mental health professionals and institutions has been outlined in terms of a series of filters (see Figure 3.2). The first of these is likely to be contact with the family's local GP who, consistent with his or her training, is likely to lean towards medical explanations which run the danger of encouraging the process of labelling the individual as the 'problem'. If the GP feels that the problems are serious then a variety of other professionals may also come onto the scene — such as social workers, psychiatric nurses and clinical psychologists — leading to intrusions into the family's life and their problems becoming 'public'. This may or may not be helpful. A negative example may be where a professional unwittingly takes sides with one member of the family against another or preventing the family from maintaining their ability to make their own decisions. One typical consequence of this can be the development of a dependency by the family on outside agencies to solve their problems so that they become labelled as a 'chronic problem family' (Burnham, 1980).

The initial contact with a GP or other professionals therefore has major consequences for patients and their families. The extent to which a family can maintain a boundary between the public and their private family life can determine the extent to which they can remain a functional unit or become dependent on professional involvement. At this stage professional decisions on whether to treat the individual or the whole family are significant: if the individual is referred on for individual treatment the implication is that he or she is the problem. If the family is referred on, the implication may be that the family is the problem. Until recently the focus was usually on one person, though increasingly the whole family may be included in a treatment programme (see Dallos, 1991). Failure of treatments at this stage is likely to lead to the person being further and more forcefully labelled. In extreme circumstances the final stages may be that the person is placed in some form of residential care and undergoes a programme of control and medication, at least temporarily.

4   EXPLANATIONS: MODELS OF CAUSATION

4.1   INDIVIDUAL EXPLANATIONS

Explanations of mental disorder have predominantly taken the individual as the focus of concern. This assumption is inherent in the diagnostic systems which have been the natural starting point for the study of these problems. The first steps in a 'scientific' approach are seen as a careful description and categorization of the 'symptoms' exhibited by mentally disturbed people. At the same time this represents the first step in framing the problem as an individual one. We could ask instead, as we will consider in the next section, what kind of relationships are such problems embedded in. Is the disorder a phenomenon shared by a group of people? In turn, the problems of attempting to create a reliable system of classification of mental illnesses have been enormous. The most widely used classification system is DSM–III (the diagnostic system of the American Psychiatric Association which is periodically revised) and here concern is essentially with the extent to which the problem, though perhaps activated by outside factors, is some individual or private fault as the key terms in the classifications indicate:

> *Depression (affective disorders)*: sad depressed mood, disorders of appetite — loss or gain in weight, difficulties in sleeping, changes in activity level — lethargy or restlessness, loss of interest in usual activities such as sex, reading etc., negative self-concept, loss of energy, difficulty in concentrating such as slowed thinking and indecisiveness, recurrent thoughts of death or suicide.
>
> *Schizophrenia*: inability to cope with daily routines of life — disorganization, disorders of thought, rambling disconnected speech, delusions, hearing 'voices', intrusive thoughts, disorders of perception and attention, hallucinations — usually auditory, bizarre body movements, flat or inappropriate emotion responses — inappropriate laughter etc.
>
> (From *DSM–III*, 1980, quoted in Davison and Neale, 1982, pp.68–74)

These definitions can incorporate the view that mental disorders originate from some form of inherited weakness or *susceptibility* (based e.g. on studies of twins by Gottesman, 1991). But the development of the illness, and to some extent the form that it takes, is shaped by environmental factors such as the level of *stress* a person experiences and their cultural milieu. It is argued that there are fundamental individual differences in patterns of response to stressful events such as family conflicts, demands arising at school or work or from relationships, loss such as bereavement, and so on.

We are left with the apparent social relativity of mental disorders. In different societies and in different periods, certain sorts of behaviour may have been treated as abnormal but holy, or worthy of exorcism; they may have been encapsulated in the quite different institutional arrangements of spirit possession in some societies, becoming a religious hermit in others, or mental hospitalization in our own (Littlewood and Lipsedge, 1989).

4.2   ENVIRONMENT: VULNERABILITY AND STRESS

Attempts have been made to link mental disorder to damage from stress resulting from a history of destructive emotional experiences and deprivation in childhood. The contributory factors include having a mother and/or a father who also suffered from a serious mental health problem, loss of one or both parents in childhood, complications at birth, and attentional/learning abnormalities developed at an early stage in the children. These approaches were developed with the idea that some children, owing to their circumstances, are at 'high risk', and a longitudinal study of a sample of high-risk and low-risk children was carried out which produced some evidence to support this model. It was also suggested that a passive, depressed style of behaviour is formed in the face of impossible and unresolvable conflict (Gottesman, 1991).

Brown and Harris (1978) attempted to assess the impact of a variety of environmental stress factors on the formation of depression:

A vulnerability factors	B provoking agents which include
• three or more young children at home;	• a recent bereavement;
• lack of an intimate relationship;	• separation;
• poverty;	• onset of unemployment;
• unemployment;	• illness;
• early loss of parents; and	• crisis;
	• more positive but disruptive changes such as unexpected pregnancy.

Brown and Harris go beyond a simple focus on individual inadequacy and start to offer a picture, at least for depression, in which mental disorders are linked to a range of social factors. The vulnerability factors suggest how depression might be prevented and here they cite intimacy as a key factor. However, it is not quite clear how relationship problems might be linked to depression and we will consider this later. It is worth noting that various forms of change, even positive events, are seen as potentially provoking factors if they can cause a disruption of the normal predictable daily flow of events.

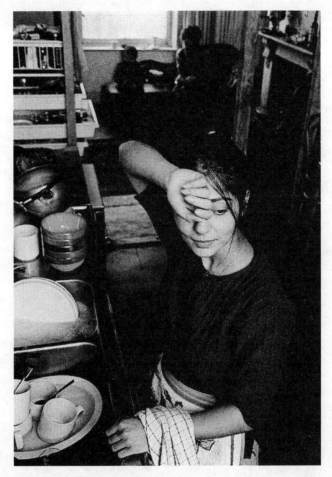

The stress of everyday life

4.3   PUBLIC CONCERNS: CLASS, GENDER AND ETHNIC DIFFERENCES

If mental illnesses, such as schizophrenia and depression, can be predominantly seen as arising individually, one might expect no major differences in their distribution according to class, gender or 'race'. However, as with the distribution of so many social 'goods' like education, housing, income and general health, social class, defined by occupation, is closely associated with mental disorder. As long ago as 1958, in their substantial epidemiological study in New Haven, Connecticut, Hollingshead and Redlich (1958) found a much higher rate of mental disorder in the most menial, unskilled and low paid Social Class V than in the skilled manual, clerical, professional and managerial classes (See Table 3.1). Having related the general incidence of mentally ill people in each class to the proportion of the general population in each class, they produced

Table 3.1 Mental disorder and social class (prevalence) rates per 100,000, adjusted for age and sex

Social class	Prevalence rate
Class I–II	553
Class III	528
Class IV	665
Class V	1,668

Source: *Social Class and Mental Illness: A Community Study* by Hollingshead and Redlich. Copyright © 1958 by John Wiley & Sons, Inc., p.210.

prevalence rates that could be compared on equal terms. This becomes even more illuminating when the distribution of patients presenting different symptoms is considered (see Figure 3.3).

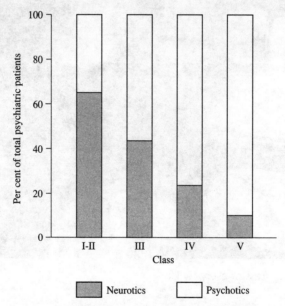

Figure 3.3 Percentage of neurotics and psychotics among total psychiatric patients — by class (age and sex adjusted)

Source: Gottesman, 1991

We can see that the serious mental disorders (psychoses) are much more likely to be found in people belonging to the lowest socio-economic classes. The pattern suggests that upper classes suffer fairly moderate levels of disorder, perhaps owing to tensions and strains of competition leading to mild neuroses and psychosomatic complaints such as ulcers, anxiety, sexual problems and so on. By contrast the severe disorders are suffered by those with least material and other resources. Of course, things are not as simple as that. We cannot conclude that poverty drives one mad. They are associated, but madness may reduce one to poverty by the loss of job, income, marriage and residence, i.e. downward social mobility. Such data is not free of problems itself. Wealthier people may be treated privately but health insurance doesn't cover prolonged illness so they will tend to end up using public services. However, as the range of alternative treatments has been developed, different social classes have tended to be admitted to hospital and given the most powerful drugs or advised to use 'talking cures' while living at home or supported in the general community. American state hospitals have become dumping grounds for the most disadvantaged (Orford, 1992); this, as now in Britain, has ethnic implications.

Having introduced social class, we shall devote most of the examples to illustrate this matter of selectivity from the ethnic differences observed in Britain over the last twenty years and some obvious differences between men and women, which Brown and Harris's research may already have raised in your minds. It is also important to appreciate that things may not be what they seem and that to raise a vital question is not to provide its answer. You should be aware of the sorts of methodological problems that have to be overcome when offering answers and even in establishing associations, let alone causal relationships, between factors that may explain the existence of different patterns of diagnosis, treatment and the prevalence of illness in these sectors of the population.

ACTIVITY 2

Tables 3.2 and 3.3 have been drawn from an article comparing the mental hospital admissions of people born in different countries or parts of the world. The data was first analysed in 1971 and then assembled in 1981 so that a comparison could be made over the decade. By choosing the same years as the census, the researchers could establish the rates of hospitalization for every 100,000 of the population born in each country but living in England. The data is therefore standardized in this respect and you do not need to worry that there are far more English born people in England than there are, say, Indian born. The tables we have selected refer to 1981. The first table is for women and the second for men, so gender differences can be detected. The main diagnostic categories of mental illness and related disorders are also listed so that reasons for hospital admission are also given. The tables simply show admission rates to hospital. They do not evaluate the diagnosis, nor do they show what alternative services may or may not have been available, nor who was admitted informally and who was detained. And they do not explain the differences or similarities in rates. Look along each row and down each column.

1   Look at the countries of birth. What sorts of groups or categories can you discern? Are any sufficiently similar to suggest broader distinct categories with reference to mental hospitalization?

Table 3.2 Rates of mental hospital admissions in England per 100,000 population, 1981. Females

Country of birth	All diag- noses	Schizo- phrenia[a]	Other psy- choses	Depres- sion[b]	Neu- roses[c]	Person- ality dis- orders etc.	Alcohol[d] abuse	Drug abuse
England	485	58	27	166	56	35	18	3
Scotland	806	88	42	260	94	62	98	4
Wales	603	69	40	213	63	37	30	4
N. Ireland	834	111	52	266	80	52	90	8
Ireland	1167	174	50	410	111	80	133	8
Caribbean	589	235	40	152	25	42	9	0
India	331	89	17	118	27	18	8	2
Pakistan[e]	229	32	3	96	47	15	1	0
Italy	434	138	18	149	42	33	4	4
Poland	755	212	40	279	75	18	12	0

Table 3.3 Rates of mental hospital admissions in England per 100,000 population, 1981. Males

Country of birth	All diag- noses	Schizo- phrenia[a]	Other psy- choses	Depres- sion[b]	Neu- roses[c]	Person- ality dis- orders etc.	Alcohol[d] abuse	Drug abuse
England	320	61	16	79	28	30	38	5
Scotland	670	75	29	120	43	51	253	17
Wales	404	59	25	100	31	31	55	5
N. Ireland	784	103	28	143	44	50	261	17
Ireland	1023	158	36	197	62	62	332	13
Caribbean	502	259	28	65	6	22	27	13
India	310	77	8	68	22	16	73	3
Pakistan[e]	216	94	8	68	19	5	6	0
Italy	267	64	7	83	25	18	14	16
Poland	490	132	36	111	28	6	60	2

[a] Schizophrenia and paranoia

[b] Affective psychoses and depressive disorders

[c] Includes 'neurotic depression'

[d] Alcohol psychosis and alcohol dependence and nondependent abuse of alcohol

[e] Includes Bangladesh

Source: Cochrane and Bal (1989) p.4, and Table 3.

2   Make a note of any mental disorder or country of origin and/or gender differences that seem to stand out because they are particularly large or small.

3   Do they suggest any gender-based or ethnic pattern to you? By ethnic we refer here to differences of culture and/or pigmentation but not necessarily to ethnic minority status which may also be worth noting.

4   Are there further questions that you think arise from your observations? If so, what further information would you need to try to answer them?

(To help you analyse these tables, you may find it useful to circle the highest figures in each column.)

DISCUSSION

Here are some observations. One could group whites and blacks if that seemed useful but it would conceal such differentiation as to be misleading. The same is true of grouping the U.K. with Ireland or the Roman Catholic countries of Europe etc. But we will use some forms of aggregation for parts of the discussion.

Taking all diagnoses, it appears that all Scottish, Welsh and Irish immigrants, male and female, have far higher rates of admission than native English people. By contrast most other 'whites' and Asians have lower rates. English men and women have similar rates of schizophrenia but the women have higher rates over all and much higher rates of depression and neuroses and less alcoholism. Most migrant categories have higher rates of schizophrenia than the English but this experience is almost five times as likely in the case of Caribbean men and women. By contrast depression is markedly less prevalent in hospitalized Caribbean men and women although the overall pattern follows that of all diagnoses. Scottish and Irish men and women are far more likely to be admitted for alcohol abuse than those born in India, Pakistan and Bangladesh — you can probably identify several other differences.

Several questions arise with reference to the effects of immigration, with reference to ethnicity, and possibly to a more general category of culture. Others arise in relation to gender, some of which have already been discussed in the context of Brown and Harris's research. But there are others which indicate the danger of investing too much meaning in one set of figures. For example, the data are based on diagnosis on admission to English hospitals, but many people are not admitted to hospital but use GPs or other psychiatric services. Could the English overall rates be low or those of the Caribbean particularly high in schizophrenia because of different referral rates to hospital? We know that the latter are much more likely to be detained compulsorily, especially by a police section order (McGovern and Cope, 1987).

You may also have raised questions about the database itself. Is hospital the only option given to some people when alternatives are offered to others? How much cultural diversity may be concealed by 'country of origin'? The term Caribbean is used because the census categories are based on country of origin, but this may mask divisions which already exist within those countries, e.g. between people who see themselves as of African or Asian descent. Given that people migrated from different places at different times, and that British Commonwealth citizens are now virtually excluded (but free access is available to EC nationals) the age of those born abroad will also differ. Standardization by age for each country of birth is therefore also necessary and effectively reduces the rates of mental hospitalization for all countries below that of England with these major exceptions (Cochrane and Bal, 1989, p.4, Table 2). The Scottish and Irish rates remain much higher and so, although less high, do the Caribbean rates. At a time when some authors are writing articles in medical journals with titles like 'Is schizophrenia disappearing?' the high rates for this diagnosis in those of Caribbean origin require explanation (Der et al., 1990).

Cochrane and Bal summarize the findings of their comparison between 1971 and 1981 as follows:

1   Although overall rates of hospital admissions had generally fallen this was less the case with schizophrenia. Migrant rates fell but still remained higher than native English rates. Caribbean rates were much higher. Only in the case of Pakistani and Bangladeshi women did rates fall below the English rate, an observation also worth investigation.

2   Rates of depression increased due to changes in diagnostic recording, with Irish, Scots and Poles remaining relatively high.

3   Drug abuse rates remained similar except for a sharp increase in Caribbeans and Italians.

4   Alcoholism increased in both men and women generally, but especially in the case of Indians, Northern Irish and Poles.

5   There was a decline in recorded personality disorders but Irish and Scots remained the highest.

6   Neuroses fell especially in the case of Northern Irish and Pakistani and Bangladeshi women.

7   Young Caribbean men were especially liable to be admitted with a diagnosis of schizophrenia and, although Caribbean women were more evenly distributed by age, their rates of admission were also far higher than those of English people.

4.4   CULTURE, PSYCHIATRY AND A MULTI-ETHNIC POPULATION

From the previous section, we have selected two issues for specific consideration. The first is the diagnosis and hospitalization of Caribbeans, especially young men. The second is the relative absence of Pakistani and Bangladeshi women and their declining admission to hospital with mental disorders. Both raise questions about the whole of society, psychiatry as such, and the operation of mental health and other services, but we shall only follow up the first in this section, leaving the second for consideration with reference to services alternative to hospital in Section 5.

The relationship between ethnicity, psychiatric disorders and hospitalization is quite complex but what stand out are the persistent and disproportionately high rates of schizophrenia amongst those originating from the Caribbean (Harrison et al, 1988, 1989), particularly those born in the United Kingdom. Migrants generally become more like their host population over several generations so this is a dramatic divergence. From a specific comparison of second generation Afro-Caribbeans and young whites in Birmingham at their first admission with schizophrenia, McGovern and Cope (1991) observed that these young people were, like the first generation, admitted at a higher rate, for longer stays in hospital and with more active symptoms. In addition they found that 'The Afro-Caribbeans admitted to hospital with this diagnosis (schizophrenia) do seem to be more isolated, to have greater contact with police and forensic services, and to avoid voluntary treatment' (McGovern and Cope, 1991, p.99). In a series of articles published in 1989, Glover (1989a, b, c) also found much the same patterns but also that the Afro-Caribbean rates were themselves differentiated, in the case of Jamaicans being higher than those from Barbados and Trinidad. He concluded 'Do they reflect greater or different morbidity or different management? To the extent that they reflect morbidity differences, are these rooted in biological or social influences and do these influences operate in infancy, childhood or adulthood?' (Glover, 1989a, p.55).

From their clinical experience, Littlewood and Lipsedge argued that

> ...mental illness is rooted in biology and culture, in the individual and society. What is important is not whether mental illness should be regarded as a biological or a social phenomenon, or whether a particular individual is 'really ill', but how different levels of interpretation interact and how they are derived from each other. The question is not whether a patient is 'orientated to reality' but to which reality and why.
>
> (1989, p.xv)

From a set of cases it was concluded that great problems are posed for Western psychiatry in, for example, cases where patients use religious beliefs and ideas as their idiom of expression, e.g. Margaret, a young Nigerian woman, complained of being tormented by evil forces sent by a 'babalawo' (sorcerer) and was initially treated as schizophrenic. Psychiatry's own system of meanings and explanations, as in the case of schizophrenia, may in some cases be in direct competition with such religious beliefs (Littlewood and Lipsedge, 1989, p.245). They also argue that much can be understood as an acute psychotic reaction to the experience of racism, institutionalized through work or lack of it, home and living standards, and general exclusion and deprivation. Alienation from the host society is also reflected in a lack of integration into its services. Only the most florid reactions then get acted upon and at a much later stage of mental disturbance. The filter process described in Section 3 is bypassed or truncated and misdiagnosis of schizophrenia may result as well as compulsory hospital admission. Heavier drugs may be used but the 'talking cures' including family therapy, and less institutional forms of treatment, are generally offered to whites who will understand the norms of such services. This form of two-tier service for the purposes of social control may be further exacerbated by the fact that most consultant psychiatrists are white, if not necessarily English, many of those in junior medical posts are of Asian origin, and that the junior nursing ranks are also often predominantly filled by people of migrant origins, often black.

Two quite different questions must be put. Both involve racial factors but with quite different implications. Is there any racial stereotyping which leads to different diagnoses and different treatment pathways for different ethnic groups? Is there a marked degree of cultural insensitivity which results in different conditions being labelled in the same way for all ethnic groups?

Through the use of hypothetical cases accorded different gender or ethnic characteristics, several studies have concluded that psychiatrists don't operate in a cultural vacuum although, when made to do so, they tend to diagnose the text book state (Loring and Powell, 1988, Lewis et al., 1990). In the U.S.A. male psychiatrists tended to diagnose women as depressed with additional emotional problems, even when none of the latter symptoms were listed. Violence tended to be imputed to black men, and both black men and women were seen as having paranoid personalities. Black psychiatrists followed the white professionals' line but tended to assign even less severe diagnoses to white cases. Quite apart from different treatment patterns, these stereotypes become reified in official statistics. As Fernando (1989) argued, predominant white psychiatric perceptions provide the model for general perceptions of mental illness. '... a false sense of confidence in objective measures can be dangerous when it ignores the possibility of bias (or misperception) and when it helps to maintain that bias through both treatment and statistical reports' (Loring and Powell, 1988, p.19).

From this brief look at some statistics on social differences, one can see how the 'private' problems of individuals may be significantly related to much more general 'public' phenomena. Gender, 'race' and socio-economic circumstances can be seen as combining to produce on 'underclass' of mentally disturbed people. We now need to ask what part is played by the family, or family life, in transmitting or moderating these social and cultural factors? We also want to consider modes of explanation at an intermediate level of analysis which focus on the contribution of the family itself, namely the dynamics or internal tensions which may contribute to the development of such disorders.

4.5   MODELS OF FAMILY DYNAMICS

Freud (1960) in his formulation of the Oedipus complex set the scene for an approach to mental illness which focuses on the family as causing mental illness largely through the damaging effects of sexual conflicts and inability to resolve incestuous feelings. Families were seen as having the task of 'socializing' their children through the process of 'repressing' their sexual instincts, so that they would emerge as 'normal' and 'healthy' citizens able to participate effectively in society. Despite Freud's family based formulations, most treatments derived from his ideas were individually focused. Many psychodynamically trained therapists from the 1950s onwards started seeing patients along with their families in the hope that this would shed light on how problems were caused and help with the more 'difficult' cases who did not respond to individual treatment (Ackerman, 1958; Dallos, 1991).

The family models stressed that disturbances in family relationships resulted in a fractured or distorted view of reality. With most of the early approaches the focus is on the mother child relationships (Bateson, 1956, Wynne et al., 1958), with a dangerous consequence that blame is attached to mothers as victimizers, with children regarded as victims. The double bind hypothesis for example, suggested that schizophrenia arose from a pattern of contradictory and confusing communications, directed at a child by his mother (Dallos, 1991). Subsequently, attention moved from the mother child–pair to threesomes and the idea of children with symptoms serving as 'scapegoats' for marital and other family conflicts (Jackson, 1957). A danger with these models was that they simply shifted the focus of 'blame' from individuals to families without taking account of the range of external stress factors, such as socio-economic, gender and racial inequalities. There was a major change in the 1970s towards viewing families as parts of wider systems involving the extended family, the workplace and interaction with professional systems. This re-emphasized the contribution of social and cultural values, as transmitted through the attitudes and practices of the professional in causing mental health problems. Therapists working with families were encouraged to reflect upon their positions on issues of gender, class, race. It became recognized for example, that women are often relatively powerless but at the same time there is a cultural expectation for them to provide the child-rearing and nurturing functions. Given this position of family responsibility without real power problematic consequences can follow for a mother: frustration, mixed emotions and even ridicule from her children (Madanes, 1981).

4.6   FAMILIES: VULNERABILITY AND STRESS

A great debate has raged as to whether mental illness is to be regarded as basically an organic illness with physical causes or one that is socially induced. The family models described above are at the extremity of the social end of this spectrum. Testing such models is not easy because the experience of growing up in a particular family environment is so subjective. It is almost impossible to decide objectively what it might feel like to be a particular child in a family, how it feels to become involved in the family disputes, alliances and loyalties and so on. Interestingly, a recent approach is gaining ground, possibly in part because it offers something to both sides in this professional argument, by suggesting that mental illness results from both an organic vulnerability in the patient and the level of negative emotions arising within the family. The suggestion is that in families where there is a high level of conflict, over-involvement and expression of negative emotions (EE = expressed emotion) there is a much greater chance that their mentally ill relative will relapse and have to be returned to hospital. These negative emotions are seen as something more than the family's response to the behaviour of their mentally ill member since not all families display high EE. The high EE may reflect fundamental patterns of relating in some families. But, when families are 'educated' to change these patterns to ones with more positive and less emotionally over-involved styles of relating, it has been found that the chances of their relatives staying out of hospital are dramatically increased (Leff and Vaughn, 1985). Furthermore, it has been found that such changes in EE accompany effective family therapy (Vostanis et al., 1992).

Surprisingly, however, the connections between the earlier studies of stress and social class have not been articulated. It is only a small step to suggest that families in the lowest socio-economic groups, ethnic minorities and single-parent families are likely to experience the greatest levels of stress in our society and consequently that this will give a

'Tell me Dr. Eichhorn, if I marry Alex, will I become part of the solution or part of the problem?'

negative colour to their interactions and limit their ability to cope with conflicts that are an inevitable aspect of family life. Nevertheless, it is dangerous to offer simplistic interpretations of the effects or definitions of stress. As we saw in the Camberwell studies, the effects of provoking factors are mediated by the nature of the family, its economic resources and the timing of the events. The Brown and Harris (1978) study does suggest, along with these theories based on family models, that families are likely to be more vulnerable after experiencing losses, rapid changes as at transitional or family life-cycle stages or crises of various sorts. If a serious event emerges to provoke their distress, such as an illness or apparently unusual behaviour in one of their children they may be less capable of dealing with it and consequently descend down a plunging spiral of distress and illness (Haley, 1980; Dallos, 1991).

5   TYPES OF INTERVENTION

5.1   PSYCHIATRY AND ANTI-PSYCHIATRY

Throughout this chapter we have made constant reference to some of the main categories of mental illness and to those in the medical profession under whose responsibility they fall in the guise of patients, namely psychiatrists. Since the conditions were regarded as 'illnesses', it followed that they should be treated by doctors. However, as outlined in Section 2, not only are psychiatrists responsible for programmes of treatment but also, with approved social workers and some others, they have legal authority to detain people in certain circumstances against their will and decide how long they will be kept in hospital. Like all doctors they also hold advisory powers over discharging patients but informal patients may make their own decision to leave against advice. The vast majority of mental patients in hospital are admitted informally or lapse into informal status after the expiry of the short detention sections which are used for emergency admission and initial treatment.

But, of course, informal patients are usually well aware of the potential powers of psychiatrists to detain them if they do not agree to admission and treatment. Such section orders may last up to six months and can be renewed after review. Patients may appeal against detention to their hospital managers and to a Mental Health Tribunal but only a few do so. However, although dangerousness to themselves or others is generally considered a sufficient reason for detention and hence a bone of contention when it is seen to be used with apparent ethnic bias, mental patients cannot now be held in general hospitals unless they are considered suitable cases for treatment. To put it frankly, mentally ill people are much more likely to be found in contemporary British prisons than undisturbed people are to be imprisoned in mental hospitals.

Until relatively recently, one of the most common forms of intervention in cases presenting serious problems of mental illness was the removal of

'Not much of a psychiatric unit, though, is it?'

such people from their families and local communities to a place of 'asylum', a psychiatric hospital. Within this setting they could experience a variety of treatments, which included various forms of medication by psychotropic drugs, individual psychotherapy and group therapy, behaviour training through 'token' economies, and expressive or task-related art or occupational therapy. Irrespective of the different aims and forms of these treatments, they generally shared the common practice of disconnecting patients from their local communities.

Following a flurry of psychiatric hospital building in the Victorian era, their population has gradually been reducing (148,000 in 1954 to 59,000 in 1991, *Social Trends*, 1992, p.139). Concerns developed about the damaging effects of prolonged medication in the 1960s and 70s but the whole medical concept of mental illness, as well as that of hospitalization, was challenged by what came to be termed an anti-psychiatry movement. Russell Barton (1959) coined the phrase 'institutional neurosis'. Erving Goffman (1961) presented mental hospitals as one of a type of 'total institution' alongside prisons, boarding schools etc. and the 'career' of a mental patient as one of moral degradation. Even more forcefully Thomas Szasz (1971 et al.) condemned the use of public mental hospitals as unauthorized prisons. And a group of psychiatrists in the U.K., inspired by R.D. Laing, questioned the validity of biologically based theories and medical diagnoses of mental illnesses and insisted on a broader ecological analysis of how these problems might arise. They argued that the causes of schizophrenia and depression were located in destructive family relationships which themselves arose from the ways in which families internalized patterns of oppression evident in the wider society (e.g. Laing, 1969; Cooper, 1967).

This movement introduced a climate of change and innovation. First, the whole family was given treatment instead of individual patients on their own. Second, a number of therapeutic communities were created which attempted to provide a supportive environment to counteract both the damaging effects of family experiences and the wider society. Third, there was an increase in the range and activity of voluntary agencies such as the Richmond Fellowship, Mind and the Schizophrenia Fellowship which attempted to provide support for patients and/or their families. Fourth, there was a serious attempt to empower mentally disturbed people and their families and to question the underlying assumptions and power bases of the medical model and psychiatry. One of the outcomes of the anti-psychiatry movement was a politicization of mental disorder and its location within debates about systems of oppression in society.

Although often considered as a movement, the anti-psychiatrists can also be seen as both disparate in their goals and often very narrowly focused in their field of application. It was argued that what was primarily under way in implementing the reduction of psychiatric hospitals and attendant problems of institutionalization was the reaction of those in power to the colossal costs of the welfare state in all its guises. No future was seen in denying the anguish and problematic reality of mental illness but there was hope in some form of social-communitarian support for sufferers (Sedgwick, 1982):

> Deinstitutionalization of the mentally ill, while securing the negative right to be free of organized interference in one's life, has all too often meant the denial of the positive right to care and attention. As a result, for the majority of those affected with chronic mental illness, what has changed is the packaging rather than the reality of their misery.
>
> (Scull, 1977, p.174)

We shall return to this discussion in our consideration of alternatives to mental hospitals in Section 5.3.

5.2   FAMILY MODES OF INTERVENTION

It would be hopeful to be able to write that family-based models of intervention, such as family therapy, are a co-ordinated development arising from critiques of the hospital-based system of treatment but this is not the case. To some extent the models of intervention arose as a result of the anti-psychiatry movement but, in Britain, although family therapy has received some support from NHS funding it was also seen as a threat to psychiatry rather than a valuable adjunct. Interestingly, some of the major early developments in family therapy were in precisely this field of serious mental illness but, paradoxically, it is also where it has met and continues to meet resistance.

Family-based forms of intervention follow directly from the models of explanation described earlier. We can broadly differentiate between two

The reality of deinstitutionalization

approaches: the first is family therapy and the second psycho-education. Family therapy has usually involved asking other family members to accompany the person labelled as mentally ill to a hospital or day-hospital for a one-hour session of therapy, usually at intervals of one or two weeks for a set period. Most forms of family therapy intend to take a 'neutral' stance and do not blame the family for what has happened. This position seems less contrived or contradictory if we remember that there is a vast pool of untreated 'mental illness' in the community. However, families nevertheless often do feel blamed and may find it difficult to change their culturally shared view that 'mental illness' is simply a disorder with organic origins suffered by just one of their members.

One important development in family therapy has been a shift from the common focus of guidance on keeping families together and intact to one in which families may be helped to make separations. One view was that the frequently observed state of dependence of a psychotic child on the family kept them together, safeguarded family secrets of covert conflict and thereby reduced the risk of the potential disintegration of the family. The goals of family therapy have, therefore, been to help families resolve some of their conflicts and consequently liberate their disturbed relatives from the need to display symptoms. A second development has been the use of family therapy to enable the family to more readily accept a member leaving home, so that a disturbed child, for example, can gain independence and establish normal relationships. Considerable successes have been reported by therapists working with families in this way (Palazzoli et al., 1978) but some questions remain about the extent to which such an approach can also serve to locate the blame within the family. Consequently ammunition is provided for social policies which do not provide adequate resourcing of community care and make little or no attempt to recognize the burden that such families bear and eventually feel obliged to shoulder (Orford, 1992).

> The parents of a psychotic offspring suffer from chronic grief over the tragic loss of the well child they once had and the need to abandon hopes for the future of that child. The grief may be dealt with by denial of the illness; intrusiveness and hypercontrol of the patient; and the inability to maintain appropriate parental distance, which tends to impair the marriage, work and friendships of the parents ... the dilemma they confront is at heart an ethical one — what does one owe one's children and how is one to lead a meaningful life?
>
> (Grunebaum, 1984, p.241)

There is danger, then, that family therapy can promote social policies which essentially 'blame' families and of course families are not unaware that such covert accusation is taking place. Consequently, they may question the need for them to attend for family therapy. Increasingly, family therapy is regarded as one aspect of community care policy and as providing support for all the family members — not simply the one who has been identified as disturbed.

The following case study illustrates some of the issues involved in a family therapy approach with the Martin family described earlier in Case Study 3.

'Enid, why can't we get depressed as a family?'

ACTIVITY 3

Before you read through the next part of the case study of the Martin Family, return to Case Study 3 on p.91 and consider the possible ways that Terry's situation might have deteriorated or improved without intervention at the family level. To what extent do you think taking a family therapy approach runs a risk of 'blaming' the family for having 'caused' Terry's problems? What do you think might have been a useful approach to take with the Martin family?

CASE STUDY 4   THE MARTIN FAMILY INTERVENTIONS

Following Terry's release from prison the suggestion was made by a family friend, who was also a psychiatric social worker, that they attend for family therapy (typically the referrals are through G.P.s, social workers or other psychiatrists). The family therapy was carried out by a team who are part of the local N.H.S. psychiatric rehabilitation service, whose remit is to help patients with chronic problems to re-integrate into the community. This often involves assisting them to utilize the support of their families. In the fortnightly one-hour sessions there was no overt sign of any anger in the family and contrary to expectations Terry was not aggressive, and was contrite and confused about why he had acted the way he had. The family communicated an acute sense of 'failure' at what had happened. Terry felt he had not been able to live up to his parents' high expectations and had felt very rejected by them. His parents, in turn, felt they had made a mess of things with Terry and engaged in so much self-criticism that they seemed unable to act in any clear and consistent way with him. There appeared to be a shared pattern of denying emotions in the family. The parents found it hard to express anyanger at the way Terry had terrorized them. And Terry felt rejected by his parents.

Some discussion otheir mutual expectations, feelings and beliefs took place, but within a framework of making some practical and realistic decisions about how they could help each other and operate more amicably as a family. They were encouraged to make some clear arrangements about meeting Terry, in order to pre-empt and disrupt the negative pattern of their previous meetings with him. They decided to have a meeting twice a week; once socially, outside the home, and another to help him with his financial worries. This plan also introduced the idea that Terry needed emotional as well as economic support from them. Some changes started to appear with no repetition of the 'urban terrorism' and they all said that they enjoyed their outings. Terry was able to express a need for parental support although the therapists anticipated that this would change in the future. The labelling of Terry's behaviour as schizophrenia slipped into disuse, medication was withdrawn and he has continued to live independently with this level of support from his parents which they all regard as quite 'normal' and acceptable.

Source: Dallos, R. (1993)

Many families of course do not have the resources, financial stability, education, contacts with professionals and so on that Terry Martin's family had. Despite these resources, it seemed clear that without an intervention at the family level Terry's situation could have progressively deteriorated.

5.3   PRIVATIZING CARE, ALTERNATIVES TO HOSPITAL AND FAMILY SUPPORT

Every epidemiological study of mental illness rates in the general population, using some standard and tested form of psychiatric diagnostic mode of assessment such as that developed by Wing et al. (1974), indicates that the vast bulk of people admitting to symptoms of psychiatric disorder either have no contact with any medical practitioner, or are only in touch with their GP who may or may not recognize such a disorder and treat them accordingly. When community care policies were introduced in the 1960s they were primarily orientated to the discharge of long-stay patients from hospitals to alternative services — hostels, day centres, group homes, even workshops. People discharged from mental hospitals or the psychiatric units of general hospitals were generally left to their own devices, or those of their relatives, some of whom founded the Schizophrenia Fellowship to fight the authorities who refused to hold their sick relatives in hospital but gave neither them nor their carers more than minimal support after discharging them.

Although the British government's national policy had shifted from expanding the range of services in the late 1970s to the actual closure of mental hospitals in the 1980s, regional and local district implementation was piecemeal, a few new elements being added to an increasingly fragmented service. About 20 per cent of current NHS expenditure is devoted to mental health services of which half is spent on maintaining about ninety large mental hospitals. The other half is used to fund 98 per cent of the actual services which are provided for patients living in the community or entering psychiatric units of general hospitals for short-term acute treatment. The problem is how to turn that expenditure around so that most of it is spent on the majority of patients, and in particular on patient care and support outside hospital, whilst maintaining a priority for people exhibiting symptoms of severe mental illness.

Community based models have been operating, or were at least initiated many years ago. As early as 1968, Dingleton mental hospital in the Scottish Borders had reduced its new admissions to a handful by setting up joint crisis intervention teams with local authority social work departments and general practitioners. These were geared to provide family visits and home consultations followed by domiciliary support. At the other end of this period of intended service development was the programme implemented in South Devon in the 1980s. This consisted of local community mental health centres for reception, consultation and group therapy, support for voluntary social centres, hostel provision for those chronic patients transferred from the old hospitals (which were soon developed into a range of rehabilitative and supported lodgings), an extensive small nursing home provision for the many elderly people who only enter the net of psychiatric services during their final years of life, and a psychiatric unit at the general hospital.

Much more radical has been the attempt to reform mental health services in Italy. Unlike British legislation, which as we have seen makes little reference to types of service and practical intervention and is primarily concerned with legal safeguards against compulsory admission, and the proper administration of the tiny proportion who are detained, the Italian reforms in the *Law 180* of 1978 did include service-related directives. The intention of the law was to transform the mode of national provision on the lines already carried out in Gorizia and Trieste by Basaglia and his colleagues in Arezzo and elsewhere. The Italian legislation specifically introduced procedures which would phase out the mental hospitals by preventing new admissions and set up new, staffed local mental health organizations within the new N.H.S. which could arrange a range of local community services (Basaglia, 1981).

Basaglia had aimed to reduce the hierarchical divisions of staff, as well as the gulf between them and their patients, by setting up socially supportive local centres where staff were available for patients to call on as they wished rather than the staff providing set services which *they* thought the patients should have. But to implement Basaglia's ideas required staff imbued not only with the relevant egalitarian ideals but also some idea of their actual implementation. Unfortunately both medical and nursing training in psychiatry was at schools with very different aims. Anti-psychiatry therefore took the form of a new movement to formulate the new law and its implementation. There are districts like Arezzo, which has a twenty-four hour multidisciplinary team service with a few emergency and acute general hospital beds for its own use, a greatly reduced asylum, substantial sheltered housing of various kinds, social clubs, cooperatives of ex-patients in waged work, and a domiciliary crisis service. But there are also districts in which substantial asylum funding still continues and patients are illegally admitted to hospital while funds allocated by the central government for new services are returned without expenditure (Boswell, 1986).

A criticism often directed at new community mental health services, particularly in the United States where they have operated for nearly thirty years, is that they meet new needs for a different category of patient and provide the opportunity for participative group therapy and talking cures whilst ignoring the people who are most severely disturbed and present the greatest disruption to their families and society at large. Those with nowhere to go and no-one to turn to have been left to exist in bed-and-breakfast resort ghettoes, common lodging houses in big cities, and to some extent on the streets or in prison. Or they have been admitted to the more traditional medically dominated hospital services. We have already discussed this with reference to the alleged selective diagnosis and hospitalization of black people in Britain in Section 4.4.

Special problems are presented by the situation of carers, usually other members of the family or household of the person who is mentally ill. They are as closely bound to ideas about the causes of mental illness, and professional role definitions, as they are to the felt or latent needs of those closely associated with mentally ill people. In addition, professionals who see themselves as advocates for the latter, particularly those seeking more independence, may see their interests as quite different from, or even in competition with, those who may be seeking peace and quiet at home. Even for active carers, professional or paid care at home may seem to threaten the little that lay family members feel they can do, however laborious and even damaging this care may be to their lives and/or incomes.

In this respect the different perspectives within the practice of family therapy are themselves of great interest. Berkowitz (1984 and 1988) has contrasted:

A   the involvement of family members in seeking the explanation of one member's mental illness, where their relationships are seen as at least partly to blame for the condition; and

B   seeking a viable solution to that member's problems, which may require less contact, or more support, to relieve the anxiety and burden experienced by other members of the family.

Family therapy has been criticized for being expensive in staff time and resources since the work is usually done in a team. It is also suggested that it has not proved its effectiveness in more serious cases. The first argument is probably more valid, but even this should be set against the enormous cost of hospitalization and continued medication. However, in an ethos which demands cuts in hospital services these arguments hold considerable sway, so increased attention has been directed at how families may be empowered or 'educated' to manage the mental illness of their members. The work on expressed emotion described in Section 4 has been valuable in this context. It has been found that relapse rates decreased dramatically among patients when their families were given educational programmes about the 'nature' of schizophrenia, as well as a supportive form of family counselling and assistance to reduce their levels of expressed emotions.

The treatment would in most cases continue medication but with the intention of reducing it gradually to a minimal level.

Falloon et al., (1986), analysing the impact and form of his domiciliary service based on psychiatric support for GPs in Buckingham, has claimed dramatic differences between people treated in the conventional forms of individual patient-centred psychiatry, with persistence rates of 83 per cent, and 50 per cent long-term remission from symptoms in the case of patients whose families have been trained in methods of structured problem solving. While one could argue that, for people hitherto so disregarded as family members, any attention is likely to have positive effects, differences of this magnitude suggest very significant differences between the effects of different treatments. (See also Berkowitz, 1984.)

Family therapy, such as one of the authors practises, involves teamwork with psychiatric nurses, psychiatrists and a psychologist, who organize a programme of rehabilitation. However, such a service may be separated from the 'acute' service which deals with mental health crises and is responsible for providing hospital care and medication. It is assumed that someone undergoing an acute phase of illness needs to be stabilized before any rehabilitation or family work can be started. As a result families may be seen relatively late in the progression of an 'illness', by which time the medical label has been attached and it may be much more difficult to reframe the problems as interpersonal or as due to wider societal factors.

With this proviso, what are the basic requirements of a community-based mental health service? Common characteristics have been developed in the U.S.A., Australia, and Italy. These include a seven-day week and twenty-four hour service; multidisciplinary teamwork in local areas with specific case management and staff responsibility for particular patients; a range of local day services as well as home support through a crisis-resolution service; open referral of patients by themselves or via any other agency and active intervention after initial stabilization to prevent further deterioration at home or at work. A service of this kind, with particular relevance to the treatment of ethnic minorities, was introduced in the

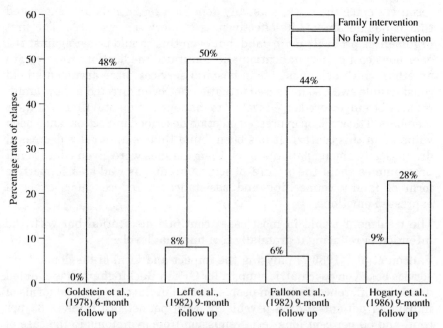

Figure 3.4 Rates of relapse from recovery back to schizophrenic episodes from four studies in the United States and England examining the protective effects of family therapy interventions versus no such interventions in schizophrenics who were continuously maintained on antipsychotic medicines.

Source: Gottesman, 1991, p.159

Sparkbrook area of Birmingham in 1987 when a community mental health team began working from a disused community centre. Of its population 50.6 per cent came from New Commonwealth countries in 1981 and a further 11.1 per cent from Ireland. The multidisciplinary team was selected to include several relevant language speakers and thereby aims to conduct every initial assessment in the patient's own language.

Once the twenty-four hour on-call service was operating, two-thirds of the patients could be treated at home, where three-quarters of them had been assessed. Although just over a third of those who were admitted to hospital had initially been assessed at home, the majority had been assessed on admission, at another medical centre or in police custody. Asian patients born abroad were significantly more likely to be treated at home as were those with children at home. But those admitted to hospital tended to be younger, single, living alone and to have shown some violence in the episodes that had led to their hospitalization (Dean, 1990). This is obviously not a service that could dispense with using hospitals, but its clinics also operate through GPs' health centres and day care is provided in different ways. Home treatment records are left in patients' homes and initially daily visits are paid by doctors and nurses with the result that the situation settles more quickly and relatives can discuss their problems — to which emergency hospitalization is seldom conducive – with each other as well as with medical staff. Patients who fail to attend clinics for injections or other appointments are actively followed up.

Comparative research currently in progress suggests that admissions in Sparkbrook have been reduced and fewer compulsory admissions are made by the police because problems are picked up earlier. And the common criticism of *laissez-faire* regimes that increase the burden laid on other carers has not been recorded there. Although their anguish was general, the stress felt by relatives was considerably less common in the case of those receiving home treatment than those treated in hospital, and even the burden experienced by other family members was more widely felt by those with relatives in hospital. In general relatives were more satisfied with home treatment than hospital admission. It may well be the case that the second phenomenon that was summarized from the 1971–81 comparison of hospital admissions in Sections 4.3 and 4.4, the fall in the rate of Pakistani and Bangladeshi (i.e. mainly Muslim) women admitted to mental hospital beds, may be addressed by this form of ethnically sensitive and domiciliary service. Rather than being put away privately or sent back to their country of origin their problems may be addressed where they arise without the cultural threats posed by mixed wards and group therapy etc.

The implications of these alternative modes of providing services for severely disturbed people and their families are far reaching. They represent far more active intervention than other more permissive or selective forms of service. But they are also supportive at the point where problems actually arise and become unbearable, within families or when difficulties arise at work or in finding or maintaining a home. The run-down of hospital beds does not represent a caring community but a way of saving money. If that money is used to resource more appropriate, and appreciated, models of care and treatment, then it could be termed a community service. If this also operates in such a way that problems do not generally escalate to the point that they cannot be contained, the service may even be acting in a preventive way. And that, by any calculation, would be better value for money!

ACTIVITY 4

Make a note of the features of these community mental health services we have just been discussing.

Do they seem to address some of the problems raised by compulsory detention or stigmatization which were taken up in the movement for reform attendant upon anti-psychiatric criticism?

If not, how do you think these differences might be reduced or even resolved?

---

6   CONCLUSIONS

As we have seen, the subject of mental health is complicated by confusion, disagreement and dilemmas. Even if the will to fund and implement policies for a variety of services exists, there may be limits to our intervention. The framework of discourse within which different theories are held has fundamental implications for such intervention. Above all the idea persists that mental illness is just that, an 'illness', for which a physical cause will ultimately be found. We have shown how researchers, like Brown and Harris, have preferred a redefinition of mental illness which shares some features of a physical illness, such as a clearly identifiable list of symptoms and a pattern of development etc., with other factors arising from social conditions and stress.

But the division between those committed to views of social causation as opposed to those wedded to medico-biological explanations not only persists but seems to create a kaleidoscope of modes of intervention. The language of discourse is itself a straitjacket. We would like to have avoided the term 'mental illness' but it is difficult to find suitable alternatives, especially when so many of those involved in service provision and debate are in health services. 'Mental health problem' is less specific, wordy and no less medical in implication. In time perhaps some of the diagnostic labels like schizophrenia and depression will be replaced by reference to specific changes in mental states which do not simply imply illness.

The association of explanations and services with families has also been confusing. On the one hand, family therapy approaches have provided some considerable hope and have shown some success in assisting families where mental health problems have arisen. On the other hand, family therapy has been placed in a difficult position if other forms of support are seen to have been withdrawn. This can appear to put both the blame and the burden of care on to families. They can become regarded as a kind of sub-class of 'undeserving' people who should take responsibility for the illness they have caused themselves. Intervention with such families, however, needs to include opportunities for education and above all employment to ease their poverty and help people who have suffered mental illness to gain a sense of self-respect. There is a powerful dilemma here. It may appear to be more compassionate and to place less blame on a family, if the form of intervention taken by the support services is to target one member as being ill and to simply offer that member help and support rather than to offer the whole family therapy. Yet this very definition of treating one of them as 'ill' can serve to label and 'produce' the separation implicit in the status of being 'ill'. It may also explain part of the apparent 'success' of community mental health services when positively applied to domiciliary care and the treatment of patients at home.

But questions also arise as to which interventions are most appropriate for particular types of illness. Diagnostic measures have been developed with claims to universal applicability, i.e. that they are culture free. When applied to epidemiological studies in different countries, the results suggest that schizophrenia, for example, is found universally with little variation in the rates for men and women, irrespective of race, culture, religion etc. Depression however, which is much more common, is subject to substantial variations. Should one therefore assume that intervention at a social and political level — in the form of greater community support for mothers with young children, better housing or more opportunities for employment — is more relevant to the prevention of depression?

If so, how do we respond to the very different rates of schizophrenia between some of the ethnic groups resident in Britain and the differences in the ways in which they are admitted to hospital? Some argue that schizophrenia is so socially disruptive that it will eventually always lead to hospitalization. It is also more commonly seen as an illness with organic causes which can reduce the attention given to ways of supporting those suffering from it. But the evidence from the active community mental health services suggests that schizophrenia can also be supported in the community and that other family members prefer this to hospitalization, which presents its own burden to them as well as the patients. And they have needed to use hospitals far less than other traditional forms of mental health services.

The combination of community support with family psycho-education, of the sort described in the use of the model based on expressed emotions, also suggests the importance of education about mental illness for the general population as well as for families. Although popular distinctions are usually made between people one knows, who have 'nervous break-downs', and others assumed to be 'really mad', the association of the latter with dangerousness persists. Certainly, the longer they remain beyond the intervention and potential support of any service, the more likely these people are to become unbearable to family and community. The detachment of some ethnic groups from the potential range of informal supportive services may help to explain their different rates and modes of hospital admission. But this can only be changed by the intervention of a different kind of local service agency. Mentally ill people are most danger-ous to themselves rather than the general public. Nearly one in ten of those with schizophrenia attempt suicide at some stage and such thoughts are one of the primary accepted symptoms of clinical depression. As Foucault (1967) suggests, perhaps our fear of mentally ill people reflects the fear of our own vulnerabilities. They face us with our own nightmares.

REFERENCES

Ackerman, N.W. (1958) *The Psychodynamics of Family Life*, New York, Basic Books.

American Psychiatric Association (1980) *DSM–3: Diagnostic and Statistical Manual of Mental Disorders*, third edition, Washington D.C., American Psychiatric Association.

Audit Commission (1986) *Making a Reality of Community Care,* London, H.M.S.O.

Barton, R. (1959) *Institutional Neurosis,* Bristol, John Wright.

Basaglia, F. (1981) 'Breaking the circuit of control', in Ingleby, D. (ed).

Bateson, G. (1956) *Steps to an Ecology of Mind*, New York, Ballantine Books (2nd edn 1972).

Beck, A.T. (1967) *Depression: Clinical, Experimental and Theoretical Aspects*, New York, Harper and Row.

Berkowitz, R. (1984) 'Therapeutic intervention with schizophrenic patients and their families: a description of a clinical research project', *Journal of Family Therapy,* 6, pp.211–33.

Berkowitz, R. (1988) 'Family therapy and adult mental illness: schizo-phrenia and depression', *Journal of Family Therapy,* 10, pp.339–56.

Boswell, D.M. (1986) *Report on Italian Community Mental Health Services, with Particular Reference to the Implementation of the 1978 Mental Health Service Law 180 in Different Regions*, Strasburg, Council of Europe.

Brittan, A. and Maynard, M. (1984) *Sexism, Racism and Oppression*, Oxford, Blackwell.

Brown, G.W. and Harris, T. (1978) *The Social Origins of Depression*, London, Routledge and Kegan Paul.

Burnham, J. (1980) *Family Therapy*, London, Tavistock.

Busfield, J. (1986) *Managing Madness: Changing Ideas and Practice*, London, Hutchinson.

Central Statistical Office (1992) *Social Trends 22*, London, H.M.S.O.

Cochrane, R. and Bal, S.S. (1989) 'Mental hospital admission rates of immigrants to England: a comparison of 1971 and 1981', *Social Psychiatry and Psychiatric Epidemiology*, 24, pp.2–11.

Cooper, D. (1967) *Psychiatry and Anti-psychiatry*, London, Paladin.

Dallos, R. (1991) *Family Belief Systems, Therapy and Change: a Constructional Approach*, Buckingham, Open University Press.

Dallos, R. (1993) *To be or not to be: Madness and the Family's Construction of Choice*, (Forthcoming).

Davison, G.C. and Neale, J.M. (1982) *Abnormal Psychology*, New York, Wiley and Son.

Dean, C. (1990) 'Home treatment for acute psychiatric illness', *British Medical Journal*, 301, pp.1021–3.

Der, G., Gupta, S. and Murray, R.M. (1990) 'Is schizophrenia disappearing?', *The Lancet*, 335, pp.513–16.

DSM–III *see* American Psychiatric Association (1980).

Falloon, R.H., Pederson, T. and Al-Khayyal, M. (1986) 'Enhancement of health giving family support versus treatment of family pathology', *Journal of Family Therapy*, 8, pp.339–50.

Fernando, S. (1989) *Race and Culture in Psychiatry*, London, Croom Helm.

Ferreira, A.J. (1963) 'Family myths and homeostasis', *Archives of General Psychiatry*, 9, pp.457–63.

Finch, J. (1989) *Family Obligations and Social Change*, Cambridge, Polity Press.

Foucault, M. (1967) *Madness and Civilization*, London, Tavistock.

Freud, S. (1960) *Totem and Taboo*, London, Routledge.

Glover, G.R. (1989a) 'The pattern of psychiatric admissions of Caribbean-born immigrants in London', *Social Psychiatry and Psychiatric Epidemiology*, 24(1), pp.49–56.

Glover, G.R. (1989b) 'Differences in psychiatric admission patterns between Caribbeans from different islands', *Social Psychiatry and Psychiatric Epidemiology*, 24(4), pp.209–11.

Glover, G.R. (1989c) 'Why is there a high rate of schizophrenia in British Caribbeans?', *British Journal of Hospital Medicine*, 42(1), pp.48–51.

Goffman, E. (1961) *Asylums: Essays on the Social Situation of Mental Patients and Other Inmates*, Chicago, Aldine.

Goldberg, D. and Huxley, P. (1980) *Mental Illness in the Community: the Pathways to Psychiatric Care*, London, Tavistock.

Gottesman, I. (ed.) (1991) *Schizophrenia Genesis*: the origins of madness, New York, W. H. Freeman and Company.

Griffiths, Sir Roy (1988) *Community Care: Agenda for Action,* London, H.M.S.O.

Grunebaum, H. (1984) 'A response to Terkelsen: schizophrenia and the family'; *Family Process,* 22, pp. 200–3.

Haley, J. (1980) *Leaving Home: the Therapy of Disturbed Young People,* New York, McGraw-Hill.

Hardwick, P.J. (1989) 'Families' medical myths', *Journal of Family Therapy,* 11(1), pp.3–29.

Harrison, G., Holton, A., Neilson, D., Owens, D., Boot, D. and Cooper, J. (1989) 'Severe mental disorder in Afro-Caribbean patients: some social demographic and service factors', *Journal of Psychological Medicine,* 19(3), pp.683–96.

Harrison, G., Owens, D., Holton, A., Neilson, D., and Boot, D. (1988) 'A prospective study of severe mental disorder in Afro-Caribbean patients', *Journal of Psychological Medicine,* 18(3), pp.643–57.

Hollingshead, A.B. and Redlich, F.C. (1958) *Social Class and Mental Illness: a Community Study,* New York, Wiley and Son.

Ingleby, D. (ed) (1981) *Critical Psychiatry: The Politics of Mental Health,* Harmondsworth, Penguin.

Jackson, D. (1957) 'The question of family homeostasis', *Psychiatry Quarterly Supplement,* 31, pp.79–99.

Jones, K. (1972) *A History of Mental Health Services,* London, Routledge and Kegan Paul.

Laing, R.D. (1969) *The Politics of the Family and Other Essays,* London, Tavistock.

Leff, J. and Vaughn, C. (1985) *Expressed Emotion in Families: its Significance for Mental Illness,* New York, Guilford.

Lewis, G., Croft-Jeffreys, C. and David, A. (1990) 'Are British psychiatrists racist?', *British Journal of Psychiatry,* 157, pp.410–15.

Littlewood, R. and Lipsedge, M. (1989) *Aliens and Alienists: Ethnic Minorities and Psychiatry,* London, Unwin Hyman.

Loring, M. and Powell, B. (1988) 'Gender, race and DSM–III: a study of the objectivity of psychiatric diagnostic behaviour', *Journal of Health and Social Behaviour,* 29 (Mch): pp.1–22.

McGovern, D. and Cope, R. (1987) 'The compulsory detention of males of different ethnic groups, with special reference to offender patients', *British Journal of Psychiatry,* 150, pp.505–12.

McGovern, D. and Cope, R. (1991) 'Second generation Afro-Caribbeans and young whites with a first admission diagnosis of schizophrenia', *Social Psychiatry and Psychiatric Epidemiology,* 26(2), pp.95–9.

McGrath, M.E. (1984) 'Where did I go?', in Gottesman, I. (ed).

Madanes, C. (1981) *Strategic Family Therapy,* San Francisco, Jossey Bass.

Orford, J. (ed) (1987) *Coping with Disorder in the Family*, London, Croom Helm.

Orford, J. (1992) *Community Psychology: Theory and Practice*, London, Wiley.

Palazzoli, M.S., Cecchin, G., Prata, G. and Boscolo, L. (1978) *Paradox and Counter Paradox*, New York, Jason Aronson.

Parker, G. (1990) *With Due Care and Attention: a Review of Research on Informal Care,* London, Family Policy Studies Centre.

Piercy, B.P. (1985) 'Making the best of it' in Gottesman, I. (ed).

Porter, R. (1987) *A Social History of Madness: Stories of the Insane,* London, Weidenfeld and Nicolson.

Royal Commission on the Laws Relating to Mental Illness and Mental Deficiency (1957) *Report*, Cmnd. 169, London, H.M.S.O.

Scull, A.T. (1977) *Decarceration: Community Treatment and the Deviant: a Radical View,* Cambridge, Polity Press (2nd edn. 1984).

Sedgwick, P. (1982) *Psycho Politics*, London, Pluto.

Szasz, T.S. (1970) *Ideology and Insanity: Essays on the Psychiatric Dehumanisation of Man,* New York, Doubleday.

Szasz, T. (1972) *The Myth of Mental Illness*, London, Paladin.

Terkelsen, K.G. (1983) 'Schizophrenia and the family: 11. Adverse effects of family therapy', *Family Process,* 22, pp.191–200.

Vostanis, P., Burnham, J. and Harris, Q. (1992) 'Changes in expressed emotion in systematic family therapy', *Journal of Family Therapy,* 14, 1, pp.15–29.

Wing, T.K., Cooper, T.E. and Sartorius, N. (1974) *Measurement and Classification of Psychiatric Symptoms,* Cambridge, Cambridge University Press.

Wynne, L., Ryckoff, I., Day, J. and Hirsch, S. (1958) 'Pseudo-mutuality in the family relations of schizophrenics', *Psychiatry*, 21, pp.205–20.

CHAPTER 4
OLD AGE

JOHN BALDOCK

I INTRODUCTION

To write about old age is to engage in controversy. People, both lay people and experts, disagree about almost every aspect of old age: when it begins, whether it is good or bad, a burden or a benefit, whether it is to be desired or to be feared. A brief discussion amongst a group of friends, probably like-minded about many things, will soon reveal a huge variety of belief and opinion about being old. Being old can include the best part of one's life and the worst. People's conceptions of old age are the repositories of their hopes and fears. It is a time we can now all reasonably expect to pass through, although, paradoxically, we are very poor at preparing for it. Old age will often be the most unpredictable and testing part of our lives and, because people are fearful of it, they are intolerant of images of it that do not fit their own. These differences are a reflection of the huge spread of experience that the term has to encompass.

How social policy can and does affect the experience of old age is similarly broad and uncertain. Old age is not essentially a social problem and not obviously the business of social policy. Yet the quality of our old age will be partly the product of social policies aimed at other parts of our lives. Indeed that so many of us can look forward to a long old age represents a victory over the diseases and traumas that in the past prevented a large proportion of the population completing a natural lifespan and which still cut short the lives of many in the Third World. When today old age is conceived of as a problem it is largely because of its association with images of disability and dependency. This association is, however, often a false one. Even many very old people retain all or much of their autonomy. Only just over half of those aged seventy-five and over report that their activities have been limited in any way over the last month (OPCS, 1989).

Yet the images of infirmity and dependency are not wholly wrong either. Built into the very idea of old age is that it is to be closer to death and, before death, frequently comes infirmity. No amount of 'positive thinking' can do away with these connotations. They are part of the meaning of terms like 'old woman', 'old man' and 'old age'. For most people old age will bring frailty and dependence at some point or other even if it is only for a very short time. What many people fear is that they cannot know how much dependence and for how long. At the level of the individual the disabilities of age are largely unpredictable. Neither are they equally allocated. For example, it is the unpredictability of the dependence that may come with age that makes it different from that due to youth or disability. In the case of the needs of children or those with permanent disabilities the future is much more certain and everyone can operate on that basis. In contrast to be old is to know that a stroke, a fall or the onset of dementia might quite suddenly change one's life. Becoming old brings great uncertainty and unfairness and these two themes of unpredictability and inequality will often recur in this account of responses to old age. They are important reasons why the relationships between old people, their families and the state are both complex and varied.

In order to work, social policies have to make broad assumptions about whole groups of people. Within limits, this is feasible in the case of categories such as, for example, the unemployed, single parent families and young delinquents. In contrast, it is a constant theme of this chapter that a real problem for social policy is that old people cannot be treated in this way. It is, for example, very difficult to deduce the needs of old people from general social characteristics such as class, education, income, race and gender. As one gets older the crude social determinants of one's life merge with the accidental and with individual personality to produce unique outcomes. The ratio of the significance of the social to the personal shifts in favour of the latter. The older a person is the less that can be predicted about them. Consider by way of illustration the following. To know simply someone is one year old is to know, with a high degree of probability, a great deal about them. To know someone is twenty-five, white, male and a graduate would still allow some intelligent guesses about their health, their occupation, their income and even their interests. But one can know a great many of the social characteristics of a seventy-five year old and yet presume little about their needs. Would they be well or ill, fully fit or slightly disabled, clear headed or confused? Will they be married or single, living at home or in a hospital or some other institution? Will they be rich or poor, depressed or content, have a long or a little time to live? As we get older so individual differences have time to accumulate and generalizations become less reliable. This is one of the errors of what is sometimes called 'ageism', the tendency to discriminate against people on the basis of their age. Ageism is particularly vicious and simplistic in its prejudices against old people. Yet the older a person, the less any presumption about them is likely to be true and the more social intervention is likely to fall foul of individual differences.

ACTIVITY I

Make a list of the positive and negative attributes of old age. Then consider how you constructed this list. Is it a product of distinct events in your own life? Do you think these images of old age are widely shared in British society?

'Being old can include the best part
of life and the worst'

2   THE POSITIVE ASPECTS OF OLD AGE

Because this chapter concentrates mainly on the burdens and disadvantages of age and social policy responses to them, it is appropriate first to
spend a little time on longevity's more positive aspects. As has already
been pointed out, the fact that most of us can expect a substantial portion
of fit and able life after retirement is itself a triumph for which social
policy can claim some credit. As recently as the 1930s life expectancy for a
man in Britain was less than sixty years and for a woman less than sixty-
five. Three-score-years-and-ten may be the classic definition of the natural lifespan but it is only in the second half of the twentieth century that
attaining it has become a mass phenomenon. The scale of the change is
vividly caught by Ronald Blythe.

> If a Renaissance or Georgian man could return he would be as much
> astonished by the sight of the two or three thousand septuagen-
> arians and octogenarians lining a south coast resort on a summer's
> day in their preponderantly white and palely coloured clothes, as he
> would by a television set. Astonished and maybe shocked. His was a
> world where it was the exception to go grey, to reach the menopause,
> to retire, to become senile and to acquire that subtle blend of voice,
> skin and behavioural changes which feature so largely in our long-
> lived times.
>
> (Blythe, 1981 pp. 11–12).

Indeed, as the statistics show, it would be not just someone from Renaissance or Georgian times who would be surprised but a Victorian or Edwardian too.

One of the consequences of the relative newness of a longish retirement as a normal expectation is that the manner in which it should be lived is relatively unscripted or ordered by social conventions. Most obviously, freedom from the obligation to engage in paid work or to take responsibility for dependents, provides many people, men much more than women, with great choice as to how to fill their days. They are no longer bound by the need to abide by the rules and conventions of time-keeping and behaviour that employment or family responsibilities require. Their lives are less structured by outside forces and institutions. However, it must be remembered that this freedom is less evident for many women. For them the labour of housework and caring for family, frequently for their husbands, often for their grandchildren, continues into old age just as it has done throughout their lives. It is no accident that the television comedy series 'Last of the Summer Wine', portraying the footloose pranks of a gang of active retirees, is about three men and not three women. Quite realistically, the elderly women in the series are almost always engaged in some sort of work.

Nonetheless, it is clear that many people do find, in early retirement at least, a time of exceptional freedom in which the manner of their lives is less socially determined than ever and in which the full force of their individuality can express itself. Again, Ronald Blythe vividly portrays the quality of this time:

> Life is good and buoyant then, and we want it to last. With a new house in a new place and, subsequently, a new circle, there can come a new energy which breaks into new interests, often with more forcefulness than that which inaugurated our working days, for we still retain the poise given us by the seniority of work from which we have just retired. Under modern conditions too, the sixties to the early seventies are often very healthy years. As Montaigne observed, 'The greatest vice the sages see in us is, that our desires incessantly grow young again; we are always beginning again to live'. Our studies and desires should sometimes be sensible of old age; we have one foot in the grave, and yet our appetites and pursuits spring up every day.
>
> (Blythe., 1981, p.21)

This is the time of life that Peter Laslett dubbed the 'third age' and contrasted with the 'fourth age' of dependency and disablement that leads to death (Laslett, 1989). He has called this third age 'the crown of life — the period of self-fulfilment'.

Yet it takes skill and resources, both personal and material, to make the most of this time. Some people are too worn out and empty to do so and Laslett argues that it should be the task of social policy to help people to

Portraits of age

make the most of this stage of their lives. Here there is not the space to consider the many novel policies that have been suggested. The pressure on public welfare budgets means few of them are likely to come to fruition. What this section seeks, in doing no more than allude to the debate about the third age, is to emphasize the breadth and ambiguity of the term 'old age'. It is open to a huge range of social constructions, both in terms of the varied reality it must encompass and in terms of the hopes and fears we all invest in it.

3   SOCIAL POLICY AND ITS CONSEQUENCES FOR OLD PEOPLE

Over the last forty-five years, during the life of the post-war welfare state, the impact of government action on the welfare of old people has been profound although largely as an indirect consequence of policies aimed at the whole population. The contribution of the state to the welfare and care of older people is largely a by-product of policies that affect their whole lifetime well-being rather than the specific needs of old age. In this sense, too, the current social problems of old people today are a consequence of the social policies of the past, and of their successes as well as of their failures. The welfare of retired people is crucially determined by their health, their incomes and their housing, not just in old age but across their whole lifetimes, and in all three social policy plays a fundamental role. There is general agreement that improvements in the material quality of people's lives are the major cause of the drop in mortality and the increased average life expectancy that have characterized this century. In particular, the fact that most people (but certainly not all) can afford satisfactory diets and are adequately housed is substantially due to the near universalism of state pensions, the expansion of publicly-subsidized occupational pensions and to the enormous direct and indirect state investment in housing. People are living longer because their material welfare is better and that in turn is in part a consequence of a huge range of state interventions in social and economic life. Yet the ultimate welfare outcomes of this 'progress' are not unambiguous in their effects on old people and their families. The gains have been substantial but they bring in their train new costs and problems. In particular, the role of social policy and the boundaries of public and private responsibilities are still uncertain and subject to fundamental renegotiation.

Post-war provision for old people was built upon the Beveridge principle of universalism. In the four main areas relevant to retired people (incomes, health care, residential homes and home care) the state would seek to provide a decent minimum available to all. But in practice the minimum was often less than decent and, instead of being a source of fundamental social citizenship, the social services became a foundation of inequality. The 'social division of welfare' (Titmuss, 1963; Sinfield, 1978), the ways in which social policy interventions tend to replicate and even accentuate existing economic and social differences, has become more pronounced in its effects on the retired than any other group. Both the poorest and the richest in society are disproportionately represented amongst old people. On the one hand, massive state subsidies to those able to buy their own houses and accumulate private savings and occupational pensions have created a growing class of elderly who wield considerable economic power both in the market and in their families (Forrest and Murie, 1989; Hamnett, 1991). On the other hand, those whose working lives have been afflicted by low pay, unemployment and disease-inducing jobs find themselves in old age destined to live on the official poverty line, dependent upon declining public social services and with nothing to offer their families but their dependency (Walker and Walker, 1987). Women, in particular those whose pension entitlements are derived from their husbands, can find that growing older is closely associated with growing poorer (Walker, 1987). These cumulative processes, whereby the rich tend to get richer and the poor poorer as both get older, have been exacerbated by recent changes in social policy. Since the mid-seventies, economic constraints and political ideology have meant that universalism is giving way to residualism. State services are increasingly minimal benefits targeted on those who cannot afford or find private provision. Only in the National Health Service has the universal principle of equal treatment for all been sustained, and even here many now argue it is under threat as a result of the recent changes which introduced internal markets into the system (Paton, 1990).

The greatest and most blatant source of disadvantage faced by old people is the low incomes many have to live on. In 1980 the median couple, faced with the retirement of the main wage earner, experienced a fall to 54 per cent of their pre-retirement income (Gilbert et al., 1989 p.110). Four out of ten households headed by a person over retirement age rely entirely on state benefits for their income. But these benefits do not provide the decent income Beveridge envisaged and have effectively become poverty benefits. At its peak at the end of the 1970s the state retirement pension for a couple reached only 45 per cent of average earnings (HMSO, 1991a; 1991b). Since then state pensioners' incomes have been in decline relative to those in work. The problem for the substantial minority who have not been able to accumulate private sources of (state subsidized) income is that the government now no longer expects that the universal state pension, a cornerstone of the Beveridge welfare state, will be their principal source of income and is allowing its value to fall in relative terms. In 1980 the government altered the system under which the state pension was uprated annually in line with wages and replaced it with indexation to prices. It was argued that increasing numbers of retired people had adequate savings and occupational pensions and could and would wish to provide for their welfare privately.

In 1991 the maximum state retirement pension was £46.90 a week for a single person and £75.10 for a couple (£20 less than if it had continued to be uprated annually in line with wages). It may be that in the longer term the accumulation of occupational and personal pensions will add substantially to these 'poverty pensions'. That depends very much on whether the private pensions industry can match inflation. So far, however, for many, the much heralded private provision amounts to little. Six out of ten pensioner households have a private or occupational pension or some savings to supplement their incomes but these sources often constitute tiny additions. In 1987 the average occupational pension was £23.30 a week, 14 per cent of average earnings at the time (HMSO, 1991b). Because a few people get very large pensions this means that more than half of occupational pensioners were receiving less than this average. Another problem is that a significant minority of people, those whose working lives are characterized by intermittent and part-time employment, are unlikely to have occupational pensions anyway. As recently as 1988 25 per cent of men retiring from full-time work did not have an occupational pension (OPCS, 1990a). Even the state retirement pensions of many people are incomplete because either they or their partners did not enjoy sufficiently regular employment during their working lives in order to have a full social security contribution record. In 1989, 1,441,000 single pensioners and 329,000 couples (that is just over 20 per cent of all pensioners) were receiving means-tested income support to supplement their state pensions and were therefore, by definition, living on the poverty line (Department of Social Security, 1991).

4   CRITIQUES OF THE EFFECTS OF SOCIAL POLICY

Over the last twenty years much of the writing and research on the social and psychological circumstances of older people has been very critical of the role of the state and social policy in industrial societies. This literature might broadly be called the new 'radical social gerontology' (e.g. Walker, 1980; Townsend, 1981; Phillipson, 1982). Its criticisms have focused on three related issues: the creation of the 'structured dependency' of all old people, the generation of systematic inequalities amongst old people and the social construction of a negative image of age itself. The literature dealing with these issues is large and the arguments are vigorously contested. Here we can merely summarize the implications of these debates for the family life of old people and for social policies that impinge on it. The main point to be made here is that there are no obvious or easy lessons for practical policy intervention to be derived from this research and theorizing.

One way of grasping the ideas of the radical gerontologists is to notice how they deal very directly with ideas about old age that are current in everyday conversation. Thus, the concept of 'structured dependency' is essentially what people mean when they observe that by simply reaching the age of retirement they find themselves thrust into a different and less eligible social category despite the fact that they as individuals feel quite unchanged in their skills, abilities and needs. The phenomenon of mass retirement from the labour market at a particular age is very much a twentieth century one. The 1901 census found almost 60 per cent of men aged sixty-five and over to be in employment. By 1981 the figure was only 10 per cent and there is little doubt that the 1991 census will show a further fall (Johnson, 1989, p.64). The pattern for women is essentially the same: in 1981 only 8 per cent of women aged sixty and over remained in paid employment despite the huge growth in female participation in the labour market. Rather in the same way as the nineteenth century saw the creation of the social category of childhood extending well into physical maturity, with all the implications that has had for families and social policy, so the twentieth century has seen the creation of a category of retired person which applies long before the onset of physical frailty and dependency. This, argue some researchers, is for many a forced dependency. The state, employers and trade unions, often with the best of intentions, have conspired to create an almost compulsory social status where one must depend on pensions and savings and fall back upon the family for personal support. As has already been shown, the condition of retirement amounts, for the vast majority, to a substantial reduction in their financial welfare. Add to this the fact that effective exclusion from the primary labour market does not simply bring financial costs but social and mental ones too. People are abruptly cut off from a major source of social interaction and support. For many people work is the main basis of their social life and their chief source of social status and self-image. In retirement they find they have to seek these largely from within the family and their local communities and at a time when their ability to contribute may have been sharply reduced.

Clearly the above characterization of retirement is an extreme one. It has already been argued that for many retirement is welcomed and enjoyed and that, for those who have been able to accumulate adequate pension entitlements and savings, it is also a time of financial security. Yet, however positive people's responses and however rich their resources, there is no disguising the socially compulsory nature of the status of pensioner and the enforced dependencies that it brings for people. This structured dependency, the creation of a social status of less worth and eligibility, is the paradoxical achievement of twentieth century social and economic policy.

Closely related to the operation of structured dependency are the inequalities that appear to be particularly associated with age. Again the work of social researchers has tackled the issues that people routinely comment on: that old age is different for men and women; that the inequalities of class and ethnic origin are accentuated with age and become more crucial to how life is lived. There is, for example, a large literature on the relationship between gender and age. Women are more likely to live alone, to become socially isolated, to be poor, to be entirely dependent on state benefits — three-quarters of pensioners on income support are women (Department of Social Security, 1991) — or to experience direct financial dependency on others (Peace, 1986). At the same time, for women, reaching the age of retirement often does not mean a reduction in their workload or responsibilities. Housework and care for others — be it spouse, grandchildren or even very elderly parents — are likely to continue. On the other hand, the very nature of their 'women's duties' means that age does not necessarily bring isolation and disengagement. Women are more likely to have strong emotional and functional ties with other members of their families, particularly daughters. Thus the gains and losses are not easily evaluated. Not only are there great varieties of experience between different women but between individual women's experience at different stages of their 'old age'. A reasonable income, strong social contacts and high self-esteem in early retirement can deteriorate to poverty, isolation and depression in very old age. In the face of this variety it is invidious to attempt some kind of social audit of advantage and disadvantage between the sexes.

ACTIVITY 2

As you read the next section consider to what extent old age is a time when people, particularly old women, become 'socially invisible'. Do you think society disregards their wishes and even their physical presence? Do they lose power and rights?

Social researchers are under immense pressure to reach general evaluative conclusions but in this area they are more likely to reflect a prevailing academic ideology than their observations. Compare, for example, two studies thirty years apart: Peter Townsend's *The Family Life of Old People* (1957) and Janet Ford and Ruth Sinclair's *Sixty Years On: Women Talk*

About Old Age (1987). Both provide exceptionally sensitive portrayals of the way in which social differences between the sexes are often accentuated with age. Despite the lapse of thirty years the accounts of old people's lives reported in the two studies are astonishingly similar. But the conclusions drawn are much more peculiar to their time. Ford and Sinclair conclude that

> while all older people are subject to the discriminatory and demeaning processes of ageism, women suffer additional disadvantages because of their low status, their traditional role(s), their lack of economic power and because the majority of them live alone... In so far as the world of the old is predominantly the world of women, they are at particular risk of the outcomes of... stereotyping exploitation, disregard and humiliation.
>
> (Ford and Sinclair, 1989, p.74)

Townsend, on the other hand, observed how men

> could not match in range or quality the wives' bonds with relatives, particularly daughters and no longer could contribute much to their welfare... Those unable to help their wives or female relatives in domestic and family activities were left without many ways of justifying their lives... This was why so many men talked of their retirement as a tragedy. They were forced to recognize that it was not their working life that was over, it was their life. 'In the sweat of thy face shalt thou eat bread till thou return unto the ground.'
>
> (Townsend, 1957, pp.146-7)

These are powerful and deeply felt conclusions and they are not untypical of the literature on ageing. Research documenting the dependencies and inequalities of age is bound to produce strong reactions and, from there, to generate a presumption in favour of public policy remedies. This is partly because of the way the research has demonstrated how ineluctable and remorseless are the processes which lead to unhappy outcomes. Where they occur, the inequalities of age — low income, poor health, severely handicapping disabilities, the burdens of care and family obligations, discrimination and feelings of exclusion and low selfworth — have usually accumulated over people's whole lifetimes and in ways that are deeply embedded in the social organization of society. Individuals can do little to prevent them. There is, however, a danger of the research literature being used to create new stereotypes and inappropriate policies. Social research produces general statements about risks and probabilities to which there may be many individual exceptions. Very rarely can clear and obvious social policy remedies be deduced from research findings about the social behaviour of large numbers of people.

Work on the needs of the elderly amongst the minority ethnic communities is an illustration of the limits to the usefulness of social research as a guide to social intervention. It has been shown that black old people have higher probabilities of illness and disability (Bhalla and Blakemore, 1981), of poverty (Cook and Watt, 1987), of language and communication difficulties with public services (Norman, 1985), of poor housing and of residence in inner cities (Johnson et al., 1983), of more rigid gender divisions within the home (Donovan, 1986) but that their social isolation is likely to be less and family and community support greater. However, all these findings are poor guides to service provision. The work of the Birmingham Community Care project in the inner city areas of Sparkhill and Sparkbrook (Evers et al., 1990) shows how, while these generalizations are, in a statistical sense, true, there is an infinite variety of exceptions. Indeed it is often those who are the exceptions to the rule that social services should attend to. Thus, contrary to the general pattern of research-based expectations, they found old people of Asian origin who were isolated and without family or community ties, Muslim sons who provided personal care to female elderly, black families where the cultural rifts between ageing parents and children were major obstacles to care giving, instances where expectations of domiciliary services were unrealistically high and others where to ask for help was seen as over-whelmingly stigmatizing. In essence what they discovered were not homogeneous ethnic minority communities whose particular character-istics and needs could in principle be calculated and met with suitably designed services but rather communities and families in rapid transition both economically and culturally. Almost any presumption about need and likely response had a high chance of being inappropriate in individ-ual cases. Indeed the difficulty for those who would design services for old people from minority communities is this very variety and the speed at which it is changing. Certainly the numbers of old people from the ethnic minorities will be proportionately the fastest growing group over the next thirty years but the problems and disabilities of age will come to people from minority communities at very different stages in their understand-ing of and acceptance by the wider society. Amongst members of the minority communities, social and cultural variety, and diversity of response to social provision, are likely to be as important as any charac-teristics and needs they have in common. Unfortunately the dominant shared factor is likely to be their experience of racism and the probability that they will recognize it in the available services. There is a very thin line between the provision of services that are sensitive to cultural differ-ences and those that make racist assumptions.

Paradoxically, these dangers of crude and potentially stigmatizing selec-tivity were what the British welfare system was designed to avoid. The post-war Beveridge welfare state is now blamed for many ills, and in particular for making unwarranted assumptions about the nature of the family and women's role within it. The needs of old people and especially of old women and of female carers were rendered invisible. It has been a long battle to make them apparent. These outcomes are quite explicable in terms of the masculine prejudices of Beveridge and of the class from which he came, but they are also the product of a more defendable central purpose which was to avoid services that made assumptions about the way people choose to live.

The Beveridge Report had its ideological origins in the minority Poor Law report of 1909. There Beatrice Webb, George Lansbury and their fellow Fabians argued for what was called 'administrative functionalism', a system that organized social services 'to do a specific job and not to provide for the needs of a specific group' (Rodgers, 1969, p.62). They specifically sought to reject the ideas of social work and the Charity Organization Society which attempted, on the basis of 'scientific research', to tailor service provision to the particular problems of the indigent and their families. Henceforth the dominant form of state assistance was to be the provision of a minimum income. Beveridge was opposed to what he called the 'Santa Claus state' (Harris, 1977, p.414) and believed that, once provided with sufficient resources, people should be allowed to spend and live as they wished, 'free from supervision'. It is probable that the Webbs, Beveridge and the early Fabians would see the current debate, with its talk of targeting, of care management, of 'family policies' fitted to different household structures and varied cultural norms, as a return to the bad old ways of the Charity Organization Society. Yet they would surely also be forced to admit that it has been the failure of universalism to protect many retired people from hardship that has led to this change of tack.

5   HOW AGEING POPULATIONS POSE A CHALLENGE TO SOCIAL POLICY

At the end of the twentieth century, there are important reasons why ageing and old age itself can be argued to be the dominant pressure points in social policy, affecting all industrialized societies and many of the 'developing' nations too. On the one hand, in so far as old age is considered to be natural and normal and to be desired, our culture does not sanction public intervention in the detailed organization of people's lives. The condition of age is defined as essentially part of the private sphere of the individual and the family and, thus, where intervention does occur it has a tendency to be stigmatizing. On the other hand, in so far as old age is the source of great distress and burden, public support becomes very necessary and the social norms of privacy, independence and family solidarity become obstacles to sensible solutions. This is perhaps part of the reason why public policy in this area is more haphazard, inefficient, unpredictable and unequal than in almost any other. As populations age these failings are becoming increasingly manifest and unacceptable with the result that care of old people has become the cutting edge of policy innovation in modern welfare societies.

As is documented throughout this book the boundaries between the public and the private, between family life and civil society, are shifting at a time of change and pressure. This remapping is a response to uncertainty about who will perform core functions necessary for the reproduction and continuence of society. In the industrial nations at least, both the state and the family are deeply involved in the support and care of old people. As the size of the task grows so a degree of social and political renegotiation is taking place about who shall be responsible for what and who shall do what. In some of the developing nations the prospect of a substantial increase in the numbers of old people is forcing governments to consider welfare issues they have so far been able to avoid and to begin to step into an area that has traditionally been regarded as the sole prerogative of the family. Four core forces are contributing to this remapping of the relationships between state and family over the issues of old age.

Firstly, we live in an era of rapidly ageing populations. In most industrial nations the population over fifty will soon constitute the majority (OECD, 1988). Secondly, the nature of the family itself is changing, partly as a consequence of this ageing process. More people are living in single person households or in two person households where there are no children. Separation, divorce and remarriage have for large sections of the population complicated the traditional definitions of expectation and obligation between parents and children, between one generation and the next, between the old and the young. Thirdly, improvements in incomes and housing conditions have allowed many more old people to continue to live on their own rather than with others, though most have frequent contact with family and friends (see Tables 4.1 and 4.2).

Table 4.1 Living arrangements of people aged 65 and over (excluding those in residential institutions)

	1962 %		1985 %	
Living alone	--	} 55	36	} 81
With spouse only	--		45	
With siblings	7		3	
With children	32		7	
Other	6		9	

Sources: Townsend, 1968; OPCS, 1989

Table 4.2 Frequency of seeing relatives or friends: people aged 65 and over living in the community

	Every day %	2–3 times a week %	once a week %	once a month %	less than monthly %	never %
Lives alone	43	29	17	6	2	2
Lives with spouse only	29	30	25	10	4	2

Based on data extracted from various tables in OPCS, 1989

Fourthly, the same processes that are producing an ageing demographic structure are also rapidly increasing the numbers of people who are frail and dependent because of their old age. These people need care, that care can be burdensome and often it can only be adequately carried out through complex collaboration between state and family.

As we approach the end of the twentieth century, these four core sources of pressure — the ageing population, the changing nature of the family, the preference of old people to remain in their own homes and the growth in the numbers of people needing help because of their age — are, in some ways, the mirror images of the changes that were forcing renegotiation of the relationship between family and public policy at the end of the nineteenth century. Then, because of reduced infant mortality, the population was getting younger not older. It was childhood, defined as a period of dependency, that was being extended rather than old age. The structure, functions and social meaning of the family were changing because of youth not age. All these forces meant that a hundred years ago a key pressure point in social policy was the relationship between state and family concerning the care and nurture of children. New social policies emerged that shifted the balance of responsibility for educating children and for protecting them from cruelty and exploitation. The nature and limits of parental responsibility were redefined. These social policy issues, dominant at the turn of the last century, have not gone away a hundred years later but now they are issues of clearly defined renegotiation between state and family. For example, the 1989 Children Act is notable for its shift of emphasis towards an insistence that natural parents cannot shed responsibility for their child even where someone else, such as the state, has taken over daily care. By contrast, in the case of old age, much more fundamental boundaries are still to be established between state and family. What, for example, should be the balance of responsibilities between adult children and the social services when an old person needs daily help? It remains very unclear who is obliged or even likely to do what when need and emergencies arise.

ACTIVITY 3

Refer to Tables 4.1, 4.2 and 4.5 and note down the level of live-in assistance, contact and regular help given by children, sisters/brothers and relatives to those aged sixty-five and over. What do these figures suggest about the obligations people feel they have for an elderly relative?

---

6   THE CARE NEEDS OF FRAIL OLD PEOPLE

There is considerable debate about whether improvements in life expectancy mean less or more ill-health and dependency. It may well be that the paradoxical effect of social policy has been to increase social need in old age. More people are living longer and are dependent on others for help for longer. This issue is the subject of a currently unresolved debate in the gerontological and medical literature. Some, most famously J. F. Fries (1980, p.130), have argued that not only are people living longer but they will be ill and dependent for less time. He sees the period of reasonably healthy independence extending well into what was formerly seen as old age and the time of dependence before death as shorter than before. Others, while not disputing that more people are living longer, point out that there is no strong evidence of age-related morbidity declining and that we are moving towards societies in which a huge proportion will be suffering from chronic and dependency-inducing diseases, some over very long periods of time.

These competing scenarios pose quite different prospects for both the family and the state. If older people remain fit and healthy for longer and are, on average, only briefly dependent, then their ability to contribute positively to family life is much greater. There will be potential for a transfer of resources and even labour downwards to the benefit of younger members of the family. Old people may also become an increasingly important source in the formal labour market and the much heralded pensions-burden may be less of a problem. On the other hand if the more pessimistic scenario is correct then the implications for families and social policy are likely to be much more negative and burdensome.

However, at the moment there is no reason to adjust the age-dependent forecasts of dependency that make up the core data of most discussions of the implications of ageing populations. Our evidence of changes over time in the amounts of disability from which people report themselves to be suffering comes from large scale surveys like the annual *General Household Survey* and from smaller, one-off studies. These show little of the improvements common sense might predict. Whether people consider themselves able to perform particular activities (like wash, cook or dress for instance) tends to be strongly affected by cultural attitudes and changing assumptions about what is normal. For example, men and women report very differently on an issue such as being able to make a cup of tea! Put another way, measures of disability are strongly affected by peoples' expectations of the roles they are to play in family life. However, bearing in mind these provisos, reported levels of disability at particular ages are not falling and some research has even found that they are rising (OPCS, 1990a, p.61).

One of the most commonly cited projections of current levels of disability and dependence onto future population estimates is that calculated by Melanie Henwood and Malcolm Wicks (see Table 4.3).

Table 4.3 Elderly people (thousands) in the UK

	1985 (base)	1991	2001	change (between 1985 and 2001
(a) Unable to bath unaided				
65–74	217	219	210	–7
75–84	352	379	395	+43
85+	208	272	356	+148
All 65+	777	870	961	+184
(b) Unable to get in/out of bed unaided				
65–74	48	49	47	–1
75–84	75	79	82	+7
85+	47	61	80	+33
All 65+	170	189	209	+39

Source: Henwood and Wicks, 1984, p.16 (figures updated 1992 by M. Henwood)

In Table 4.3 the two categories estimated are a good indication of (1) those who will need help on a daily basis and (2) those who will need almost constant surveillance. What this data shows is that we are at the moment living through a time of very substantial proportional increases in the numbers of old people who need intensive support. At the same time the absolute numbers are not overwhelming: it is clearly not beyond the resources of an affluent industrial society to deal adequately with this need were the will and the means found. Neither, from a policy point of view, are the numbers unpredictable as, for example, they tend to be when planning the demand for schools or teachers. Policy makers get considerable advance notice of the projected numbers of old people. Yet these very certainties are at the root of what might even be described as the current squabble between state, families and old people themselves about who is going to be responsible for what in the care of old people. The very predictable increases in the numbers of old needing care have pushed current patterns of support into crisis.

7   THE CRISIS IN CARE

The implicit post-war promise of a comprehensive safety net of support for the frail and disabled has never been fulfilled. State and family have tended to operate as distinct alternatives to one another. For the large majority of the dependent elderly, it has traditionally been the case that they were either cared for at home by their families, or by the state in an institution. There has been little role for intermediate forms of care where state and family collaborate and cooperate. Movement conventionally takes place between the two extremes of care solely by the family and care solely by an institution. When one form of care breaks down, or is not available, the other takes over (see Figure 4.1). It is only recently, as governments pursue policies to construct a 'mixed economy of welfare' that we are beginning to see signs of social policies that recognize the central role of the family and seek to support or relieve informal carers by working explicitly in partnership with them.

One consequence is increasing use of residential care. The proportion of people aged sixty-five and over in institutional care in Britain is relatively low by European standards. For example, in 1985 the level in Sweden was 9 per cent, in the Netherlands 14 per cent, but in Britain only 5 per cent (Kraan et al., 1991). However, in Britain over the last decade the rate of institutionalization has been rising relative to the numbers and age-composition of elderly population and this is in part a reflection of a 'flight' from poor home care services (Laing, 1991). Unable to find places in hospital or state residential homes, old people and their relatives have turned to the private sector. The extraordinary growth in the for-profit residential care industry, a 300 per cent increase in beds during the 1980s, has been fuelled both by the absence of alternatives and by the fact that 50 per cent of residents are funded, wholly or in part, by the state through the social security system. Under the current rules of the system, which applied until April 1993, any person entitled to income support will also receive the cost of their board and lodging, up to certain limits, if they

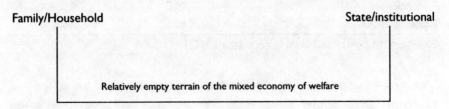

Figure 4.1 Forms of care

enter a residential home. This has effectively meant that any old person with assets of less than £3,000 can enter a private residential or nursing home, with no test of need other than the willingness of the proprietor to admit them, and that person's costs will automatically be paid by the state. For those with more than £3,000 there is an incentive to 'spend-down' or 'pauperize' themselves so that they too can be paid for in full by the state. Those with capital between £3,000 and £8,000 have had to pay a proportion of residential care costs, those with more have had to pay all their costs. The growth in the use of residential care has happened almost accidentally and has been described by government reports as a perverse effect. Nonetheless there is evidence that few people enter private residential care who do not need it and its growth is proof of pent-up demand (Gibbs and Bradshaw, 1988).

Current levels of public provision of care services to people in their own homes are not sufficient to constitute a reliable alternative to institutional care. Tables 4.4 and 4.5 are taken from the *General Household Survey*, the only large-scale national source of data, and give an indication of where old people who remain in the community get help from, particularly those who cannot perform domestic tasks or who need assistance in performing daily living functions. What emerges is the importance of family care and to a lesser extent the role of state services. There is very little evidence of commercial or voluntary help with personal care tasks.

Table 4.4   Use of public care services by all people 65+ with no problems with domestic activities, and by those who are unable to perform at least one domestic activity* (1985)

	Percentage of sample	
	65+ no problems	65+ one or more problems
Casualty or outpatient dept of hospital in last year	16.7	11.6
Hospital in-patient in last year	10.3	10.8
Saw doctor in last month	34.3	21.6
Home nurse in last month	2.7	9.8
Home help in last month	5.7	11.9
Day centre or lunch club in last month	7.0	4.4
Meals on wheels in last month	1.6	4.4
Paid help	4.0	10.0
None of above	10.5	16.2

Based on data extracted from various tables in OPCS, 1989

*Activities = shopping, cleaning, climbing stairs, laundry, cooking and making tea.
Number in sample = 3,386

Table 4.5   Regular sources of help for people 65+ who cannot perform activities*
of daily living on their own

Help received from	Percentage of sample
Spouse	28
Other household member	17
Relatives	20
Paid help	1
Nurse, social worker	45
Other	2
No one	1

Based on data extracted from various tables in OPCS, 1989

*Activities = move about house, get out of bed, negotiate stairs, bathe, walk out-
side, cut toe-nails, wash face/hands

Number in sample = 579

It is now not possible to simply ask for more resources for the public
system (or even for a proposed mixed system) because it has been shown,
in a whole series of studies, that those funds that do exist for care of the
frail elderly are very poorly used. For example, the Personal Social Services Research Unit at the University of Kent in 1990 completed a large-
scale survey of how ten local governments in England and Wales allocated
their resources for the home care of old people over a period of two and a
half years (Davies et al., 1990). The results were in many ways most
puzzling. There seemed to be no rational pattern to the allocation of the
work the social workers and other professionals were doing. Some old
people with very high dependency (what was called 'critical interval
need'), who needed help very often and very unpredictably, were actually
getting very low levels of support from the social services. At the other end
of the spectrum, some low-level need people (with 'long interval need')
were getting high levels of expensive state input. In between were people
with a whole range of needs who appeared to be getting quite random
allocations of help. A further complication was that across a group of
people with a similar level of need, it was not possible to show that those
getting a lot of service help had measurably better welfare outcomes than
those getting very little.

The existing system of care, already very inadequate, during the course of
the 1980s, crossed a threshold of political and social acceptability. One
result was to force the government to initiate a substantial reconstruction
of public provision which emphasized a mixed economy of support for old
people outside institutions and in the community. Another, closely related
consequence, was to stimulate innovation and experimentation with new
ways of supporting the frail elderly. Together these responses promised a
very different, and possibly better, world of care for old people in the
future. However, these new forms of care also entail risks. They often
involve questionable assumptions about the amount of caring work that
will be done by families and particularly by women.

ACTIVITY 4

Make a list of the arguments for and against the family, as opposed to the state, shouldering the responsibility of caring for old people.

---

8   THE GROWING RESPONSIBILITY OF THE FAMILY

It has long been understood by researchers in this field that by far the largest part of care for old people in the community is provided by families (e.g. Townsend, 1957) and that little account has been taken of this reality by public policy. Numerous studies have shown how poorly integrated social services are with informal care and how insensitive they can be to the needs of carers (Pitkeathly, 1989; Lewis and Meredith, 1988; Qureshi and Walker, 1989). There is some evidence that the provision of public support tends to be inversely related to the supply and commitment of informal care, particularly when that care is provided by women (Parker, 1990; Twigg et al., 1990). Yet this understanding about the central role played by informal carers only began to play a central role in policy debate in the 1980s. It did so for two reasons.

The first was that the issue was taken up by feminist social researchers who began to theorize about and document in detail the work and burden of caring (e.g. Finch and Groves, 1980; Stacey, 1981; Graham 1983). Secondly, came the realization on the part of government and policy makers that quite small reductions in the supply of family care could have substantial costs for the public sector if it had to fill the gap (Audit Commission, 1986). As a result more recent policy documents like the Griffiths report (1988) and the White Paper, *Caring For People* (Cm 849, 1989), have been far more explicit about the need to work with and support the family in its caring role.

Another problem was that our knowledge of the work of caring was until recently essentially anecdotal. We knew that some people, women in particular, were bearing extraordinary burdens but there was no hard evidence to show how typical they were, or how many like them existed. The data then available was based on very small samples obtained by individual researchers. More recently, however, this situation was corrected by two very large-scale studies. In 1985, the *General Household Survey*, which is a national sample of over 12,000 households, included detailed questions on caring for dependent adults (Green, 1988). It was discovered that one adult in seven (14 per cent or over 6 million people in Great Britain) was supplying 'some regular service for a sick, handicapped or elderly person living in their own or another household'. 3 per cent of people gave twenty hours a week or more to this caring role. Although women were more likely to be carers than men, and in particular were more likely to be doing heavy caring, the gender divisions were not as great as some had previously expected. The value of this caring work was estimated as between £15–24 billion a year; more than the state expenditure on the National Health Service (Family Policy Studies Centre, 1989).

These findings were confirmed and supplemented by the National Disability Survey which looked at the sources of support for disabled people living in the community (OPCS, 1990b). More than 60 per cent of the disabled were found to be over retirement age. It was also found that only 7 per cent of the disabled were in institutions and that the vast majority were supported by their families. Disability was rated along a scale of one to ten and amongst those in the severest categories, nine and ten, 86 per cent were cared for informally in private households. The formal sector was found to be supplying very little help with self care (4 per cent), or with household activities (12 per cent).

This raw demographic data needs to be put into the context of a more sociological understanding of the changing role of the family in modern Britain. The surveys are snapshots in time, indicating those involved in caring in one week or one month in a particular year and as such tend to give the impression that the people affected are a minority. In fact the data indicates that the chances of any adult becoming the carer of another adult at some point in their lives is very great and is increasing. Most of us will be carers of adult dependents at some point in our lives, but the incidence of this burden is very much dependent on other social characteristics like income, education, ethnicity and, most of all, gender.

High rates of marriage and family formation throughout the post-war period coupled with substantially increased life expectancy mean that the three generational and even the four generational family is common. The different generations in these families may not live together in the same households but there is much evidence that regular contact and support between the generations remains very high (Willmott, 1986). For example, amongst women with children who work, well over half of the consequent substitute childcare is done by grandmothers (Martin and Roberts, 1984). Caring and other forms of support, such as the transfer of money and property, is almost always a product of kinship and it is becoming even more explicitly central to the planning of public policy at a time when the family as an institution is undergoing rapid change and is clearly under strain. Social research makes it clear that social policy should not assume that traditional social definitions of family obligation, and particularly of women's obligations to care, will be sustained in the future.

The divorce rate in Britain is one of the highest in the world: four out of ten marriages now fail. One child in four now lives in a reconstituted family or with a lone parent (Kiernan and Wicks, 1990). It is not clear whether these children will feel the same obligations to care for their elderly parents, or that their parents will expect it. It must be said that research does still appear to show that a majority still accept that children have a duty to care for their elderly parents (Finch and Mason, 1990). This is reflected in the remarkable statistic that in Britain, outside institutional care, 23 per cent of single women over eighty live with their children (CSO, 1987). Finch and Mason found that 57 per cent of their sample of adults disagreed with the proposition that children had no obligation to care for their parents, but at the same time 39 per cent did agree with this view. It seems that cultural ideas about caring obligations relate almost solely to children and parents (very few extend this obligation to other members of the family), that these ideas are not universal throughout the community and that they are changing.

In particular, there is evidence that filial obligations to care are not seen as absolute and unconditional (Finch, 1989). Rather they are to be assessed in terms of a daughter's or son's other obligations and duties and the quality of the relationship between child and parent. The rule that children should care for their parents is not incontestable but is perceived as a starting point for negotiation within families. Furthermore, over half the sample in Finch and Mason's study believed that where there was an available alternative to family care, such as state care or paid-for care, then that was to be preferred. These contingent definitions of family obligation are particularly under threat from the growth of married women's employment. In Britain today 75 per cent of married women with children aged over ten are in work (OPCS, 1989). This is not just a product of economic necessity. It is clear that many women today regard employment as a right and do not accept traditional assumptions about a woman's 'natural role' in relation to the home and care. This view is likely to receive material confirmation in a society where low birth-rates mean an inevitable decline in the number of young people available to enter the labour market and in which eight out of ten new jobs will be filled by women (Moss, 1988). There are real reasons to believe that many more women will have other commitments to weigh against their 'obligation' to care and that public policies that assume some particular model of family life are in danger of being socially oppressive or simply of not working.

In summary, the available data shows the role of the family in the care of old people is becoming more complicated, varied and ambiguous. Traditional assumptions and practices remain strong and important. Family care remains by far the most important form of social care for old people. However, public policy makers need to be very careful about relying on these institutions. Family practices are much more varied than they used to be. The values of kinship obligation have to compete with others to do with work and independence. Patterns of household formation are similarly more varied and the consequent arrangements more fragile and, in that sense, less reliable. Public policy about caring must operate in much more varied and uncertain territory.

An obvious policy response to this uncertainty about family obligations is for the state to intervene directly through law and enforcement to regulate behaviour. This is indeed what is done in a number of European countries. The right to be cared for and the obligation to care or to pay for the care of one's relatives can be found enshrined in law in the form of the principle of subsidiarity, e.g. in the German Social Assistance Act. 'This Act refers to the "subsidiarity principle" whereby first of all the individual in need of assistance is responsible for changing his/her situation, then the immediate family and, only after exhausting these possibilities, the bodies for social assistance. Thus the notion not only of self-help, but of family responsibility is stated explicitly and dominates attitudes and feelings in such a way that help from outside the family is not taken for granted' (Jamieson, 1990).

ACTIVITY 5

Go back to the notes you made for Activities 3 and 4. Now add to your notes reasons why family obligations tend to be uncertain and contingent.

It is clear that in Britain many families do not take state assistance in old age for granted either but the absence of a legal framework that specifically defines family responsibility means that the state has little formal power to intervene and regulate the 'malfunctioning family'. That it should seek very openly to do so would clearly offend established definitions of civil liberties. The European laws of subsidiarity sound quite shocking to the British. Yet there are disadvantages to the more voluntaristic approach. Where the state cannot punish the uncaring family it tends perversely, in Britain, to discriminate against those that do care in the allocation of resources (Twigg et al., 1990). The carers movement has highlighted the way in which many of those doing a great deal of caring receive no support at all and that to get public help with the caring task requires the hard-hearted ability to refuse to do anything for one's beloved to the point where the social services are forced to intervene. This is a game of bluff that few relatives can bring themselves to play.

Government policy documents and legislation, such as the Community Care White Paper of 1989 (Cm 849) and the Community Care Act of 1990, recognized that this was a dangerous and expensive way to continue in the face of changing social mores and increasingly organized opposition from carers. Explicit collaboration with informal carers has now become a central plank of new legislation governing community care. The changes, which will come into operation during the first half of the 1990s, might be argued to amount to a substantial renegotiation of the relationship between the state and the family in dealing with old age.

9 THE NEW AGENDA FOR SOCIAL POLICY: FAMILY CARE AND COMMUNITY CARE

The effective collapse of the established 'system' of care for frail old people in the face of demographic pressure and public unacceptability has now led to a time when a quiet but significant three-cornered battle is currently being waged over how things are to be done in the future. The combatants are: firstly the state, which holds most of the cards; secondly the elderly, who hold almost none at all because of the lack of political solidarity amongst retired people in Britain, and to some extent the future elderly; and thirdly those who are and might be carers, few of whom appear to realize the high incidence of the caring role. The contest is over who is going to do the work and who is going to pay for it. The most public manifestation of this battle so far is the 1990 Community Care legislation which was somewhat hidden from public view because it was tagged onto much more visible National Health Service changes (Wistow and Henwood, 1991). Nonetheless the changes that have been set in train will become very visible during the 1990s. Where it deals with social care, the National Health Service and Community Care Act 1990 is in no sense incrementalist. It sweeps away the established modes of public care for old people with a cavalier confidence which would be astonishing in most other areas of public policy.

A core idea in the government's conception of the new order is that the state should not provide services itself but rather enable the family and the community to do so. A language of enablement and distancing of direct responsibility was very apparent in the British government's White Paper on community care (Cm 849, 1989). Two words that appear with extraordinary frequency are 'enable' and 'promote'. 'Promoting choice and independence underlies all the Government's proposals' (Section 1.8). 'The Government has endorsed Sir Roy Griffiths' recommendation that social services authorities should be "enabling" agencies. It will be their responsibility to make maximum possible use of private and voluntary providers, and so increase the available range of options and widen consumer choice' (Section 1.11). Private (for profit) provision will be encouraged by a central government requirement of local authorities to draw up plans to make 'maximum use of the independent sector' (Section 1.12) and by effectively restricting state subsidy to those below the poverty line (income support level). The White Paper recognizes 'the great bulk of care is provided by family, friends and neighbours' (Section 1.9) and argues that 'helping carers to maintain their valuable contribution to the spectrum of care is both right and a sound investment' (Section 2.3).

One way of encouraging the private and the informal (family) sectors to do more care work is to provide allowances that add to the care-purchasing power of people in need. This is a pattern of development that can be observed in most industrial countries and it has complex implications for the relationships between old people and their families. It is an area in which recent Conservative governments have substantially expanded welfare provision: benefits **paid to** those with disabilities grew during the

1980s from a value of around £100 million to over £1.5 billion a year. They fit well with the Conservative Party's view that welfare provision should involve consumer choice and supplier competition and that the disabled should be provided with money rather than services. The positive potential involves such things as overdue recognition and compensation for care work and a reduction in feelings of indebtedness. But monetizing family care has dangers too. It has been argued that governments are creating a new class of care worker paid at sub-market rates and with none of the protection that the same work might bring in a more formal setting (Baldock and Ungerson, 1991).

The most important of the cash benefits involved is the Attendance Allowance (also known since 1991 as the Disability Living Allowance where it applies to those under 65), a benefit of between £10 and £42 a week (up to April 1992), that is paid to people simply on the basis of their degree of dependency and is intended to help them pay for help. It is not related to income and it is not taxed; in other words it is needs-tested not means-tested. The benefit is now paid to over 700,000 people at any one time. However, research shows that relatively few people actually spend this income on paying for care they would not otherwise have received (Horton and Berthoud, 1990). There appear to be three reasons for this 'disappointing' outcome. Firstly, disability remains strongly correlated with poverty: many recipients simply spend the benefit on food, heating and housing. Secondly, there is no established supply of care services in return for payment at the levels that the care allowances would allow. Thirdly, families do not respond to their members' needs in a straightforward market manner.

Where an old person is receiving the Attendance Allowance, a relative who is under sixty-five and has foregone employment in order to care for him or her for at least thirty-five hours a week may receive the Invalid Care Allowance, worth £31.25 a week up to April 1992. At its inception in 1976 this benefit was not available to married women, the assumption being that they had not foregone paid work in order to care. This exclusion was ruled illegal by the European Court in 1986 but the Invalid Care Allowance is still not paid to carers over retirement age. In 1989, 121,000 people were receiving this benefit on an average day (Department of Social Security, 1991). As yet there is no research evidence that the availability of the Invalid Care Allowance does in fact add to the numbers of people available to care.

There are good reasons for doubting that the family can be organized by the state into a new and low-cost tier of the labour market. Research shows that the level and quality of informal care in a community is not easily influenced, managed or bought. It is the outcome of complex patterns of kinship, tradition and reciprocity (Wenger, 1984; Bulmer, 1987) which are unlikely to be readily amenable to policy manipulation. Attempts to tamper with complex cultural forms can be dangerous; they tend to react in unpredictable ways. There is the risk of killing the goose that lays the golden egg. Encouraging the informal sector to take on additional loads might even lead to a reduction in the willingness to care, though there is currently no evidence for or against such a proposition.

The very character of personal dependency, the way it emerges and develops, means it cannot be treated like other more routine forms of demand in the economy. Simply adding small amounts to dependent people's purchasing power is unlikely to call forth an increased supply of care. The variety and individuality of dependent people's needs and the speed and suddenness with which they change make it very difficult to turn care into a simple market commodity. A great deal of time must be spent not just on doing the caring tasks but on management and coordination that fits the available care to needs which are likely to appear abruptly and change unpredictably. Research has shown that many family carers already operate as case managers, often combining various public and private sources of help in imaginative ways and against considerable odds (Balbo, 1987; Ungerson, 1987). There is a danger that professional attempts to intervene in this arena with money and contracts might lead to conflict with carers. The work of the Personal Social Services Research Unit at the University of Kent has shown that the, relatively invisible, 'managerial' functions are the most expensive and the cost of fulfilling them through the market or by the state is likely to be prohibitive (Davies and Challis, 1986).

ACTIVITY 6

What are the main reasons why 'enabling' families to provide care may not result in a better service for elderly people?

---

10 CONCLUSION: THE THREATS TO THE CITIZENSHIP OF OLD PEOPLE.

It is a basic tenet of democracy that all people share an equal status of citizens in their society. That is to say, we all enjoy certain legal, political and social rights and these apply in the same way to all of us. Social policy, as it has developed, can be seen as gradually extending these rights, particularly in the social sphere. However, if a group of people, such as old people, are perceived by substantial numbers to be less worthy or entitled than others, then it is difficult for social policies to work effectively. Social Policies only take on their full meaning in the context of the social values and behavioural norms that define the rights of particular sections of the population to support from their families and community. Unless that right to help is deeply embedded in the culture of a society, social policies designed to help a category of people can be undermined and thwarted. The place of old people, particularly those who are dependent, in the system of rights and obligations that define citizenship is not clear. They and their carers often seem less eligible than others for public support (than say children, people in work or certain categories of the unemployed). There are a number of established, conventional explanations of why this is.

One is that it is a principal function of the written and unwritten rules of citizenship to distinguish the public from the private and to protect the private from interference. As has been documented throughout this book, the private is largely located within the family. The needs of old people, and the welfare of their carers, remain largely family concerns within which the state intervenes only marginally. Indeed, with the decline of the public pension system this conception is in some ways being encouraged by government. People may feel that the difficulties they face in old age do not entitle them to ask for help from the state or the community. Research has frequently shown that old people and their carers often do not ask for the services and benefits to which they are technically entitled because they believe for some reason they should not. They do not actually feel entitled, or they find asking embarrassing and demeaning (Ungerson, 1987; Wenger, 1984). In this view they are not necessarily wrong or confused. They may be demonstrating their long years of experience and understanding of how their society really works.

Frail old people in particular are caught between established social values and their dependency. Their adulthood requires them to be self-sufficient and autonomous, that they should not demand favours without being able to reciprocate. Their kin, particularly women, are caught between traditional norms which emphasize obligations to care and more modern expectations about their entitlement to autonomy and leisure. Many of them are less willing to take on the role of carer just because they are women and the needy person is a relative. Thus the major caring institution in society, the family, is becoming less predictable as a source of support for us when we grow old. Yet social policies are being enacted which explicitly rely on the family continuing to be the major source of care for old people. The management and delivery of public care services for old people seem to be about to take real account of the contribution of the family just a moment too late, when the values that have made it care for its elderly are dissolving. These values were perhaps more congruent with a society in which death was less frequently preceded by long enfeeblement and in which care work was almost always women's work. Is it now the case that the rapid growth in the numbers of very old people has caught industrial societies in a cultural time lag? Are policy makers misjudging the caring capacity of the family? If so, the current public policy stance, which distances the state from proactive intervention and which encourages a more *laissez-faire*, mixed welfare approach, may be particularly ill-timed for those who are old and those who hope to be so.

REFERENCES

Atkinson, A. B., (1969) *Poverty in Britain and the Reform of Social Security,* Cambridge, Cambridge University Press.

Audit Commission (1986) *Making a Reality of Community Care,* London, HMSO.

Balbo, L. (1987) 'Crazy quilts rethinking the welfare debate from the woman's point of view' in A. Showstack Sassoon (ed), *Women and the State,* London, Hutchinson.

Baldock, J. and Ungerson, C. (1991) 'What d'ya want if you don't want money? A feminist critique of paid volunteering' in M. McLean and D. Groves (eds), *Women's Issues in Social Policy,* London, Routledge.

Bhalla, A., and Blakemore, K. (1981) *Elders of Ethnic Minority Groups,* Birmingham, All Faiths for One Race.

Blythe, R. (1981) *The View in Winter: Reflections on Old Age,* Harmondsworth, Penguin Books.

Bulmer, M. (1987) *The Social Basis of Community Care,* London, Allen and Unwin.

Cm 849 White Paper (1989) *Caring for People: Community Care in the Next Decade and Beyond*, London, HMSO.

Cook, J. and Watt, S., (1987) 'Racism, women and poverty' in C. Glendinning and J. Miller (eds.), *Women and Poverty in Britain,* London, Tavistock.

CSO (1987) Central Statistical Office, *Social Trends No. 17,* London, HMSO.

Davies, B., Bebbington, A. and Charnley, J. (1990) *Resources, Needs and Outcomes in Community Based Care: a Comparative Study of the Production of Welfare for Elderly People in 10 Local Authorities,* Aldershot, Gower.

Davies, B. P., and Challis, D. (1986) *Matching Resources to Needs in Community Care*, Aldershot, Gower.

Department of Social Security (1991) *Social Security Statistics 1990,* London, HMSO.

Donovan, J. (1986) *We Don't Buy Sickness, It Just Comes,* Aldershot, Gower.

Evers, H., Badger, F., Cameron, E. and Atkin, K. (1990) *Community Care Project Working Papers,* Birmingham, Department of Social Medicine, University of Birmingham.

Family Policy Studies Centre (1989) *Family Policy Bulletin No. 6,* Winter 1989, London, Family Policy Studies Centre.

Fennel, G., Phillipson, C. and Evers, H. (1988) *The Sociology of Old Age,* Buckingham, Open University Press.

Finch, J. (1989) *Family Obligations and Social Change,* Oxford, Polity Press.

Finch, J., and Groves, D. (1980) 'Community care and the family: a case for equal opportunities?', *Journal of Social Policy,* 9, pp.487–511.

Finch, J. and Mason, J. (1990) 'Filial obligations and kin support for elderly people', *Ageing and Society,* 10, pp.151–76.

Ford, J. and Sinclair, R. (1987) *Sixty Years On: Women Talk About Old Age,* London, Women's Press.

Ford, J., and Sinclair, R. (1989) 'Women's experience of old age' in P. Carter, T. Jeffs, and M. Smith (eds), *Social Work and Social Welfare: Yearbook 1,* Buckingham, Open University Press.

Forrest, R. and Murie, A. (1989) 'Differential accumulation: wealth, inheritance and housing policy reconsidered', *Policy and Politics,* 17, 1, pp.25–39.

Fries, J.F. (1980) 'Ageing, natural death and the compression of morbidity', *New England Journal of Medicine,* No. 303, p.130.

George, V. & Howards, I. (1991) *Poverty Amidst Affluence: UK, USA,* Aldershot, Edward Elgar.

Gibbs, I. and Bradshaw, J. (1988) 'Dependency and its relationship to the care needs of elderly people', *British Journal of Social Work,* 8, pp.577–93.

Gilbert, G. N., Dale, A., Arber, S., Evandrou, M. and Laczko, F. (1989) 'Resources and old age: ageing and the life course' in M. Jefferys (ed.), *Growing Old in the Twentieth Century,* London, Routledge.

Graham, H. (1983) 'Caring: a labour of love' in J. Finch and D. Groves (eds).

Green, H. (1988) *Informal Carers: General Household Survey 1985,* OPCS, Social Survey Division, series GH5 No 15, supplement A, London, HMSO.

Griffiths, Sir R., (1988) *Community Care: Agenda for Action. A Report to the Secretary of State for Social Services,* London, HMSO.

Hamnett, C. (1991) 'A nation of inheritors? Housing inheritance, wealth and inequality in Britain', *Journal of Social Policy,* 20, 2, pp.509–36.

Harris, J. (1977) *William Beveridge: a Biography,* Oxford, Oxford University Press.

Henwood, M and Wicks, M. (1984) *Forgotten Army: Family Care and Elderly People,* London, Family Policy Studies Centre.

HMSO (1991a) *Social Security Statistics 1990,* London, HMSO.

HMSO (1991b) *Annual Abstract of Statistics 1991,* London, HMSO.

Horton, C. and Berthoud, R. (1990) 'Informal Care in Europe' in A. Jamieson and R. Illsley (eds), *Contrasting European Policies for the Care of Older People,* Aldershot, Avebury.

Jamieson, A. (1990) 'Informal care in Europe' in A. Jamieson and R. Illsley (eds), *Contrasting European Policies for the Care of Older People,* Aldershot, Avebury.

Johnson, M., Cross, M. and Cardew, S. (1983) 'Inner city residents, ethnic minorities and primary health care', *Postgraduate Medical Journal*, No 59, pp.664–7.

Johnson, P. (1989) 'The structured dependency of the elderly: a critical note' in M. Jefferys, (ed), *Growing Old in the Twentieth Century,* Routledge, London.

Kiernan, K. and Wicks, M. (1990) *Family Change and Future Policy,* York, Joseph Rowntree Memorial Trust.

Kraan, R., Baldock, J., Davies, B., Evers, A., Johansson, L., Knapen, M., Thorslund, M. and Tunissen, C. (eds) (1991) *Care of the Elderly: Significant Innovations in Three European Countries,* Frankfurt/Boulder, Campus/Westview.

Laing, W. (1991) *Empowering the Elderly: Direct Consumer Funding of Care Services,* London, Institute of Economic Affairs.

Laslett, P. (1989) *A Fresh Map of Life: the Emergence of the Third Age,* London, Weidenfeld and Nicolson.

Lewis, J. and Meridith, B. (1988) *Daughters Who Care: Daughters Caring for Mothers at Home,* London, Routledge.

Martin, J. and Roberts, C. (1984) *Women and Employment: a Lifetime Perspective,* London, HMSO.

Moss, P. (1988) *Child Care and Equality of Opportunity,* Consolidated Report to the European Commission, Brussels, the European Commission.

Norman, A. (1985) *Triple Jeopardy: Growing Old in a Second Homeland,* London, Centre for Policy on Ageing.

OECD (1988) *Ageing Populations: The Social Policy Implications*, Paris, OECD.

OPCS (1980) *Mortality Statistics*, London, HMSO.

OPCS (1985), *see* Green, H. (1988).

OPCS (1987) *The General Household Survey 1985*, London, HMSO.

OPCS (1989) *The General Household Survey 1986*, London, HMSO.

OPCS (1990a) *The General Household Survey 1988,* London, HMSO.

OPCS (1990b) Office of Population, Census and Surveys, *Disabled Adults: Services, Transport and Employment,* Disability Survey Report No. 4, London, HMSO.

Parker, G. (1990) *With Due Care and Attention: a Review of Research on Informal Care,* 2nd edn, London, Family Policy Studies Centre.

Paton, C. (1990) 'The Prime Minister's Review of the National Health Service and the 1989 White Paper Working for People' in N. Manning and C. Ungerson (eds), *Social Policy Review 1989–90,* London, Longmans.

Peace, S. (1986) 'The forgotten female: social policy and older women' in C. Phillipson and A. Walker (eds), *Ageing and Social Policy.*

Phillipson, C. (1982) *Capitalism and the Construction of Old Age,* London, Macmillan.

Phillipson, C. and Walker, A. (eds) (1986) *Ageing and Social Policy,* Aldershot, Gower.

Pitkeathly, J. (1989) *It's My Duty Isn't It?*, London, Souvenir Press.

Qureshi, H., and Walker, A. (1989) *The Caring Relationship: Elderly People and Their Families* Macmillan, London.

Rodgers, B. (1969) *The Battle Against Poverty: From Pauperism to Human Rights,* Volume 1, London, Routledge and Kegan Paul.

Sinfield, A (1978) 'Analyses in the social division of welfare', *Journal of Social Policy,* 7, 2, pp.129–56.

Stacey, M. (1981) 'The division of labour revisited or overcoming the two Adams', in P. Abrams et al. (eds), *Practice and Progress: British Sociology, 1950–80,* London, Allen and Unwin.

Titmuss, R. M. (1963) *Essays on the Welfare State,* London, Allen and Unwin.

Townsend, P (1957) *The Family Life of Old People,* London, Routledge and Kegan Paul.

Townsend, P. (1968) 'The structure of the family' in E. Shanas, P. Townsend, D. Wedderburn, H. Friis, P. Milhol and J. Stehouwer (eds.), *Old People in Three Industrial Societies,* London, Routledge and Kegan Paul.

Townsend, P. (1981) 'The structured dependency of the elderly: a creation of social policy in the twentieth century', *Ageing and Society,* 1, pp.5–28.

Twigg, J., Atkin, K. and Perring, C. (1990) *Carers and Services: A Review of Research,* London, HMSO.

Ungerson, C. (1987) *Policy is Personal: Sex, Gender and Informal Care,* London, Tavistock.

Ungerson, C. (ed) (1990) *Gender and Caring: Work and Welfare in Britain and Scandinavia,* Hemel Hempstead, Harvester Wheatsheaf.

Walker, A. (1980) 'The social creation of poverty and dependency in old age', *Journal of Social Policy,* 9, pp.49–75.

Walker, A. (1987) 'The poor relation: poverty amongst older women' in C Glendinning and J. Miller (eds), *Women and Poverty in Britain,* Brighton, Wheatsheaf.

Walker, A. and Walker, C., (eds) (1987) *The Growing Divide,* London, Child Poverty Action Group.

Wenger, G.C., (1984) *The Supportive Network: Coping With Old Age,* London, Allen and Unwin.

Willmott, P (1986) *Social Networks, Informal Care and Public Policy,* Research Report No. 655, London, Policy Studies Institute.

Wistow, G. and Henwood, M. (1991) 'Caring for people: elegant model or flawed design?' in N. Manning (ed), *Social Policy Review 1990–1,* London, Longman.

CHAPTER 5
JUVENILE DELINQUENCY

EUGENE McLAUGHLIN AND JOHN MUNCIE

1 INTRODUCTION

At the 1989 Conservative Party Conference the Home Secretary announced that 'the family is our first defence against crime'. This idea surfaced again in 1991 following 'joy riding' disturbances on housing estates in Oxford and Tyneside. Amidst claims that the police had not acted quickly enough, the Home Secretary suggested that the question should not be 'Where are the police?' but 'Where are mum and dad?'. Kenneth Baker listed what he considered to be the common characteristics of such offenders: low achievement at school, erratic and inconsistent parenting, parental neglect, family criminality and personality factors. In so doing he established a clear relationship between 'problem' families, the delinquent young and the (re)production of a criminal 'underclass'. The 1991 Criminal Justice Act placed greater emphasis on enforcing parental responsibility for children's (mis)behaviour and stressed that the punishment of juveniles should take place in the community rather than in institutions. The government's first clear response however to the 1991 joy riding incidents was to establish a new offence of Aggravated Vehicle Taking — with a custodial sentence of up to five years. Subsequent to this in November 1992 the government announced that it was considering setting up a new type of institution for young offenders to detain a hard core of persistent young offenders.

Contradictions such as these have long been a hallmark of juvenile justice policy. The rhetoric of community and family-based intervention, whilst gathering strength since the 1960s, has always had to sit uneasily alongside a system that is designed to punish juveniles through custodial confinement. The 1991 Act marked the latest in a long line of initiatives ostensibly aimed at controlling delinquent behaviour. These have ranged from the building of specialist reformatories in the nineteenth century through to the establishment of community based treatments and systems of punishment in the 1960s and 1970s. Yet these initiatives have never replaced the custodial option. Rather they have become additions to a seemingly ever expanding juvenile justice system.

Throughout the history of juvenile justice the role of the family has been a paradoxical one. Sometimes the family has been seen as a contributing factor to delinquent behaviour; at other times it has been seen as offering the best potential for curbing it. This paradox — that not only does family background and parental conduct provide the key to explaining the causes of delinquency, but it also may offer the best solution to the problem of delinquency — is something which has dogged every effort of politicians, reformers and legal and welfare professionals for the past two centuries.

This chapter is designed to help you come to a more informed understanding of these debates. We should make it clear at the outset that there are several contested 'readings' of the historical development of juvenile delinquency and the juvenile justice system. However, our 'reading' is centrally concerned with firstly exploring how delinquency came to be defined as a social problem; and secondly charting how the state and voluntary organizations have subsequently attempted to solve the problem. Within this we would argue that the role of the family is pivotal. 'Delinquency' does not simply refer to criminal behaviour, but to a lack of 'proper' moral values and habits. Thus the concept of juvenile delinquency also conjures up images of delinquent families in which parents have failed to bring up their children responsibly or have neglected them. The juvenile justice system has a history of responding both to the criminal and to the deserted. Its stated aim is to punish, but also to protect; to control, but also to care; to take away parental rights but also to encourage parental responsibility.

Throughout this chapter we must ask why the recurring concern for juvenile misdemeanours and law-breaking? Do juveniles really commit more crimes than adults (official statistics suggest that the peak ages for offending are 15 to 18) or is it simply that their deviant behaviours are more visible and thus more easily detected, apprehended and processed through the courts? Is the concern with young people merely the surface manifestation of a deeper concern for social stability, moral discipline and the nation's future?

2   THE CONCEPT OF JUVENILE DELINQUENCY

Modern systems of justice clearly differentiate between juveniles and adults. In England and Wales, for example, the criminal justice system has separate arrangements for these three non-adult age groups: those aged under 10; those aged 10–15; and those aged 16 and 17. At 18 young people reach the age of majority. This primary classification system has arisen because of a general belief that children and young people are different from adults, more innocent and less capable of criminal intent. For this reason, in addition to the dominant ideology that all lawbreakers should be made responsible for their misdemeanours there is an alternative ideology that for some sections of society, such as the young, a number of mitigating factors should be taken into account when examining their transgressions against the law. With regard to young people these mitigating factors are thought to be social disorganization, family breakdown, inadequate parental control (or care) or more generally 'inadequate socialization'. As a result, juvenile offenders today are usually dealt with separately from adults — in separate courts, community punishment and treatment schemes and institutions. They are treated differently because they are viewed as being in need of both protection (as innocents) and discipline (as yet to be civilized individuals).

This distinction between juvenile and adult is firmly ingrained in twentieth century systems of justice, but it is a relatively new concept. The concept of the juvenile offender and the juvenile delinquent, with all that that implies for criminal justice and penal policy, is barely 150 years old. It is in fact a Victorian creation.

In this section we will be: (1) exploring how and why such concepts came into being; (2) tracing the impact such concepts had on the evolution of the criminal justice system in the nineteenth and early twentieth centuries; and (3) highlighting how notions of 'the family' are firmly embedded in disputes over the problem of juvenile delinquency.

2.1   THE ORIGINS OF DELINQUENCY

Although concern existed about criminal activity prior to the nineteenth century, little attention was paid to any particular problem caused by the young. However, with the publication of the first Home Office statistics on the extent and nature of crime in 1805 — and a number of unofficial enquiries produced by magistrates — teachers and church officers began to give specific consideration to delinquency as something separate from crime *per se*.

Recognition of the juvenile offender as being in some way different to the adult was also emerging coterminously in the field of penal reform. The emphasis placed upon separation, classification and categorization highlighted age differentials and led to various conclusions being drawn about the position of the young in relation to the penal system. A high recidivism rate tended to suggest that imprisonment with adults strengthened the criminal habits of the young.

The concept of delinquency however presupposes much more than actual criminal behaviour and how to deal with convicted offenders.

Given a set of common-sense (middle class) presuppositions about the true nature of family life, childhood and the increasing accumulation of empirical data organized directly around these presuppositions, it is not surprising that a specific set of conclusions surrounding the nature and causes of delinquency was to emerge in Victorian society. A view of childhood as an essentially innocent and dependent state requiring nurture and discipline on the part of parents led to a certain definition of delinquency in particular, but also of youthful behaviour in general. It was not just criminal behaviour that was of concern to the nineteenth century reformers. Whilst there was a recognition that economic and social conditions were connected with the criminal propensities of the young, this was subordinated to a consideration of the *moral* dimension of the problem. The terms which emerged to describe the problem were 'unnatural independence', 'contamination' and 'parental neglect and irresponsibility'. Delinquency became firmly associated with the conditions of working class family life. Victorian concern also encompassed orphans, the illegitimate, the deserted, the independent young and anyone who appeared to fail to live up to middle class assumptions of normal family life. Victorian social investigators and reformers were able to produce such damning reports of the conditions of existence for economically independent working class children because the realities of slum childhood

Alternative images of
Victorian childhood

violated their sense and image of their own protected and dependent
childhood (May, 1973, p.16). Concern was directed not only towards these
children, but towards the failings of their parents — the apparent absence
of supervision and control; the failure to imbue their children with proper
moral habits.

It should also be noted that middle class anxieties about the moral habits
of the working classes locked into a discourse about 'Englishness' and

'civilization'. Cunningham (1991) has argued that by the middle of the nineteenth century a racially informed language had been constructed to describe the children of the poor. There was a common image of these children as 'street Arabs' and 'savages'. Pearson (1983) has made a similar point, in his discussion about the origins of the word 'hooligan', noting that 'the "Hooligans" were understood as an entirely unprecedented and "un-British" phenomenon; indeed, we must allow that it was most ingenious of late Victorian England to disown the British Hooligan by giving him an "Irish" name' (Pearson, 1983, p.75).

For much of the last century fears were expressed that the Irish (defined as a culturally inferior race) and their children would 'contaminate' the English working classes with their 'wild' lawlessness and criminality (Davis, 1991, p.58). As we shall see later on in this chapter, race continues to be a feature of contemporary debates about delinquency and criminality.

By the turn of the century, the identification of young people as being especially troubled and thus potentially troublesome took another significant turn. In particular the concept of *adolescence* constructed within the rapidly developing disciplines of social psychology and child psychology gave traditional concerns about young people 'both a more profound substance and a new legitimacy' (Hendrick, 1990, p.11).

This discovery of adolescence also coincided with renewed anxieties about working class youth. In the 1880s amid the emergence of a juvenile labour market and statistical increases in juvenile crime, concern was expressed that the urban working class family was not fulfilling its regulatory functions and that the wage earning capacity of working class youth enabled them to buy freedom from parental control (Springhall, 1986). This had particular consequences for working class girls. Whilst it is undoubtedly the case that the delinquent activities of young working class males was of primary concern, anxieties were also expressed about the independent nature of young working class women. It was believed that too much female autonomy was socially undesirable and connections were made between the independence of working class girls, sexual precocity and prostitution. Thus 'Female delinquency, very much a secondary question, revolved almost completely around sexuality. State intervention was directed to the reconstruction of girl's "domesticity" — either as mothers, or as domestic servants' (Clarke, 1981, p.253). In a later section there will be further discussion of how nineteenth century attitudes about the nature of female delinquency are still pervasive in the contemporary juvenile justice system.

2.2 THE MANAGEMENT OF DELINQUENCY: NINETEENTH CENTURY LEGACIES

Reformist conceptions of childhood and adolescence and their interpretations of delinquency tended to relieve the young from full responsibility for their actions and emphasize the role of family, family life and socialization in the formation of obedient and respectable citizens. When the family failed, the state must intervene — not merely to punish but also to compel responsible behaviour on the part of parents. It was believed to be quite appropriate for the state to intervene in working class family life to ensure that children were being educated, moralized, and disciplined in the correct fashion. Victorian philanthropists (such as Mary Carpenter) thought that in this way they could break the chain according to which the neglected and deprived children of today would become the criminal and depraved children of tomorrow. Mary Carpenter and her supporters also believed it was not necessary for a child to have committed a criminal act to justify intervention and control. Her recommendations for Reformatory schools for the 'depraved' and industrial schools for the 'deprived' came to fruition in the 1854 and 1857 Acts. Both were designed to provide conditions for the exercise of a sound moral and religious influence, the inculcation of industrious habits and the creation of a position of dependence in order to restore children to a 'true position' of childhood.

This reformist vision, whilst gathering strength throughout the nineteenth century was, however, not without its critics. An influential body of opinion continued to argue that the punishment should fit the crime and not be mitigated by personal circumstances; that juveniles should be treated the same as all other offenders; so that 'the idea of pain might be instantly associated with crime in the minds of evil-doers'. This recurring tension between the differing interpretations of delinquency — one determined by parental conduct (thus absolving juveniles from responsibility), the other put down simply as wilful behaviour (thus reinforcing individual responsibility) — meant that reformist proposals were subject to legislative compromise. At the turn of the century, the principle that juveniles were less responsible than adults and should not be subject to the full majesty of the law was influential in the introduction (in 1907) of separate court procedures for juveniles — the juvenile court. However the following year specialist detention centres — borstals — were also inaugurated. Whilst the reformist rhetoric was one of training, the impact of humanitarian welfarism was not such that juveniles were excluded from systems of punitive justice. In other words, the reformatory system was merely grafted onto the existing institutions of punishment and justice and did not replace them.

It is from these definitional, ideological, institutional and legal disputes that twentieth century preoccupations with working class youth grew. Having invented the delinquent and established the principle of a child's diminished responsibility, penal and welfare professionals and reformers have continually struggled to deliver adequate and appropriate responses. Disputes over the management of delinquency continue to centre on the nineteenth century preoccupation with issues like: Should juvenile offenders be held personally responsible for law-breaking? Should they be reformed or punished? Should they be subjected to welfare or classical justice based interventions? In short, are they deserving of care and protection or control and discipline? By defining delinquency as being caused by a lack of *moral* care, however, the issue not only concerns identified offenders, but also working class childrearing practices in general. Throughout this period, the necessity for some form of intervention became assumed and eventually, unquestionable.

ACTIVITY I

To conclude this section make notes on the following questions:

1   Why is delinquency viewed as a moral, rather than simply a criminal, matter?

2   To what degree are welfare and punitive interventions interlinked and interdependent? Do welfare initiatives necessarily herald a more liberal, less punitive means of dealing with young people in trouble?

---

3   THE WELFARE APPROACH TO DELINQUENCY

In the 1950s and 1960s principles of welfare began to challenge the hegemony of a criminal justice approach. Delinquency came to be viewed as a temporary problem residing in families who had been 'left behind' in the advancement of post-war prosperity and meritocracy. Welfare agencies were to be central in tackling the problem, not by locking children up, but by educating families in child rearing and rehabilitating the residue of young people who came to the notice of the justice system. As criminality became defined as a problem of individual maladjustment or family pathology, it made no sense to punish offenders. Rather it was argued that the juvenile court needed to be transformed into a rehabilitative clinic, through which the state could offer a family service, employing professionals to treat the problem of those sentenced by the court or considered 'at risk'. This argument was bolstered by the emergence of a new body of social psychological knowledge which contributed the main framework for understanding post-war delinquency (see Rose, 1991).

Sociological studies also identified 'marginal' families and deprived communities (Sprott et al., 1972, p.36). These studies viewed the family as being a central bulwark against delinquency, emphasizing notions of defective discipline, inadequate supervision, lack of moral and social education and the need for effective parental control over the leisure pursuits of their children. It was also argued that when young delinquent males 'moved towards a family of their own, they become once more subject to the social controls of the local community and the national society' (Willmott, 1972, p.87). Therefore, marriage for young working class males was viewed by sociologists as being central to the social control of delinquency.

Thus, the point of intersection of these disciplines was the family. Delinquency was a 'symptom' of deeper troubles and these deeper troubles lay with the family.

Families that were inadequate in socializing their youngers; families that failed to adapt to the new surroundings; families that neglected children through pursuit either of newly available affluence or newly popular leisure activities; families who ignored approved childrearing methods; families who had too well-established links with criminal subcultures — all these were 'criminogenic' families whose members could be expected to be 'delinquency prone'.

(Hudson, 1987, p.15)

3.1   THE TREATMENT MODEL

This discourse provided support for those demanding a moving away, once and for all, from notions of guilt, individual responsibility and punishment towards diagnosis, treatment and prevention in dealing with troublesome youth. A forceful case was constructed for treating disturbed, delinquent and deprived children alike. This was based on the assumption that the child was not a totally separate, responsible individual. Deprivation at home could lead to various forms of maladjustment and court proceedings and punishment were considered to be completely inappropriate and indeed potentially damaging. It was argued that families, as well as children, needed professional help and care.

ESSENTIAL PROPOSITIONS OF THE TREATMENT MODEL:

1   troublesome behaviour and 'misconduct' have antecedent causes which explain them; past conditions and situations are emphasized, individual choice is ignored;

2   these causes can be (and have been) discovered;

3   their discovery has made possible the treatment and control of such behaviour;

4   'troublesome' children share pathological conditions which make them fundamentally different from the law abiding;

5   'trouble' or 'misconduct' gets 'worse' without 'treatment';

6   'treatment' has no harmful side effects;

7   involuntary 'treatment' is not punishment.

(Morris et al., 1980, p.34)

Collinson (1980) has argued that this renewed focus on the family in the post-war period was sharpened because of the expectation that it should extend its competency, most obviously, given the educational changes, in its responsibility for the child for a longer period prior to work. It is no coincidence, therefore, that the focus on the family emerged at a time when public and private responsibilities were being redistributed. An ideal type of the normal social democratic family had been constructed which had clearly demarcated responsibilities both internally and in relation to society. But, some families were not living up to this ideal and were not fulfilling their responsibilities and by the late 1950s multiple-problem families and neighbourhoods had been identified. The psychologists, sociologists and welfare workers were in agreement that state intervention was necessary to deal with this malfunctioning residue.

There followed, in the 1960s, a renewed political debate about juvenile delinquency in the form of the Longford Report and two White Papers. In many respects these embodied the beliefs of advocates of the welfare approach. The Longford Report distinguished between most minor juvenile crime, which the committee viewed as 'an incident in the pattern of a child's normal development' not justifying intervention, and more serious forms of crime which the committee believed were symptomatic of a deeper malaise, making intervention necessary. The Report stated confidently that: 'it is a truism that a happy and secure family life is the foundation of a healthy society and the best safeguard against delinquency and anti-social behaviour' (1964, p.16). It recommended that a family service should be set up to play a central role in delinquency treatment and prevention.

Thus a major shift was proposed to recognize formally that the object of state intervention was not the delinquent but the family life that produced this behaviour in children. The juvenile court was to be replaced by family courts in which parents were to be centrally located both within proceedings and in the work of the social services. The traditional concepts of criminal justice — individual responsibility, guilt, innocence and punishment — were to be replaced with care, protection, welfare, treatment and rehabilitation. Magistrates were no longer to be involved in detailed decision making about appropriate treatment — this was to be the preserve of social services professionals.

Central to the welfarist approach was the increased involvement of local authority social workers. Their role was to prevent delinquency by intervening in the family life of those considered at risk of delinquency (e.g. non-school attenders), to provide assessment of a child's needs and to promote non-custodial disposals in court. Attendance centres and detention centres were to be 'phased out' in favour of community based Intermediate Treatment (IT). The ideology embedded in the proposals was that, 'it was now the task of professional social workers, aided by social science, to identify and where possible to correct the problems that were preventing families and individual family members from experiencing the full benefits of citizenship in the Welfare State' (Taylor, 1981, p.64).

The 1969 Children and Young Persons Act embodied many of these proposals. The Act stipulated that all 10–13 year old offenders should be dealt with by care proceedings rather than by criminal ones, and that 14–16 year olds should be preferably dealt with in care proceedings. Home Office approved schools and remand homes were to be amalgamated with local authority children's homes and all were to be renamed 'community' homes and run by local authority social services departments. Probation orders were to be replaced by supervision orders operated by social workers. Attendance centres, detention centres and borstals were to be discontinued as new 'intermediate treatment' facilities became available. The Act was heralded as the most progressive and decriminalizing instance of post-war penal policy.

3.2 WELFARE IN TROUBLE

The stated aim of the various welfare proposals was to keep children out of courts, out of custody in the community and to provide treatment and care. However, the 1970s saw more children removed from their families than ever before and punishment re-emerging as an overarching concern of the juvenile justice system (see Figure 5.1).

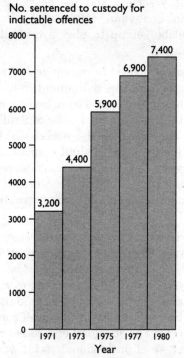

Figure 5.1 Males aged 14–16 years sentenced to custody, 1971–80

Source: Allen, 1990, p. 31

Custodial sentences rose at four times the rate of juvenile crime in the 1970s. What had gone wrong? Part of the reason for this lay in the fact that key sections of the 1969 Act were not implemented during the 1970s. The Conservative government, which had been elected in 1970, was opposed to state intervention in the life of the child through a welfare rather than a judicial body (Bottoms, 1974). Ministers made it clear that they would not implement those sections of the Act which would raise the age of criminal responsibility and replace criminal proceedings with care proceedings. In addition, magistrates opposed the further blurring of the distinction between the deprived child and the delinquent child and the infringement of certain of their powers by social workers. They responded to this seeming undermining of their role by becoming more punitively minded.

The most important development was that instead of replacing the old structures of juvenile justice as the framers of the Act had intended, the welfarist proposals were grafted on to them. Intermediate Treatment was introduced but detention centres and attendance centres were not phased out. Community homes were introduced but retained the characteristics of the old approved schools. Care proceedings were made available in criminal cases, but it was still possible to take criminal proceedings against children.

The welfare approach, instead of constraining the numbers entering the system, appeared to encourage entry. This had particular consequences for young women as we shall see later. Furthermore, instead of liberalizing intervention it appeared to strengthen penal sanctions, particularly for those who were seen to have failed earlier in the system; and above all created new categories of the 'hard core' and 'intractable' delinquent: categories which, as we will see, had the most serious implications for black youth.

NET WIDENING

Because the new system was grafted onto the existing one a net widening occurred with more children being brought into the system. The police were given a key role to play by the 1969 Act since it gave the first legal recognition to the police caution. Most police forces set up juvenile bureaux and the number of cautions for 10–17-year-olds rose from 36,000 in 1970 to 104,000 in 1980. This again was supposed to divert young people from the courts but in reality it brought more into the system. The caution had a threefold net widening effect. First, although it replaced prosecution it also replaced informal warnings. Second, formal cautions had the same consequences as a conviction if they became part of subsequent court proceedings. And third, cautioning also resulted in children and young people being placed under informal supervision or on a programme placement. Intermediate Treatment programmes used it, for example, as a way to recruit clients. Decisions not to prosecute were determined in part by the assessment made by the police of the young person's attitude and social circumstances. Formal cautioning gave the police the authority to investigate the home and as Bennett (1979) has shown parental attitudes were important in influencing police decisions over whether to prosecute or not. Hence, intervention was also being extended directly to the level of the family.

And here social workers played a crucial role because, as Rutherford (1989, p.28) has noted they *routinely* recommended care and custodial proceedings for children in trouble. A significant cause of the rise in custodial sentences in the 1970s was due to social workers using

Social Inquiry Reports (SIRs) to recommend highly interventionist disposals for first- and second-time offenders, unintentionally projecting them 'up the tariff' and making them high risk candidates in the event of reoffending (Thorpe et al., 1980).

CATCHING THE GIRLS IN THE GANG

As has been previously noted, juvenile delinquency is traditionally viewed as being the preserve of young working class males and in many respects delinquent behaviour is conceptualized as being a part of growing up and a natural, even if reprehensible, extension of 'boys being boys'. This view is reinforced by statistics which show that approximately 80 per cent of all known offenders are male and that only one in nine of those brought before juvenile courts are young women. Girl delinquents, like criminal women generally, continue to be viewed as oddities and the media sensationalizes their involvement in crime.

Researchers have found that the pathway for girls through welfare-oriented juvenile justice systems is different to that of boys. Their studies suggest that very different ideological assumptions, many of which are familial in orientation, govern young women's experience of juvenile justice. They are judged not against a yardstick of 'boys being boys' but against a complex definition of womanhood. This definition is tied closely to a woman's role within the private sphere of the family and the home. Notions about respectability, decency, the role of the girl in the home and the concepts of the 'good girl' and 'dutiful daughter' have been found to constitute the ideal against which young women who end up in the patriarchal and paternalistic juvenile justice system are judged (Zedner, 1991, pp.11–12).

This focus on womanhood and family continues to lead to a preoccupation with the sexuality of young women. The alarm bells about promiscuity, prostitution and teenage pregnancy begin to ring when a girl gets into trouble and the paternalism of the juvenile justice system has a greater impact on girls than on boys because of different perceptions of their respective needs. Researchers have found that girls are referred to the juvenile court for different reasons than boys. Casburn (1979) found that over half the girls in her study were brought before the juvenile court on non-criminal matters such as truancy, being 'beyond control' or being in 'moral danger'. As Hudson has argued:

> There is plenty of evidence that focusing on the welfare needs (real or supposed) of girls who come to the notice of the social control agencies has led to large numbers of girls and young women, without having committed any serious acts of criminal delinquency, being removed from home or being placed under the supervision of social workers because of adult disapproval of their sexual activity and general life style and demeanour.

> (Hudson, 1989, p.97)

Terror on streets of Stockholm
as England yobbos go on a bloody rampage

NOW EVEN GIRLS JOIN THE THUGS

Fury as louts run amok in Sweden and heap new shame on English soccer

DRUNKEN English women helped heap shame on their country in the Battle of Stockholm.

They joined in the brawling that outraged not only Sweden and Britain but the rest of the world.

The English girl pictured on this page was among the scores who were ignominiously bundled into police paddy-wagons and whisked off to the cells.

Last night a Swedish police chief said: "We've never seen behaviour like this before.

"It's the worst we've ever had to experience."

Media concern about the girls in the gang

This also leads to the family background becoming a crucial factor in the juvenile court's examination of delinquent girls.

ACTIVITY 2

Why do you think family background plays such a significant role in a delinquent girl's pathway through the juvenile justice system?

DISCUSSION

Barrett and McIntosh (1982) have shown how the family is the key source of social control over women and that the ideology that girls belong in the private world of the home, are the property of the family and should carry out the responsibilities required of dutiful daughters constitutes the basis for socializing and controlling young women. Hence, if a girl appears in the juvenile court it is proof of her participation in the public world of boys and there can be no clearer indication that the family has failed in its socialization and policing functions. As a consequence, during court proceedings Casburn (1979) found that mothers were questioned very closely about their relationships with their daughters and assessed as to whether they were providing proper role models for them.

Because of the judicial system's preoccupation with appropriate behaviour and the welfarist concern with protecting them from themselves, girls are much more likely than boys to be given care or supervision orders. If we look at Gelsthorpe's (1989) research on girls who ended up in institutional care, we can see that efforts were made by the authorities to reproduce the ideologies of the normal family and resocialize these young women. There was a general belief amongst staff that the roots of a girl's delinquency were in her family. There was also a belief that the girls should aspire to be mothers and homemakers and activity programmes reflected this belief. There were cooking sessions, sewing sessions, keep fit classes, housework and efforts were made to reproduce notions of 'normal' family life and 'normal' expressions of femininity.

The image of the 'nice girl' was essentially that of the 'natural female' as passive, sensitive, caring, and any step towards this was viewed as a step towards 'improvement' and the resolution of problems. The social control agency staff wanted the girls to care for their appearance, honour their parents (despite acknowledgement that the parents' behaviour had often contributed to the girls' admission to the agency in the first place), be non-aggressive and moderate in manners and general behaviour. Looking beyond the confines of the agency, the ultimate goal for the girls was a steady relationship, marriage, a home of their own and a family.

The role that familial ideologies play in a young woman's pathway through the juvenile justice system led Casburn to conclude:

the juvenile court process is not geared towards its professed uneasy compromise of justice tempered with welfare for girls ... our juvenile court functions as a management tool, equipped to correct and survey female behaviour which is not 'sugar and spice and all things nice' but, rather, flaunts normative expectations by challenging family authority and threatening truancy and sexual promiscuity.

(Casburn, 1979, pp.14–15, 21)

THE EFFECTS OF INTERMEDIATE TREATMENT

The net widening effect of non-custodial measures such as IT also had considerable implications for non-delinquent children generally. In 1972 the government stated that truants, non-achievers and children from families already under supervision were eligible for IT and that the voluntary and statutory youth services should deliver this service. Hence, social agencies and voluntary bodies were being co-opted into running the juvenile justice system and monitoring family life. It is significant that IT was being recommended for such use in the same time period that intervention was generally being intensified in inner city areas which were afflicted by increasing social problems. In 1972, Keith Joseph the Social Services Minister, delivered a major speech on the causes of deprivation and social problems. He postulated that there was a sub-culture of problem families whose inadequate childrearing practices produced children who were incapable of taking advantage of education, ill-equipped with work skills, lacking morality and unable to form stable relationships. When these children grew up they produced the next generation of misfits. Preventive work was necessary to break the *cycle of deprivation*. Birth control, social work intervention to improve parental behaviour, and community resources were to be the core of this preventive work.

The problem family was clearly identified as being the key to the problem of delinquency and intervention in these families as the preventive solution.

Any inner city child could effectively be a candidate for IT and social workers selected children who were known to them rather than children who were in care. 8,000 children and young people participated in IT schemes in 1976–7. However, the majority were aged 8–15 and not subject to any court order. As a result, a younger and less delinquent population was brought into the system and this was justified in terms of their having behavioural problems which could lead to delinquency. In the process, the categories of 'at risk' and 'pre-delinquent' entered official discourses.

Those children and young people who subsequently ended up in juvenile court having 'failed' IT programmes were subject to more punitive disposals even if officially it was only their first offence. The report of the Personal Social Services Council in 1977 assessed IT and recommended that intensive IT be introduced to cope with the persistently delinquent. As a result, an institutionalized and punitive form of IT was introduced for children and young people already in the juvenile justice system. As

Cohen (1985) has argued: 'in other words "alternatives" become not alternatives at all but new programmes which supplement the existing system or else expand the system by attracting new populations — the net of social control is widened'.

NET STRENGTHENING

Detention centres, borstals and approved schools were supposed to be replaced by 'alternative' community homes. However, this did not happen and the community homes which were designated played a very different role to that envisaged by the 1969 Act. They took younger children than had been originally intended and also non-delinquent children into their treatment programmes. Those defined as troublesome were quickly passed on to the secure institutions. Certain community homes thus became merely 'feeders' for the secure system. It is not surprising therefore that as the numbers of children in secure institutions increased in the 1970s the numbers in community homes declined. In 1965, for example, 25 per cent of convicted 10–17-year-olds were in detention centres and borstals, but by 1977 that figure had increased to 38 per cent (Morris et al., 1980, p.101). Furthermore, within the community homes a restructuring also took place as secure accommodation units were introduced. Overall in 1960 there had been sixty 'secure places' in local authority residential establishments, whereas by 1981 there were at least 537 officially approved secure places available. As Cawson and Martell have noted:

The constant passing on of children to others considered more 'expert' or specialized, the perpetuation of myths about 'diagnosis', 'treatment' or 'cure' at the expense of 'care'... and the use of therapeutic euphemisms [all indicate an] unwillingness [by officialdom] to face the reality that children are being locked up for extended periods occasionally in solitary confinement.

(Cawson and Martell, 1979, p.229)

At the same time there was a decrease in the use of supervision and care orders. In 1969, for example, there were 19,759 supervision orders (formerly probation orders) compared with 15,433 in 1978 and care (formerly approved schools) orders decreased from 5,865 to 5,345 over the same period. Children who were placed under a care order or a supervision order found themselves under the total control of a social worker. Extra controls could be added to the supervision order concerning place of residence, movements could be restricted and activities could be specified. Care orders were semi-indeterminate in nature and could (in exceptional circumstances) last until a child was 18 or 19. Although they were made by the courts they were operated by local authorities whose duty it was 'to receive a child into their care and notwithstanding any claim by his parent or guardian to keep him in care while the order or warrant is in force' (Section 24, Children and Young Persons Act 1969). The length of stay was entirely dependent on an evaluation by a residential worker and a field social worker of the child's progress and their assessment of the readiness or otherwise of his/her home for the child's return.

THE RACIALIZATION OF DELINQUENCY

In the 1970s a 'campaign of counter-reform' mobilized around the notion that the changes brought in by the 1969 Act had resulted in a juvenile crime wave. Criticisms were made of the Act's weakness; its blurring of the distinction between the deprived and depraved child; the transfer of supervision from the probation service to social work departments and the transfer of magistrates' powers to social workers. As early as 1973, the government gave renewed emphasis to punishment and control. It recommended improved and increased custodial facilities for difficult juvenile delinquents; stronger powers for the magistrates in relation to what happens to the juvenile; and a redressing of the balance between the probation service and social workers.

As the 1970s progressed and the juvenile crime statistics worsened, the distinction between the deprived and the depraved child was reintroduced in the form of a general agreement between magistrates, the police, social workers and politicians. It was felt that there was a 'hard core' of persistent young offenders who should be subject to punitive and not welfare measures. In 1973 a government inquiry fully supported reintroducing the distinction between those children in need of care and those in need of strict control. Furthermore, as a result of state intervention in family life, the idea was also firmly established that there was a hard core of multiple problem families who were producing young delinquents. In many ways these problem families were increasingly held to be directly responsible for the continuing problem of delinquency.

The mounting concern about rising juvenile crime rates, 'hard core' young offenders and 'problem' families linked in with debates about the consequences of immigration for British society. A highly public debate emerged about the supposed criminality of black youth and their involvement in street crimes especially 'mugging'. The resultant moral panic about 'mugging' saw black youth emerge as a distinctive social problem and questions were asked about the causes of their supposed criminality. (see Hall et al., 1978).

Research at the time classified black youth as being educational underachievers, unemployed and alienated from, and hostile to, mainstream British society. There was, of course, a recognition that black youth was living in run-down inner city areas characterized by increasing racism and social deprivation. However, deprivation was deemed to be no excuse for, and certainly not *the* cause of, their supposed depravity. The official search for causes led straight to the internal dynamics of the black family. The black family was diagnosed as having a series of pathological features that were supposedly directly responsible for the alienation and hostility of young blacks. It stood accused of being culturally and educationally inadequate, and unrealistic in its expectations for its offspring, yet at one and the same time, the black family was said to be apathetic and over-strict in its socialization practices, overly maternal and riven with inter-generational conflict (Lawrence, 1984). In many ways the 'pathological' black family was seen as producing not only criminogenic 'outsider' offspring but criminogenic 'outsider' 'un-British' communities. Hence, all the ideas of problem families and problem communities present in previous discourses about the causes of juvenile delinquency and criminality took on a distinctly racial dimension.

In terms of what was to be done about this social problem, Fisher and Joshua (1982) argue that two approaches emerged. The first was a proliferation of welfare initiatives aimed at inner city black communities which were staffed by black youth workers and social workers whose task it was to act as surrogate parents for black youngsters and to reintegrate them again with British society, or at least to keep them off the streets and out of trouble. The welfare agencies once more were being drawn into wider law and order concerns. It is also significant to note that evidence began to emerge that if the social services intervened in a black family, the children were more likely to be made the subjects of care orders at an earlier age than their white counterparts. There were indications that a disproportionate number of black children were in the care of local authorities. Harris (1971) found that 32 per cent of girls and 52 per cent of boys in approved schools in London and the south east were from ethnic minority backgrounds. Cawson (1977) in his analysis of the reasons for committal found that the boys in particular tended to be much less delinquent than their white peers.

The second approach was much more direct and serious in terms of its social consequences. As a result of a supposed link being established between black youth and criminality, they were brought directly into contact with the police and relationships deteriorated rapidly. Such was the intensity of police operations and their use of the vagrancy laws in black communities that the Institute of Race Relations (IRR) reported:

> For such young people, in Hackney, Islington, Brixton and other areas inside and outside London, being 'hassled' by the police on their way to, and from school, or when they go out in the evening on leisure activities, has become a routine part of their existence.
>
> (Institute of Race Relations, 1979, p.34)

The continuous police pressure had serious implications for young black people not only because they were entering the juvenile and criminal justice system in increasing numbers; but also because, unlike their white peers, they were entering at the deep end of the formal system. Landau's (1981) study of the Metropolitan Police showed that for particular offences — crimes of violence, burglary, public order offences — black juveniles were treated more harshly by the police in that they were charged immediately rather than their case being referred to the juvenile bureau for a decision about whether to caution or not. As Pitts has noted 'this has the effect of projecting those young people so charged deeper into the juvenile criminal justice system and further up the tariff of penalties' (Pitts, 1987, p.129).

Because of the nature of their contact with the police large numbers of black youths were being criminalized. In comparison with their white peers young blacks were entering the juvenile and criminal justice system on much more serious offences. Therefore, they were being officially labelled and processed as being much more culpable and dangerous. Effectively they were being identified as being part of the 'hard core' of young offenders who should be removed from society. When in the late 1970s serious street battles finally broke out between black youths and the police on the streets of London all the fears and anxieties about black youth were confirmed and even harsher policing and court sentences were called for and implemented.

3.3 THE JUSTICE MODEL

By 1979 the juvenile justice system was far removed from the intentions of those who had pushed for welfarist reforms in the 1960s. The magistrates, the police and the law and order lobby made sure that their ideas concerning the causes of and cure for juvenile delinquency remained firmly embedded within the juvenile justice system. They were also in a position to ensure that social services acted to control those juvenile offenders in their care. It appeared that the heyday of welfarism was over, even though it had achieved its ascendancy more in rhetoric than in implemented policy.

The unintended consequences of the welfare model, coupled with a lack of compliance on the part of government and criminal justice personnel in turn set against a backcloth of the resurgence of law and order politics in the 1970s, led to the resurrection of a justice model of correction. The central concern was to remove all the discretionary and insidious elements of control contained within welfare practices and replace them with unequivocal legal procedures. The hope was that by emphasizing values of natural justice, fairness, due process and children's rights, the extent of intervention would be reduced and (because of legal safeguards) custody used only as a last resort.

Such was the level of disenchantment with welfare that reformers willingly agreed with the American criminologist James Q. Wilson when he stated:

> It does not seem to matter what form of treatment in the correctional system is attempted, whether vocational training or academic education; whether counselling inmates individually, in groups or not at all; whether therapy is administered by social workers or psychiatrists; whether the insitutional context of the treatment is custodial or beign; whether the sentences are short or long; whether the person is placed on probation or released on parole; or whether the treatment takes place in the community or in institutions.
>
> (Wilson, 1975, p.169)

Consequently, they began to advocate a return to principles of classical penology: that the justice system should respond to 'deeds' not 'needs' and that juveniles should be held individually responsible for their misdemeanours; protected in the courts by legal procedure rather than welfare discretion.

ESSENTIAL PROPOSITIONS OF THE JUSTICE MODEL:

1 proportionality of punishment to the crime;
2 determinate sentences;
3 an end to judicial and administrative discretion;
4 an end to disparity in sentencing;
5 protection of rights through due process.

(Hudson, 1987, p.38)

Such ideas hit at the very foundations of the welfare approach and also overlapped with the tough law and order ideas of the Conservative government elected in 1979 (Clarke, 1985). In particular the concept of 'responsibility for law breaking' neatly coalesced with Conservative arguments for increasing controls and punishment. Divorced from its political context, the 'back to justice' movement did appear to be progressive, but during the 1980s it was also quite capable of 'providing a legitimating rhetoric for right wing attempts to pass off dilemmas of unemployment, poverty and inequality as crime problems and to control by punishment what they are not prepared to cure by radical social change' (Hudson, 1987, p.164).

ACTIVITY 3

Draw up a list of the key features of the treatment model and compare these with those of the justice model. Who are the key personnel in each? How does each define delinquency? What is the purpose of their preferred modes of intervention? Finally, consider what role each apportions to the family as (a) the cause of delinquency, (b) the solution to delinquency.

---

4   DELINQUENCY AND THE FAMILY 1979–1990s

In 1979 a Conservative government took office, one which was committed to restoring law and order in British society.

The Conservatives launched a strong attack on delinquency in the run up to the election and throughout the 1980s condemned the 'soft' way that 'dangerous young thugs' were dealt with. Utilizing a neo-classical model of human motivation and liberally using terms such as 'wickedness' and 'evil', delinquency once more became a moral issue.

The Creation of the delinquent?

Much of this approach rested on the previously discussed critique of welfare approaches to juvenile delinquency with many Conservatives blaming the supposed permissiveness of the 1969 Children and Young Persons Act and liberal childrearing practices of the 1960s for the increase in delinquency.

Margaret Thatcher, the incoming Prime Minister, attacked those who had created this 'culture of excuses' and promised that her government would 're-establish a code of conduct that condemns crime plainly and without exception' (Riddell, 1989, p.171). The search for the wider social causes of crime — unemployment, social deprivation, lack of opportunity — was to be abandoned. The rhetoric of treatment and rehabilitation was to be replaced by the rhetoric of punishment and retribution. Welfarism was to be replaced by the rule of law. In October 1979 it was announced that new 'short, sharp, shock' regimes would be introduced into detention centres. As a consequence the twin principles of 'punishment of the hard core' and 'deterrence through punishment' were formally re-established within the juvenile justice system (Muncie, 1990). The 1982 Criminal Justice Act seemingly confirmed the worst fears of those who supported welfarist approaches to delinquency. Magistrates were given powers to sentence directly to youth custody centres (previously they were limited to making recommendations to the Crown court for borstal training) and those parts of the 1969 Act which advocated a phasing out of custody were officially abandoned. It seemed as if there was going to be a considerable increase in the number of juveniles 'tasting porridge'.

However, the mid 1980s and early 1990s have been much more ambiguous in terms of the treatment of young offenders than the law and order rhetoric and policy proposals of the early 1980s suggested. Since 1987 the number of juvenile offenders receiving custodial sentences has *declined* dramatically. By 1991 the government was advocating that custody should be abolished for 15-and 16-year-old girls and 14-year-old boys. So how can we account for this unexpected and dramatic shift to decarceration and deinstitutionalization? First, there has been the activation of diversionary policies; second, legislative changes; third, the curbing of professional autonomy; fourth, the construction of alternatives to custody; and finally, the reintroduction of a policy of 'bifurcation'.

4.1   PUNISHMENT IN THE COMMUNITY

DIVERSION

To some extent the fall in the numbers of juveniles sentenced to custody reflects the fall in the number of juveniles in the general population. Between 1979 and 1989 there was a 40 per cent reduction in the juvenile crime rate. However, there has also been the emergence of what is officially known as a strategic diversionary approach. The government has encouraged the use of police cautioning for first offenders and 73 per cent of known offenders aged under seventeen were formally cautioned for indictable offences in 1989. The Home Office has also stressed the

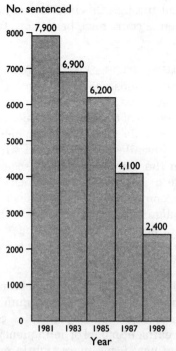

No. sentenced

Figure 5.2 Juvenile offenders receiving custodial sentences, 1981–89
Source: Based on NACRO, 1991a, p.2

dangers of net widening to police forces to make sure that Juvenile Liaison Bureaux do not repeat the mistakes of the 1970s. Therefore, some diversion from the system and not diversion *into* the system has occurred. There has also been the development of pre-court administrative tariffs as a means of diverting young offenders. If juveniles agree to undertake community activities, if families agree to take responsibility, and if reparation is agreed to, court proceedings may not be activated.

LEGISLATIVE CHANGES

Critics of the 1982 Criminal Justice Act focused on the potential that it gave to magistrates to lock juveniles up. However, it also built in a series of conditions that had to be met before this could happen. First, it provided a wider range of custodial and non-custodial options and toughened up the latter; e.g., new conditions could be attached to supervision orders. As such it was attempting to persuade magistrates to opt for punishment in the community. It also attempted to curb those magistrates in favour of custodial sentences by making justifications necessary. The 1988 Criminal Justice Act tightened restrictions further by requiring that a custodial offence could only be imposed if the offence was such that a custodial offence would be imposed on an adult. Courts were also required to specify the criteria under which custody was being recommended. Legal representation for juveniles was also introduced in the course of the 1980s.

Hence, it is argued that through this injection of justice-based principles the powers of the juvenile court have been more tightly defined and are more open to scrutiny.

CURBING PROFESSIONAL AUTONOMY

It is not just magistrates whose powers are more open to scrutiny as a result of changes in the 1980s. The curbing of social workers' discretion and the reconceptualization of their role has taken various forms. First, a strong 'alternatives to custody' ethos has taken hold amongst many social workers dealing with juveniles. Many agreed with the critiques of the welfare approach and the coercive role that social workers played previously and now take a justice-based approach. 'The position extends beyond a refusal to recommend custodial sentences in the courts, encompassing a broad campaigning role with respect to the abolition of custody. The once ambiguous, if not ambivalent, attitudes about custody held by social workers during the early 1980s have been replaced by unequivocal opposition' (Rutherford, 1989, p.29).

Many social services departments now construct their policies premised on the notions of minimum intervention, maximum diversion and underpinned by justice as opposed to welfare principles. SIRs are no longer constructed around the treatment model of delinquency and notions of family pathology. The reports now focus more tightly on the offence and the offender and this has been encouraged by the Department of Social Security.

ALTERNATIVES TO CUSTODY

There has also been the creation of a range of community based alternatives to custody that have been centred on the more serious offences. There has been increased use of community service orders and new requirements have been introduced for supervision orders to enhance their credibility with magistrates. Magistrates can specify the nature and type of programme rather than leave it to the discretion of the supervisor. Considerable emphasis was placed on Intermediate Treatment programmes in the 1980s and they are now, with local variations, broadly perceived as being viable alternatives to custody. The DHSS allocated £15 million in 1983 and 110 local authority projects had been set up offering 3,389 places by 1987. Preference is given to *intensive* IT programmes which are aimed at keeping persistent and serious young offenders out of custody. IT has been increasingly used to deal with more serious offenders and now acts as the gatekeeper to the custodial system. 'By providing constructive and credible alternatives to custodial sentences, projects were able to effectively intervene at the sentencing stage ... Given the recognition that there is a viable local resource custody ceases to be an acceptable option in all but exceptional cases' (Rutherford, 1989, p.29).

A new localized multi-agency voluntary and statutory approach has emerged to operate the IT programmes and juvenile justice teams are increasingly committed to creating 'custody free zones' in their areas. Of crucial importance is the fact that this approach has the full backing of the Magistrates Association. Hence those working in the juvenile justice system are acting in tandem: a stark contrast to the inter agency conflicts and rivalry which were characteristic of the 1970s and early 1980s.

BIFURCATION

A policy of *bifurcation* has also been a hallmark of the 1980s and early 1990s. A distinction has been made between dangerous 'hard core' young offenders — for whom custody is deemed to be essential — and 'the rest' for whom community punishment is deemed to be more appropriate. There is also less differentiation between the hard core juvenile, the young adult and the adult offender. This notion of distinguishing between different types of young offender has also resulted in the re-establishment of the distinction between the deprived and the depraved child. Under the Children Act 1989, the care order has ceased to be available to the juvenile court in criminal proceedings. In formally abolishing the care order, the government was making two ideological points. First, that a care order in criminal proceedings conflicted with the principle of determinacy in sentencing; and second, that it conflicted with the principle of the primacy of parental responsibility. Hence it is being ideologically confirmed that delinquents will be dealt with through the criminal law, not the civil law. As a consequence of this shift, the present juvenile court will be renamed the youth court and when the provisions of the Children Act 1989 are implemented, the juvenile court will no longer hear care cases. Those provisions of the 1969 Children and Young Persons Act which have never been implemented will finally be repealed.

John Pratt (1989) argues that 'a secondary form of bifurcation' unfolded in the 1980s. The conflict between the police and young blacks intensified, with regular clashes on Britain's 'front lines'. In the aftermath of the 1981 and 1985 disturbances closer attention has been paid to the treatment of black youth in the criminal justice system. In 1982 official alarm bells began to ring when it was realized that in some borstals nearly 40 per cent of youths in custody were black (Kettle, 1982). They are less likely to receive non-custodial sentences and more likely to receive longer sentences than their white peers (see NACRO, 1991b). As a result, 'the ideological distinction between the hard core and the rest seems to translate in practice to a disproportionate use of custody for black offenders, placing them firmly in the former category' (Pratt, 1989, p.245).

4.2 PUNISHING THE FAMILY?

The Conservative Party has consistently argued that in the post-war period the policies of the left eroded individual self-discipline by undermining the role of traditional social institutions, particularly the family. The permissiveness of the 1960s, combined with the impact of the overprotective institutions of the welfare state, created an underclass which abandoned self-restraint and self-reliance for free licence and dependency upon the state. The most obvious result of this was the production of a generation of selfish and violent young delinquents.

As far as the Conservatives were concerned it was of central importance that the family as a social institution fulfil its socialization role and that parents be forced to take their responsibilities seriously. Throughout the 1980s, the government attempted to push parental responsibility to the fore in many of their policy proposals.

The government also reintroduced the concept of responsibility into debates on juvenile criminality. The 1990 White Paper *Crime, Justice and Protecting the Public* which informed much of the 1991 Criminal Justice Act, stated that crime prevention begins in the home. 'When effective family control is lacking, children are more likely to grow up without self-discipline and a sense of concern for others. They are more likely to commit crimes' (Home Office, 1990, p.40, para. 8.1).

The major changes in sentencing arrangements proposed in this White Paper were directly related to the government's belief that parents should take responsibility for their children's actions. The central concern was with 'troublesome' 10–15-year-olds. The government believed that parental responsibilities for this age group should be enhanced because: 'Parents should know where their children are and what they are doing, and be in a position to exercise some supervision over them' (Home Office, 1990, p.41, para. 8.8). As a result the 1991 Act empowers the courts to:

- compel parents to attend court if their children are in trouble;
- make parents responsible for the financial penalties incurred by their offspring because 'it brings home to them the reality of the consequences of their children's behaviour and the implications for their actions';
- bind over parents as a strong incentive to improve their supervision of their children.

Hence the family has been given a central role in keeping children under the age of 16 out of trouble and will be held responsible if children do get into trouble. In principle the government's approach echoes earlier suggestions. For example, all of the welfarist proposals of the 1960s stressed the importance of parental care, guidance and duties in preventing delinquency. However, earlier approaches to the problems of delinquency recognized that the welfare state would have to intervene in order to help socially inadequate parents fulfil their responsibilities. By contrast the current approach and the neo-classical principles underpinning it utilizes criminal sanctions to discipline parents into carrying out their responsibilities. Good parenting has become a law and order issue and punishment is being located within the family.

Punishment in the community and the stress on parental responsibility places young offenders firmly in the home and this can be reinforced by curfew restrictions being placed on young offenders. As a consequence the home has become the site of punishment and the young person's parents the prison warders. This relocation of the site of punishment from the detention centre to the home also means that the home is open to surveillance by those responsible for operating curfew restrictions and IT programmes.

This home-based surveillance system is being reinforced by upgraded electronic tagging and tracking proposals. In May 1989 the government announced that it was implementing three experimental electronic tagging schemes for those on bail in an attempt to reduce overcrowding in remand centres. The 1991 Criminal Justice Act affirmed that tagging would be extended to 16-year-olds in order to enforce curfew requirements (Nellis, 1991). The government has also supported 'tracking' programmes as part of intensive supervision. '"Trackers" maintain vigilant contact with offenders by telephone or in person up to three times a day, checking their whereabouts, planning daily schedules and discussing proposed activities' (Allen, 1991).

ACTIVITY 4

What are we to make of this current shift towards punishment in the community and punishment in the family and what are the implications of such shifts for juveniles, families and the justice system? Do you think they mark a radical departure from previous practice, or are they simply another addition to the growing list of available means to control young people's behaviour?

---

5   CONCLUSION: BLURRING THE BOUNDARIES BETWEEN THE PRIVATE AND THE PUBLIC

The notion of the family as a private arena is one that is firmly embedded in British social and criminal justice policy. Yet although its autonomy is to be protected, the mixed messages of policy also include some which say that the state has the right to intervene if people are not fulfilling their responsibilities (**Muncie and Wetherell, 1992**). This ambiguity is clear in the emergence of delinquency as a social problem and successive restructurings of the juvenile justice system. Indeed the issue of delinquency provides us with one of the clearest examples of the willingness of the state to intervene in and regulate family life. As we saw in Section 1, the defining of certain behaviours as delinquent was originally closely connected with the emergence of a particular family form — that of the Victorian nuclear ideal. It was non-compliance with this ideal, initially because of economic and cultural constraints, that enabled working class childrearing practices and consequently the existence of delinquent individuals and families to be identified. Since then intervention in family structures and patterns of child upbringing have been legitimized in the interests of social stability, the reproduction of a willing workforce, mass education, the nation's future and the inculcation of correct morals and values. Such rhetoric has, for almost two centuries, crystallized around the issues of the troubled or troublesome young.

Whilst this provides an essential continuity in successive attempts to cajole, coerce or help parents to rear their children in acceptable ways, the actual means employed to ensure that correct socialization practices are followed has gone through some significant changes. As the preceding discussion has revealed, such means have oscillated between emphasizing parental responsibility or individual responsibility, welfare or justice, incarceration or community treatment, punishment or rehabilitation, and care or control. The fact that the juvenile justice system (and discourses within it) has continually worked within these sets of binary opposites has meant that none has ever achieved complete ascendancy. Rather the apparently new and innovative have always been grafted onto old established practices and never replaced them. The continual search for a 'solution' has simply meant that the juvenile justice system has become forever expanded and complex. Consider some of the primary responses to juvenile law breaking and their ideological justifications below:

Table 5.1   Responses to juvenile law breaking/ideological justifications

Chronology	Intervention	Ideology
1800→	adult prison	punishment
1830→	juvenile prison	punishment
1850→	reformatories/approved schools/community homes	punishment/treatment
1910→	borstals	training
1950→	detention centres	punishment
1960→	community (IT)	treatment
1980→	community/family	punishment

The main point to recognize in this catalogue of interventions is that current efforts to manage delinquency are an amalgam of all of these approaches. It is still possible to find juveniles in adult prisons, albeit largely whilst they are on remand, at the same time as others are subject to curfew requirements at home. Similarly whilst in the 1990s the role of the family appears centre stage, the issue of acceptable and non-acceptable family socialization patterns has always been at the heart of the issue of whether to intervene or not. However what does make the current system worthy of comment in its own right is the fact of its continual expansion and proliferation into settings which have not traditionally been associated with criminal justice and the penal system — namely the 'private' worlds of the family and the community.

During the late 1970s and early 1980s social control theorists attempted to make sense of the shifts that were then taking place in the operation of the juvenile justice system (see Cohen, 1985; Harris and Webb, 1987).

They argued that the merging of welfare and criminal justice ideologies had resulted in a collapsing of the traditional distinctions between the deprived and the depraved; the formal and the informal; the guilty and the innocent; treatment and punishment; rehabilitation and retribution. As a result a general 'blurring of the boundaries' occurred and confusion abounded. Critical criminologists believed that they had discovered a sinister logic in the shifts. The good intentions of the proponents of welfarism had been subverted and been used to disguise the expansion of the social control system. Diversion programmes operated to divert children *into* the system rather than *away* from it and alternatives became supplements to the existing system resulting in increased rather than decreased intervention. Since the system operated under the guise of 'care', 'welfare' and 'treatment' there was the belief that it was more humane and acting in the best interests of the children. As a consequence a much more insidious control system was created because the principles of welfare were masking the fact that children were being punished in ever greater numbers within a system of 'low visibility and low accountability' (Cohen, 1979, p.351). Above all there was the belief that this control system was becoming all pervasive: from its concentration in the penal system to its dispersal in the community.

However, as we have seen, in the 1980s, there was some reversal of this blurring. Through the re-establishment of the primacy of the legal process, the restructuring of the juvenile court and the reclassification of different age groups and different types of young people, there has been a corresponding re-establishment of traditional distinctions between the deprived and depraved. Hence it would seem as if Cohen's prognosis has not been realized. But if we look closer it is not so straightforward. Pratt (1989) argues that although there has been a formal return to the principles of a justice model, substantively something very different has transpired. He suggests that a delinquency management service has emerged which is corporatist in nature. This service embodies both justice ideologies and reformulated welfarist notions and is primarily concerned with administrative decision making; the formulation of policy; and applying managerialist discourses (see Table 5.2). As a corollary:

> Instead of a concern for the protection of individual rights, we find instead an emphasis on efficiency and the primacy of policy objectives. Instead of a shift from the inhumanities and injustices of the institution, we find these features of the carceral system now being reproduced in the community — in those projects that are supposed to be alternatives to the institution.
> (Pratt, 1989, p.252)

We would argue that the 'insights' of social control theorists are crucial to understanding the shifts that have taken place in the management of juvenile delinquency in the 1980s and 1990s. Whilst at the formal level there may have been a reversal of the blurring trends of the 1970s, at the

Table 5.2   Three models of juvenile justice

Parameter	Welfare	Justice	Corporatism
Characteristics	Informality. Generic referrals. Individualized sentencing. Indeterminate sentencing.	Due process. Offending. Least restrictive alternative. Determinate sentences.	Administrative decision making. Offending. Diversion from court/custody. Alternative to care/ custody programmes.
Key personnel	Child care experts	Lawyers	Juvenile justice specialists
Key agency	Social work	Law	Inter-agency structure
Tasks	Diagnosis	Punishment	Systems intervention
Understanding of client behaviour	Pathological	Individual responsibility	Unsocialized
Purpose of intervention	Provide treatment	Sanction behaviour	Retrain
Objectives	Respond to individual needs	Respect individual rights	Implementation of policy

Source: Pratt, 1989, Table 1

substantive level there has been a dramatic blurring of the boundaries between the private and the public and the family and the community are now incorporated into the justice system. There have been concerted attempts to mobilize 'respectable' communities so that they protect themselves from 'invasion' by the feared criminal 'underclass'. The active citizenry can do this through participating in crime prevention schemes, neighbourhood watch schemes, police/community consultative panels and so on. There has been the emergence of multi-agency programmes and strategies to target those communities with a crime problem. This has resulted in a key shift in the role of social workers and youth workers. In the course of the 1980s they were increasingly expected to be actively involved in crime prevention programmes. Whereas under the 1969 Children and Young Persons Act they were defined as experts who could diagnose and treat the sickness causing crime now 'they are not to work towards the reform or "cure" of individual offenders, or even simply to help and support them, in isolation from other agencies; they are to remember that they are part of a wider system that includes all the agencies concerned with crime and its control' (Blagg and Smith, 1989, pp.vi–vii). This new community approach stresses the idea that communities, and in particular parents, must take responsibility for the social problems they create and this includes being made to participate in the control and punishment of their errant children. We shall have to wait and see whether these policies will be any more successful than the previous ones discussed in this chapter. However, concern has been expressed about the dangers of pursuing policies which place the responsibility for delinquency firmly on the family. It is argued that this will inevitably produce strains in those families which are structurally least able to cope with them. Many would argue that the parents of delinquent children need the state's help not punishment (NACRO, 1992). However, there seems little likelihood of such concern being recognized within the current juvenile justice agenda.

REFERENCES

Allen, R. (1990) 'Punishing the parents', *Youth and Policy*, no. 31, November, pp.17–20.

Allen, R. (1991) 'Out of jail: the reduction in the use of penal custody for male juveniles 1981–88', *Howard Journal*, vol. 30, no 1, pp.30–52.

Barrett, M. and McIntosh, M. (1982) *The Anti-Social Family*, London, Verso.

Bennett, T. (1979) 'The social distribution of criminal labels', *British Journal of Criminology*, vol. 19, no. 2, pp.134–45.

Blagg, H. and Smith, D. (1981) *Crime, Penal Policy and Social Control*, London, Longman.

Bottoms, A. (1974) 'On the decriminalization of the juvenile court' in Hood, R. (ed.) *Crime, Criminology and Public Policy*, London, Heinemann.

Casburn, M. (1979) *Girls will be Girls*, London, WRRCP.

Cawson, P. (1977) 'Black children in approved schools', unpublished paper, DHSS.

Cawson, P. and Martell, M. (1979) *Children Referred to Closed Units*, Research Report no. 5, London, DHSS.

Clarke, J. (1981) 'Managing the delinquent: the Children's Branch of the Home Office 1913–30' in Langan, M. and Schwartz, B. (eds.) *Crises in the British State*, London, Macmillan.

Clarke, J. (1985) 'Whose justice? The politics of juvenile control', *International Journal of the Sociology of Law* vol. 13, no. 4, pp.405–21.

Cohen, S. (1979) 'The punitive city: notes on the dispersal of social control', *Contemporary Crises*, vol. 3, November, pp. 339–63.

Cohen, S. (1985) *Visions of Social Control*, Cambridge, Polity.

Collinson, M. (1980) 'Questions of juvenile justice' in Carlen, P. and Collinson, M. (eds) *Radical Issues in Criminology*, Oxford, Martin Robertson.

Cunningham, J. (1991) *The Children of the Poor*, Oxford, Blackwell.

Davis, G. (1991) *The Irish in Britain 1815–1914*, Dublin, Gill and Macmillan.

Fisher, G. and Joshua, H. (1982) 'Social policy and black youth' in Cash-more, E. and Troyna, B. (eds.) *Black Youth in Crisis*, London, Allen and Unwin.

Gelsthorpe, L. (1989) *Sexism and the Female Offender*, Aldershot, Gower.

Hall, S., Critcher, C., Jefferson, T., Clarke, J., and Roberts, B. (1978) *Policing the Crisis*, London, Macmillan.

Harris, R. and Webb, D. (1987) *Welfare, Power and Juvenile Justice*, London, Tavistock.

Harris, T. (1971) 'Survey of immigrants in approved schools', unpublished paper, DHSS.

Hendrick, H. (1990) *Images of Youth: Age, Class and the Male Youth Problem, 1880–1920*, Oxford, Clarendon.

Home Office (1990) *Crime, Justice and Protecting the Public*, London, HMSO.

Hudson, B. (1987) *Justice Through Punishment*, London, Macmillan.

Hudson, B. (1989) 'Justice or welfare?' in Cain, M. (ed) *Growing up Good*, London, Sage.

Institute of Race Relations (1979) *Policing Against Black People*, London, IRR.

Kettle, M. (1982) 'The racial numbers game in our prisons', *New Society*, 30 September, pp.535–7.

Landau, M (1981) 'Juveniles and the police', *British Journal of Criminology*, 21: 1, pp.27–46.

Lawrence, E. (1984) 'Just plain common sense: the "roots" of racism' in CCCS (ed.) *The Empire Strikes Back*, London, Hutchinson.

Longford Report (1964) *Crime — a Challenge to us all*, London, Labour Party Study Group, Transport House.

May, M. (1973) 'Innocence and experience: the evolution of the concept of juvenile delinquency in the mid-nineteenth century', *Victorian Studies*, vol. 17, no. 1, pp.7–29.

Morris, A., Giller, H., Geach, H., and Szwed, E. (1980) *Justice for Children*, London, Macmillan.

Muncie, J. (1990) 'Detention centres and the politics of deterrence', *Critical Social Policy*, No. 28, pp.53–7.

Muncie, J. and Wetherell, M. (1992) 'Family policy and political discourse', Book 1, Chapter 2, Family Life and Social Policy, Milton Keynes, Open University.

National Association for the Care and Resettlement of Offenders (1991a) *Some Facts About Juvenile Crime*, London, NACRO.

National Association for the Care and Resettlement of Offenders (1991b) *Race and Criminal Justice*, London, NACRO.

National Association for the Care and Resettlement of Offenders (1992) *Preventing Youth Crime*, London, NACRO.

Nellis, M. (1991) 'The electronic monitoring of offenders in England and Wales', *British Journal of Criminology*, vol. 31, no. 2, pp.165–86.

Pearson, G. (1983) *Hooligan: A History of Respectable Fears*, London, Macmillan.

Pitts, J. (1987) *The Politics of Juvenile Crime*, London, Sage.

Pratt, J. (1989) 'Corporatism: the third model of juvenile justice', *British Journal of Criminology*, vol. 29, no. 3, pp.236–54.

Riddell, P. (1989) *The Thatcher Effect*, Oxford, Blackwell.

Rutherford, A. (1989) 'The mood and temper of penal policy', *Youth and Policy* No, 27, pp.27–31.

Springhall, J. (1986) *Coming of Age: Adolescence in Britain, 1860–1960*, London, Gill and Macmillan.

Sprott, W.J.H., Mays, J.B., Morris, T.P., and Spencer, J., (1972) 'Delinquency areas', in Mays, J.B. *(ed) Juvenile Delinquency, The Family and The Social Group*, London, Longman.

Taylor, I. (1981) *Law and Order: Arguments for Socialism*, London, Macmillan.

Thorpe, D.H., Smith, D., Green, C.J., and Paley, J.H., (1980) *Out of Care: The Community Support of Juvenile Offenders*, London, Allen and Unwin.

Willmott, P. (1972) 'Delinquency in Bethnal Green', in May s(ed).

Wilson, J.Q. (1975) *Thinking About Crime*, New York, Basic Books.

Rose, N. (1991) *Governing the Soul*, London, Routledge.

Zedner, L. (1991) *Women, Crime and Custody in Victorian England*, Oxford, Clarendon Press.

CHAPTER 6
THE PROBLEM OF POVERTY

ALLAN COCHRANE

1   INTRODUCTION

One measure of the success of any welfare system is the extent to which it is able to maintain acceptable standards of living for its citizens. What-ever else welfare is about, one might reasonably expect the reduction of poverty for the most vulnerable of a country's population to be a high priority. In the UK's case, therefore, it is not surprising that Beveridge's report on social insurance has frequently been seen as one of the main foundations of the post-war welfare state. After all, it explicitly promised 'to win freedom from want by maintaining incomes' (Beveridge, 1942, para 409). So, one of the main aims of this chapter is to make it easier to judge the extent to which poverty — or want — has been eradicated in the UK. At the risk of anticipating that discussion, a second aim is to clarify what makes people poor and then to examine explanations for the con-tinued existence of poverty.

Two main sets of debates have dominated recent mainstream discus-sions of poverty. One set of debates has concentrated on clarifying what is meant by poverty in 'affluent' societies, such as the UK. These debates have often been heated, since just as some definitions inexora-bly lead to the conclusion that 'poverty' is on the increase, so others make it easy simply to remove 'poverty' as a social problem at the stroke of a statistician's pen. It is not difficult to see which conclusion is likely to be more politically acceptable, whatever the party in govern-ment. Nor is it, perhaps, surprising that poverty finds no explicit expression in the official language of government statistics which deal instead with categories such as 'low income households', 'lone parent families' or recipients of particular benefits. In this sense, at least, state policies do seem to have ensured that the poor really are no longer with us.

The second set of debates is rather different in that it focuses on the explanations for rather than the existence of poverty. Here the argument is equally heated, since different explanations will also lead to quite different policy (and political) conclusions. For example, if the main explanation for the existence of poverty is either that the poor make choices which consign them to poverty, or that the policies of the welfare state encourage some people to behave in ways which leave them poor (for example by encouraging 'dependency'), then the policy conclusions which are drawn will tend to move away from the provision of welfare benefits as an entitlement. On the other hand, if the main explanation stresses the importance of structural inequalities of income between different groups, then conclusions may be drawn which point either to the need for

increased rights to benefit to compensate for inequalities, or to more far reaching attempts to challenge those inequalities.

Although these two debates frequently refer across to each other, they remain distinct enough to make it possible to look at them separately. The next section of this chapter will, therefore, consider problems of definition and debates about increases (or decreases) in poverty over time, in this case using evidence from the 1980s to develop the argument, although a similar approach could be adopted for any post-war decade. Having achieved some clarity about the 'facts' of poverty, the following section (Section 3) will look at them a bit more closely, further questioning the assumptions which underlie them and seeking to move beyond aggregate figures to consider which groups are worst affected by poverty. The next section (Section 4) will focus on alternative explanations for the persistence of poverty over time, and consider some of their policy implications.

2   WHAT IS POVERTY?

One of the problems with the notion of 'poverty' is that it seems obvious what it is until one starts to ask questions about it. Once we do, it becomes difficult not to recognize that we often have quite inconsistent ideas about it in our heads which come together to give us a 'common-sense' understanding which may itself be changing over time. But the issue of definition is not merely academic — in the pejorative meaning of the term — it is also central to policy debates about the development of welfare. This section aims to show how the definition of a problem will itself influence policy intervention, as well as introducing some of the available evidence on poverty in the UK. It also aims to give a flavour of the debates between government and what has been called the 'poverty' lobby. In order to make this easier, many of the examples of argument and evidence which follow are drawn from a short book on poverty published by one of the UK's main campaigning organizations — the Child Poverty Action Group (CPAG) — at the beginning of the 1990s (Oppenheim, 1990).

2.1   ABSOLUTE DEFINITIONS

Within mainstream policy debates the focus is generally on poor households or poor families and we shall consider some of the (frequently
unacknowledged) consequences of this focus in Section 3. One of the main
tensions in these debates, however, centres around the rather different
question of whether poverty should be measured in absolute or relative
terms.

Absolute definitions imply the identification of a basic subsistence standard of living which can be utilized in different historical periods and in
different places. With the help of such a definition it should, in principle,
be fairly easy to determine whether more people are below or above the
basic level (which could be identified as the poverty line). Trends in the
proportion of the population in poverty over time could be assessed. Absolute definitions of this sort make it possible to judge whether standards of
living have improved for particular groups over time. They also help to
highlight the continuing enormous gap at global level between conditions
in the prosperous countries of the North and the poorer countries of the
South (and even between conditions in Eastern and Central Europe and
in Western Europe).

In contrast with Victorian England it might be possible to conclude — as
John Moore, then Secretary of State for Social Security did in the late
1980s — that 'not only are those with lower incomes not getting poorer,
they are substantially better off than they have ever been before... It is
capitalism that has wiped out the stark want of Dickensian Britain'
(quoted in Oppenheim, 1990, p.9). A more systematic analysis might
discover rather more people than the Secretary of State expected in conditions not dissimilar to those of the Dickensian poor, but the general
point would probably be widely accepted. It does not, however, take us
very far in our search for a useful definition of poverty. Few of us, I
suspect, would see progress from the condition of life amongst the poor as
depicted by Dickens in *Oliver Twist* or *Hard Times* as particularly
praiseworthy. On the contrary we take it for granted that standards of
living have improved in absolute terms, and — of course — continue to
use the word 'poverty' in ways which have contemporary meaning,
whether because we have experienced or are experiencing it, or because
we see it around us. Not many of us believe poverty has disappeared. At
the end of the 1980s over 60 per cent of those interviewed for the British
Social Attitudes Survey agreed with the statement that 'there is a lot of
real poverty in Britain today' (Taylor-Gooby, 1990, p.15).

2.2   RELATIVE DEFINITIONS

So, where do we go from here? One possibility is that poverty needs to be
defined in the context of the society in which one lives — in relative rather
than absolute terms. At its simplest the necessity for this can be seen
simply by comparing the difference between what is available in different
periods: there were no televisions or radios in Victorian times, domestic
heating systems were primitive, electric lighting was only being

introduced towards the end of the period. Yet lack of access to most of these facilities would probably be agreed by most of us to be a sign of poverty in the 1990s. In other words our definition of a minimum accept-able standard of living is itself likely to change over time. Even Rowntree — who set out very strict criteria of subsistence poverty as the basis of his famous surveys of the poor in York and is frequently presented as a supporter of absolute definitions — made slightly different assumptions about what constituted subsistence in different periods (Rowntree, 1922 and 1941).

ACTIVITY I

Try to identify the main features that you would consider 'necessities' for an acceptable standard of living for a household or family.

A similar exercise was undertaken in the mid 1980s by researchers work-ing on a television series called 'Breadline Britain'. They looked for agree-ment on what constituted poverty through a survey, and two-thirds of those surveyed concluded that the following were necessities for an acceptable standard of living:

- Self-contained damp-free accommodation with indoor toilet and bath.
- A weekly roast joint for the family and three daily meals for each child.
- Two pairs of all-weather shoes and a warm, waterproof coat.
- Sufficient money for public transport.
- Adequate bedrooms and beds.
- Heating and carpeting.
- A refrigerator and washing machine.
- Enough money for special occasions like Christmas.
- Toys for the children.

(Mack and Lansley, 1985, summarized in Oppenheim, 1990, p.8)

It would be interesting to know how many of the necessities listed here coincided with those you identified. I suspect that your list would be similar, although it is difficult to get universal agreement on any list of this sort. Once a list of necessities has been agreed, however, it should be easier to make judgements about how many households are 'poor' at any one time. In this case the researchers argued that people were poor when they lacked at least three of these necessities and went on to conclude (with the help of a survey undertaken in 1983) that about one in seven people were living in poverty.

In principle using a definition like this should make it easier to achieve comparison across time as long as the basic ground rules are agreed from the start. But in practice it is more difficult, because constructing a consistent statistical series would require the list to be updated regularly (producing something like a 'poverty index' on the model of the retail price index) and government statisticians seem to have little interest in doing so (although the 'Breadline Britain' researchers themselves undertook a similar exercise at the end of the decade). Another advantage of such definitions, however, is that they help to show how different elements of deprivation come together to produce an overall experience of disadvantage (or 'multiple deprivation'). Writers and campaigners have developed this argument to challenge narrowly based subsistence notions of poverty which emphasize the minimum requirements of families and individuals for survival. They argue that a crucial aspect of poverty is the way in which it reduces the ability of people to participate in the normal lives of their communities, with stress being placed on the deprivation which results from a lack of income, rather than the low income itself. Peter Townsend has probably put this most strongly, arguing that:

> Individuals, families and groups in the population can be said to be in poverty when they lack the resources to obtain the types of diet, participate in the activities and have the living conditions and amenities which are customary, or are at least widely encouraged or approved, in the societies to which they belong. Their resources are so seriously below those commanded by the average individual or family that they are, in effect, excluded from ordinary living patterns, customs and activities.
>
> (Townsend, 1979, p.31)

The main difficulty associated with these approaches in practice is that, since it is not easy to get a consensual agreement on what constitutes deprivation or poverty, each new survey has to set out to create that consensus: the first step is always to persuade others that the index being used is indeed a reasonable one. This is particularly important for those — like Townsend et al., 1987 — who favour a broad definition, to include, for example, unpleasant conditions in the workplace (with the home being included as the workplace for most women), lack of access to certain amenities (such as refrigerators, washing machines etc.) and locational disadvantage (since living on an inner city council estate implies an unpleasant urban environment, reduced access to credit, and reduced access to well-paid employment).

Existing popular definitions of poverty seem rather more narrow than those favoured by Townsend. In 1989 only 25 per cent of those questioned in the British Social Attitudes Survey (Taylor-Gooby, 1990) were prepared to agree with a definition of poverty according to which the poor would have 'enough to buy things they really needed, but not enough to buy the things most people take for granted' (what Taylor-Gooby calls a relative definition), although more than half agreed that people were poor if 'they had enough to eat and live, but not enough to buy other things that they needed' (the 'breadline' definition). Not surprisingly, perhaps, there was almost universal agreement that those who did not have 'enough to eat and live without getting into debt' were in poverty (living below minimum subsistence) (see Table 6.1).

Table 6.1:   Definitions of poverty: percentage agreeing with each definition of poverty (1989)

Relative	25%
Breadline	60%
Below minimum subsistence	95%

Source: Taylor-Gooby, 1990, p. 8.

ACTIVITY 2

One way of highlighting the impact of poverty and the way in which its effects go wider than lack of income is to identify the cumulative impact it has on those living in particular areas or neighbourhoods. The newspaper article reprinted below, summarizes one person's interpretation of some of the problems of living in Easterhouse, a large housing estate on the out-skirts of Glasgow. After reading the article, try to jot down, *first* some of the main problems Bob Holman identifies for those living on this estate, and *second* what he sees as the main causes of those problems.

■ 'HEIRS TO YEARS OF LIVING DANGEROUSLY' BY BOB HOLMAN

A small girl ran up to me as I crossed the road to our flat in Easterhouse. The next moment only her head and shoulders were above the ground. Drain covers are frequently stolen for scrap and she had dropped several feet into an open drain. After treating her cuts and bruises I took the shaken girl home.

A screaming boy came to our door. While he was delivering leaflets, an Alsatian dog had gripped his thin thigh between its teeth. Quickly, I transported him to hospital.

An agitated mother sent for me. Playing chase in the street, her son had been knocked over by a taxi whose driver delivered him to her door and left. The boy's leg was badly lacerated. Keeping it straight, we drove him to the Royal Infirmary — I'm a regular caller — where he was detained.

Scotland has the worst child accident rate in Western Europe. Scalds, falls, fires and road collisions result in not just thousands of serious injuries but also in more than half the deaths of children aged between one and fourteen.

In Scotland, accident rates are highest in places such as Easterhouse, the Glasgow housing estate with a population of more than 30,000. In 1986, its figures of 3.9 per cent of boys and 2.1 per cent of girls injured so seriously they were kept in hospital, were nearly double those for Glasgow as a whole. So numerous are child accidents, the Scottish Office has funded a special project to reduce injuries.

Easterhouse also suffers mass unemployment and poverty. 65 per cent of its school children receive clothing grants, a sure indicator of low income.

Accidents and social deprivation are linked. In 1990, the British Medical Journal reported a study showing child deaths from head injuries as sixteen times higher in deprived areas. The children of social class V parents are six times more likely to die from burns than social class I. Those of the unemployed are three times more prone to fatal accidents. Children of the poor are at most risk of being burnt, broken, even destroyed.

So what is the link between poverty and accidents? It is not that poor parents are ignorant about risks or less caring about children. Most Easterhouse parents strive hard to protect their families. Rather, it is that factors associated with social deprivations increase the likelihood of accidents in the following ways.

Firstly, the housing of low income people is less safe than that of the affluent. Most Easterhouse residents live in blocks of flats. One in four flats is abandoned and therefore vulnerable to vandals who start fires. If fire spreads, residents may be trapped in flats which possess only one exit door.

The outside landing door of friends of mine burst into flames and spread to their door. Three floors up, they were fortunate to escape by leaping through the burning door.

Housing defects are magnified by overcrowding. A 1985 Centre for Environmental Studies report showed 24.9 per cent of households in Easterhouse to be overcrowded compared with the national figure of 3.5 per cent. That figure, thanks to the Housing Department's efforts, will now have dropped but lack of space is still a problem.

In over-crowded homes, chip pans, knives, pills and bleach are more likely to be in reach of children. And parents on Income Support, for which they receive £13.35 a week for each child, can not afford a fireguard at £22, a stairgate at £40, or £40 for a playpen.

Overcrowded flats without gardens mean, secondly, that children must play on the streets. Dog bites are frequent. Large dogs are kept for protection against break-ins but the dogs cannot be confined to small flats. The ear of one 15-year-old was almost torn off by a bull terrier.

But the most lethal environmental danger is traffic. Of course, drivers are not always to blame. As I left a youth club one night, a boy thundered by on a home-made skateboard, straight into a bus. A six-year-old was killed playing 'chicken'. These accidents occur because children are concentrated on the streets. Others are due to reckless driving.

In Drumchapel, a housing estate west of Easterhouse, a child is run over every four days; cars speed through from the affluent suburbs of Bearsden and Milngavie. Drumchapel and Easterhouse are among the lowest car owning populations in Britain yet they endure some of the highest accident rates.

The third factor is violence. In Easterhouse most families detest and avoid it. But muggings and fights are more common in locations where unemployed young people are concentrated with few opportunities to seek fulfilment. One teenager needed 14 head stitches after being set upon by a gang. A 15-year-old was left with permanent brain damage after another fight. His attacker was sentenced to three years.

Fourthly, peripheral estates tend to lack the facilities which can prevent accidents. Glasgow Corporation is re-furbishing some flats. Body Shop is sponsoring an adventure playground and, in our area, parents run a magnificent summer play scheme. But the local authority, with its borrowing requirements limited by government, is short of cash. The playground will serve just one of Easterhouse's fifteen districts. The play scheme, like youth clubs, has no permanent base.

In our area there is no community building open all the time for parents and toddlers to meet, for safe indoor activities for children, for teenagers to have a place of their own. Residents did submit an urban aid application to use a deserted tenement for these ends. Unhappily, it was burnt down.

The accident toll among children in inner-city and peripheral estates could be reduced almost immediately. Parents on Income Support should receive an annual safety bonus of £100 per child for the provision of fire guards, stair and balcony gates, socket covers, kettle guards, etc. 'Sleeping policemen' should be introduced into highly populated zones and a 20 mph speed limit should be rigorously enforced.

Such steps would reduce injuries but would not bridge the affluent/poor divide. Children of the latter will remain at income levels and in environments that place them at greater risk. In a Thatcherite free market, there must be losers. The unemployed are paying the price of many social disadvantages.

The children of poor parents will remain at greater risk to accidents, illness and reception into public care until Britain becomes a more equal society. Accident prevention must be put in the context of policies that go beyond providing safety officers and which instead ensure decent incomes and homes for all families, jobs for youngsters, and play facilities.

A pub plagued by violence has recently come up for sale. Its spacious rooms would make a safe, all-day recreation centre for the community. But the local project for which I work is hard pushed to raise money to survive let alone buy a building. The local authority is retrenching, not expanding.

Yet the London Docklands Development Corporation, which has spent £2.5 billion of public money mainly for the benefit of property bosses and yuppies, agreed to spend £100,000 on a huge party hosted by Angela Rippon. Just £100,000 would secure a centre for our community, £2.5 billion would transform Easterhouse.

Government money is available for public expenditure, but until the political will exists for it to reduce rather than reinforce inequalities,

the children of isolated council estates will continue to fall from balconies, to be scarred by fires, and to be crushed by vehicles.
(*The Guardian*, 27 November, 1991) ■

2.3   USING GOVERNMENT STATISTICS

In practice, both because there is no agreed index of deprivation and because conducting the surveys required to produce one is costly and time consuming, the most commonly used indices of poverty are rather different and are relative in another sense, too. They are constructed from available government statistics collected for other purposes. Here researchers have to explain convincingly how they can be manipulated to produce evidence on poverty. One way of doing this is effectively to appeal to 'common-sense' notions, thus also seeking to build a consensus as much as pretending to provide uncontestable 'scientific' definitions. In this sense, debates about poverty are always political, even if they are not always party political.

INCOME SUPPORT

The first commonly used approach uses supplementary benefit/income support levels for guidance and the second uses measures of average income. Using the first appears to provide a more or less consensual definition which varies over time since it reflects decisions endorsed in Parliament identifying a minimum level of income for people not in employment. (The Social Security Act 1986 which was implemented in 1988 replaced supplementary benefit with income support.) The CPAG argues that people with incomes on or less than supplementary benefit/income support levels are poor, but acknowledges that there may be problems with this definition. One problem lies within the statistics themselves. If income support levels are rising in real terms, the incomes of those receiving them will be rising too. Most of us might reasonably conclude that increasing benefit payments would reduce the incidence of poverty. But the opposite impression would be given if income support levels were being used as measures of poverty. The explanation for this is fairly straightforward, even if the result is paradoxical. Increasing the threshold for the payment of benefits would also mean that all those whose incomes were at this threshold or below would now be defined as poor (although all of those with incomes below the old income support level and between that level and the new one would actually be better off).

ACTIVITY 3

The implications of this may be clearer if we consider what happens if — as may seem more likely — benefit levels go down in real terms. What effect would you expect that to have (a) on the poor and (b) on poverty statistics?

Family on Supplementary Benefit, Manchester, 1986

Queue for benefit cheque, Grangemouth, 1990

When benefit levels rise, the incomes of the poor will rise and when they fall, their incomes will fall. But — using this statistical measure — falling benefit levels would also reduce the numbers of those *recorded* as being in poverty. All of those with incomes between the old (higher) benefit level and the new (lower) benefit level would be removed from the statistics, but they would actually be worse off. To complicate matters further, even if supplementary benefit (SB or income support) rises in line with (or faster than) the retail price index that may still not tell us whether the real incomes of those relying on it have increased or not, because the rate of inflation experienced by the poor may not be the same as that experienced by those on higher incomes, because they buy different things (Barr and Coulter, 1990, p.307).

As with any government policy the aims of income support are not necessarily straightforward, and are certainly not always consistent with the priorities of researchers or the needs of the poor. Political priorities may, for example, mean that the minimum levels of some groups are effectively set at higher levels than are those of others (in the 1980s, for example, levels of benefit paid to the unemployed were cut much more than others). Minima may be shifted because parties in government face problems (e.g. over levels of public sector spending) rather than because attitudes have changed. It is dangerous to conclude that every change which stems from party political conviction reflects a wider social consensus, particularly in periods of high political controversy.

AVERAGE INCOME

The second method defines poverty as a proportion of average income using figures on 'Households below average incomes' published by the Department of Social Security in which the average is the mean (all incomes are added up and divided by the number of incomes to produce the mean). CPAG uses 50 per cent of average household income as a definition of poverty. In so far as average income reflects what is widely accepted as a 'reasonable' standard of living, then taking what appears to be the extreme case of those earning a half or less, would seem to make it possible to identify a significantly disadvantaged group. It seems likely that there would be wide agreement that most of them could be defined as poor. A similar approach is taken by the European Commission in its studies of poverty within the European Community.

There are inherent problems with this definition, too, however. If higher incomes are rising very fast, for example, then they will pull up the average and, therefore, also 50 per cent of the average. In other words the income level at which a household was defined as poor would go up, so that the numbers defined as being in poverty would rise, too. But the standards of living of the people involved would not change: they would be able to buy the same things as they had before. Whatever the statistics told us, most of us would probably agree that levels of poverty had not increased, even if the figures showed that *inequality* had increased.

Not surprisingly, perhaps, this argument has been taken up enthusiastically by those who believe that financial incentives are required to encourage the better paid to increased efficiency. This is in turn expected to lead to a more prosperous economy, so that economic improvements will eventually 'trickle down' to the poor in terms of access to employment and income. For those who argue this, increased inequality may be a step towards the reduction of poverty, rather than evidence for its continued existence. The problem with the argument, however, is that the 'trickle down' effect has been notoriously difficult to identify in practice.

INCREASING POVERTY

It is possible to become completely immobilized by a detailed consideration of the difficulties associated with the statistical measures of poverty, even when it is apparent from daily experience that it is increasing. Yet, however one defines poverty, the statistics suggest that the numbers of people in poor households increased through the 1980s. Individuals in families with incomes at or below SB levels rose from 6.1 million in 1979 to 9.4 million in 1985 (see Figure 6.1) and up to 10.2 million in 1987 (see Figure 6.2). The gap between SB and average earnings also rose dramatically through this period (see Figure 6.3), as did the numbers who would have been defined as in poverty because they lived in families which earned below 50 per cent of the average (see Figure 6.4). Between 1979 and 1988 the poorest tenth of the population had an increase in real disposable income (after taking account of housing costs) of only 2 per cent, while the average rose by 33.5 per cent (House of Commons Social Security Committee 1991, quoted in Millar, 1991, p.24). In the 1980s there was a shift from direct (income) taxation to indirect taxation (Value Added Tax), which significantly increased the costs of necessities required by the poor to the extent that Barr and Coulter modestly conclude that there has been little rise in real SB levels over the decade from 1975, and 'it may even be that the living standard of families on SB has fallen' (Barr and Coulter, 1990, p. 307). In other words, it could be concluded that even

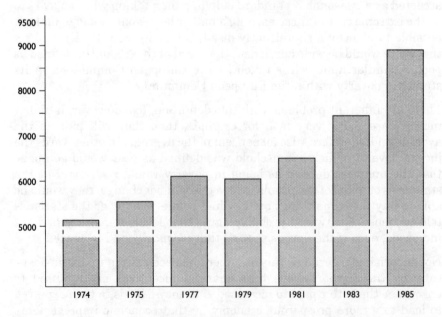

Figure 6.1   Individuals in low-income families (i.e. on or below Supplementary Benefit level) ('000)

Source: Barr and Coulter, 1990, p.313.

200

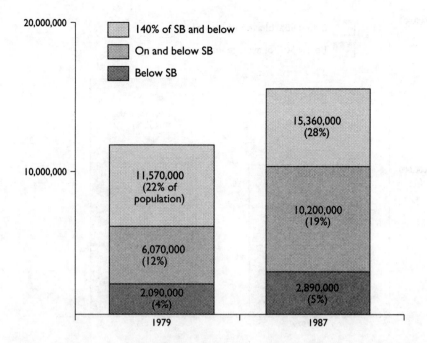

Figure 6.2   Numbers of people living in or on the margins of poverty in 1979 and 1987 (defined as 140 per cent of Supplementary Benefit and below)

Source: Oppenheim, 1990, p.22

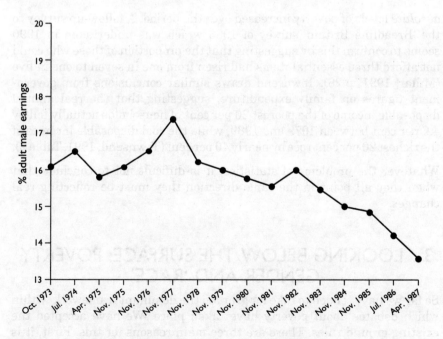

Figure 6.3   Supplementary Benefit, standard rate, as percentage of average male earnings.

Source: Barr and Coulter, 1990, p.307

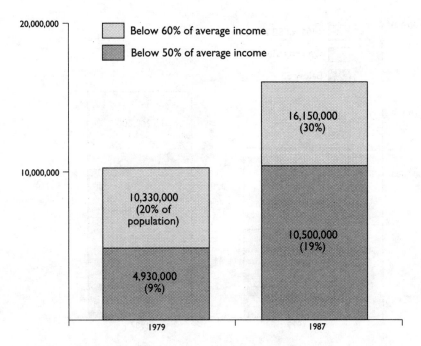

Figure 6.4   Numbers and proportions of the population living in, or on the margins of, poverty (defined as below 60 per cent of average income) in 1979 and 1987.

Source: Oppenheim, 1990, p.28

absolute levels of poverty increased over the period. A follow-up survey to the 'Breadline Britain' survey of 1983 which was undertaken in 1990 seems to confirm this by suggesting that the proportion of those who could not afford three essential items had risen from one in seven to one in five (Millar, 1991, p.26). Townsend draws similar conclusions from government figures on family expenditure, suggesting that the real annual disposable income of the poorest 20 per cent of households actually fell by 4.6 per cent between 1979 and 1989, while the real disposable incomes of the richest 20 per cent rose by nearly 40 per cent (Townsend, 1991, Table 2).

Whatever the problems of statistics, it is difficult not to conclude that when they all point in the same direction they must be reflecting real changes.

3 · LOOKING BELOW THE SURFACE: POVERTY, GENDER AND 'RACE'

So far we have tended to take for granted the dominant framework within which debates about poverty have taken place. We have accepted the existing ground rules. There are three main reasons for this. First, it is important to understand those debates precisely because they continue to dominate in policy discussions. Second, as we have seen, however inadequate, they also help to highlight the continued reality of poverty for large numbers of people in the UK. Third, it is as members of households and families that most poor people develop their survival strategies. But it is also important to acknowledge important ways in which these debates may obscure rather than illuminate some of the key features of poverty as it is lived, experienced and reproduced.

3.1   HOUSEHOLDS AND FAMILIES: THE OBSCURING OF GENDER

One of the central problems underlying the whole definitional debate on which we have focused so far is that it consistently operates with notions of households and families, and fails to acknowledge the importance of difference within families, as well as generally lumping the poor together as a more or less homogeneous category, so that both the feminization and racialization of poverty get lost in aggregate statistics. In part, of course, this can be blamed on the available statistics — after all in many cases researchers are forced to work with the statistical information produced by the government. But the problem seems to be more deep-rooted than this, both because little attempt has been made to question this aspect of the statistics and because many surveys undertaken by independent researchers (such as those associated with 'Breadline Britain') seem to take the same starting point. Poverty is defined as family poverty. The title of the leading campaigning organization in the field — the Child Poverty Action Group — seems to make the implications of this still more explicit, since families are essentially defined as collective organizations whose prime purpose is to sustain the well-being of children. So, it is the underlying assumptions which need to be questioned as much as any of the statistics. As Millar and Glendinning note, 'There are certain aspects of the way poverty is measured which are common to all poverty research, and which have the effect of obscuring gender differences in the causes, extent and experience of poverty' (Millar and Glendinning, 1987a, p.8).

How would a change of focus help? Millar and Glendinning identify five main ways in which focusing on the family unit may be actively misleading. First, because women only appear in the statistics if household income is defined as 'poor', no account is taken of the extent to which women experience significant deprivation *within* those households not defined as poor. Second, even within families which *are* defined as poor the assumption is that all members are equally poor, yet evidence suggests that women frequently make sacrifices to ensure that other family members do not suffer to the same extent. Third, the assumption that women are generally financially dependent on men is taken to imply not that they are likely to be in a weak position within households, but rather that this provides them with protection from poverty so that the low level of their own earned incomes does not matter. Fourth, no account is generally taken of work undertaken by women within the home. This may be crucial in maintaining adequate living standards yet, at present, it receives no specific financial reward. Fifth, there has been little systematic attempt to identify the different levels of support from state and other benefits, perks as well as state benefits, occupational pensions as well as state pensions, yet there is little doubt that the balance tends to work to the disadvantage of women (Millar and Glendinning, 1987a, pp.9–12). In addition it is also important to recognize that some of the assumptions underlying a focus on families may themselves be highly misleading. The increased number of single-person households, many of which comprise older women, and the increased number of lone parents, the overwhelming majority of whom are women, means that implicit assumptions about the dominance of family structures headed by male 'breadwinners' are simply untenable any longer (Coote et al., 1990; **Muncie and Sapsford, 1992**).

The possibility that the position of women within households may give them less access to resources and income than men is one which substantially undermines the traditional focus on households. Research increasingly shows that it is no longer possible to view the family as a 'black box' into which income goes to be distributed evenly among its members (Pahl, 1989). Pahl outlines a range of different ways in which families arrange their finances (from wife controlled to husband controlled with various forms of pooling in the middle), drawing the clear conclusion that 'where wives control finances a higher proportion of household income is likely to be spent on food and day-to-day living expenses than is the case where husbands control finances; additional income brought into the household by the wife is more likely to be spent on food than additional money earned by the husband' (Pahl, 1989, pp. 151–2).

The significance of differences in attitude to the domestic sphere for the analysis of poverty may not be immediately apparent, but it begins to suggest other ways in which the internal life of families affects the poverty of women within them, precisely because the needs of the family (of their children and partners) tend to be defined as their own. In poor households women frequently go without food and other resources in order to give more to their children and partners. In poor households, women have to work harder to achieve a reasonable standard — making ends meet, attempting to maintain standards of cleanliness in property which is likely to be substandard. And since this is also likely to be a losing battle, the pressures of poverty will be drastically increased. Even the fact that women tend to have greater control over household incomes when they are low than when they are higher has mixed consequences for them:

> In households where the major income comes from state benefits, women more often have responsibility for managing the money, whilst in households where the main source of income is earnings, men will more often control the finances... men retain control over income and women manage benefit: and for women poverty is a different experience, in that it draws on their skills as a manager, a 'good housekeeper', and exacts a price in terms of stress, anxiety and 'sheer hard work'.
>
> (Payne, 1991, p.35)

Frequently — contrary to the expectations one might have because of the association of lone-parent families with poverty — when relationships break up, women argue that they are in a better position, because they no longer have to cater for the expectations of men for more expensive food (such as cooked evening meals). Instead they 'report being able to buy cheaper sources of nutrition, and eat better as a result' (Payne, 1991, pp. 36–7, summarizing research by Graham, 1987b and Wilson, 1987). Coping with poverty is unpleasant in any circumstances, but it tends to be handled differently by men and women. And women are likely to have more scope to make their own decisions if they are not in two-parent households. Hilary Graham gives a graphic illustration from her research of the harsh choices which have to be made, and the different ways in which they may be made. She quotes mothers from lone- and two-parent households, discussing ways of saving money on heating. Some mothers were able to decide themselves about how to manage (and limit) expenditure on heating. It was more difficult for women in two-parent families. One lone mother explained 'I put the central heating on for one hour before the kids go to bed and one hour before they get up. I sit in a sleeping bag once they've gone to bed'. In a low-income two-parent household, matters were different: 'If we're in, I'd turn the thermostat down if we need to economize and I turn the heating off if I'm the only one in' (Graham, 1987a, p.238).

Other research evidence summarized by Payne (1991, pp.36-7) confirms that men and women tend to view the income which comes into the home rather differently. Men are more likely to retain some of their earnings for their own spending, whereas women are more likely to use their earnings for domestic purposes. This has paradoxical consequences for the analysis of poverty. Since women tend to spend more of their earnings on household needs, higher levels of women's employment suggest that fewer *households* will be in poverty. But since women retain only a small proportion of their income they may continue to be poor as individuals. One estimate suggests that if women's poverty were calculated by comparing the spending for which women were responsible to the incomes which they had (e.g. from their own employment, child benefit etc.) it would increase the numbers in poverty by around 50 per cent (Millar and Glendinning, 1989).

It is dangerous, however, to imply that the experiences of all women are the same. As we have seen, Pahl shows that different families have different arrangements for the handling and management of 'household' income, and there certainly seem to be important differences between ethnic groups within the UK. Within white families the dominant arrangements tend to leave men in control of family finances or in control of expenditure from their own incomes (which are almost always the largest source of household income). In many African Caribbean households the emphasis seems to be different. Women in these households are more likely to be in paid employment and explicitly to seek employment in order to have an independent source of income which they are able to control directly without reference to their partners (Stone, 1983). In many Asian households, which often include three generations, matters may be different again — with finances being run more explicitly as a family matter, with decision making dominated by older members, usually men. But it has also been argued strongly that older women have sometimes had an important role in this decision making, and — more recently — that increased involvement in paid employment by women has tended to increase their power within the domestic sphere (Bhachu, 1988, p.79; **Wetherell, 1992**). In one survey the threat of unemployment was explicitly seen by some young Asian women as eroding the steps they had made to greater independence although the pooling of incomes within households was also seen as a valuable source of support (Brah, 1986).

Focusing on incomes and access to incomes is useful because of the ways in which it highlights some forms of poverty. In the case of women it also directs attention to the continuing inequalities of earned income for those in paid employment, with average women's hourly earnings still being around two-thirds those of men. Women are also far more likely than men to work part-time, which sharply reinforces this difference. The hourly earnings of part-time women employees are only around 80 per cent of those of full-time women workers (Beechey and Perkins, 1987, p.150). At the end of the 1980s around 40 per cent of women in employment (48 per cent of married women) were part-time workers while the equivalent figure for men was 4 per cent (Oppenheim, 1990, p.99). But these figures, too, only raise further questions, which cannot be resolved solely in terms of earned income. One reason, for example, why women are so highly represented among pensioners in poverty is because access to full-time and higher paid employment is normally accompanied by access to pension schemes. Many women are, therefore, effectively excluded from these. Other non-monetary aspects to full-time employment include a greater likelihood of access to a range of perks, such as company cars, sick pay and other forms of paid time off. Even among women in full-time employment access to these benefits is substantially less than for men and for those in part-time employment is still lower (Economic and Social Research Council, 1986, quoted in Oppenheim, 1990, p.101, see Table 6.2).

One aspect of women's poverty can be drawn directly from the official statistics, since it is widely acknowledged that lone parent families suffer disproportionately from poverty (defined as low income) and we also know that the vast majority of such parents are women. In the middle 1980s nearly two-thirds of lone-parent families (around six hundred thousand people) were in poverty according to one calculation which sought to take account both of supplementary benefit levels and the relative position of the poor (Piachaud, 1988). Single pensioners — among whom women are also in a clear majority — constitute the other group whose members are most likely to be in poverty (see also Chapter 4 of this volume). Evidence such as this is helpful in confirming unequivocally that poverty falls

Table 6.2:   Percentage of jobs where employer provides benefits, by gender

	Male full-timers	Female full-timers	Female part-timers
Pensions*	73	68	31
Sick pay*	66	58	27
Paid time off	64	48	30
Unpaid time off	54	54	57
Company car or van	30	10	5
Free/subsidized transport	31	24	17
Goods at a discount	47	40	31
Free or subsidized meals	39	47	25
Finance/loans	21	20	12
Accommodation	14	17	5
Life assurance	39	19	5
Private health	31	22	9
Recreation facilities	40	36	24
Maternity pay	–	31	16
Child care	1	13	10

*   above basic government scheme.
Source: quoted in Oppenheim, 1990, p. 101.

unevenly on men and women. It is difficult for anyone to dismiss these differences as insignificant. But it is also clear that they understate the extent of the problem. It will come as no surprise to confirm that living to an old age is a guarantee of poverty for most of those who do it. But other life cycle stages are also associated with poverty — having children reduces income by reducing access to employment for women, whilst at the same time increasing costs. It also makes returning to the labour market at an equivalent level more difficult, thus reducing access to future pension entitlements and other aspects of welfare not delivered through the official institutions of the welfare state.

Payne argues strongly that one result of all this is that it is necessary to construct a convincing deprivation index, which takes account of more than access to resources by households and families, and their different needs at different levels of income. In addition she maintains that account has to be taken of the differences between genders and the differential impact that the absence of some facilities will have for men and women. If women spend more time at home than men, particularly when they are caring for children or other family members, for example, then it is they who will suffer most from an inability to pay the costs of heating in winter. Similarly, the absence of amenities such as washing machines and adequate cooking facilities is likely to affect women more than men, since it is women who still tend to have responsibility for the washing of clothes and cooking in most families (Payne, 1991, pp.37–40).

ACTIVITY 4

Look back at the 'necessities' you listed in answer to Activity 1. Try to assess which of these would be more important to men and which more important to women. How do you think these differences would affect the ways in which you judged whether people were in poverty or not? Do you think it would mean that more or fewer people were in poverty? Would you expect more women than men to be in poverty?

3.2   THE IMPACT OF 'RACE'

The introduction of gender makes the discussion of poverty more complex and highlights the importance of power relations within families. It raises new questions. But it is also important to note that gender divisions themselves need to be placed in other contexts. All men and all women are not the same, nor is their experience of life the same in all 'races' and classes. Poverty is the product of a dynamic interaction of various factors among which 'race' seems to play a disproportionate part, although it is difficult to explore the implications of this without the help of easily available government statistics. Research into the ways in which poverty affects Britain's African Caribbean and Asian communities has been limited, although there have been several detailed analyses of their experience in particular places.

It is, however, widely agreed that they have been affected more than other groups. The evidence for this is frequently constructed from a range of sources which come together to confirm a particular incidence of poverty. There is, for example, evidence that both African Caribbean and Asian men earn substantially less than their white equivalents (a gap of around 20 per cent according to one survey quoted by Gordon, 1991) and that both men and women are more likely to face unemployment even in times of relative prosperity with young people being affected particularly badly (see Table 6.3). In terms of employment both men and women are more likely to be in semi-skilled and unskilled manual employment than their white counterparts, although there are also substantial variations between different sections of the black population (Sarre, 1989, pp.145–7). This means that they were more affected by the economic changes of the 1980s, which have led to a significant decline in employment in these sectors. Not only have black people traditionally filled the lower paid posts within Britain's welfare state (for example, in ancillary jobs within the National Health Service), but as Britain's employment structure has moved towards a two-tier system of more secure core employment and part-time casual work (particularly in contract services) it is frequently African Caribbean and Asian women who have taken up jobs in the more peripheral, low-paid and insecure sectors (Williams, 1989, pp.179–90).

African Caribbean families are also substantially more likely to be headed by lone parents — 43.4 per cent among such families compared

Table 6.3:   Unemployment rates by sex, age and ethnic origin; average: Spring 1987 to Spring 1989, Great Britain (%)

	Men and Women aged 16 and over	Men All aged 16 and over	16 to 24	Women All aged 16 and over	16 to 24
White	9	9	13	8	11
Minority Ethnic Groups:					
All	14	15	22	13	19
West Indian/Guyanese	16	18	27	14	*
Indian	11	10	*	13	*
Pakistani/Bangladeshi	25	25	*	*	*
All other origins	11	11	*	11	*

*   Sample too small.

Source: *Employment Gazette*, Department of Employment, February 1991, Table 7.

with 11.8 per cent of white families (Hadjipateras and Slipman, 1988, quoted in Oppenheim, 1990, p.86). As we have seen lone-parent families are also substantially more likely to have low incomes. The concentration of black people in 'poor' or inner city areas is another aspect of poverty — or deprivation — which needs to be taken into account. They have had to suffer disproportionately from living in poorer housing in the large inner city council estates, from degraded urban environments created by the decline of local industries and from all the consequences of increased social polarization, including relations with the police which have tended to leave many young black people feeling harassed (see also Chapter 5).

The management of the welfare state has created additional problems for the black poor, further compounding the problems they face, not least because it has, effectively, continued to define them as 'immigrants' who are only reluctantly to be given any entitlements to welfare citizenship. The impact of immigration and nationality policies stretches far beyond the relatively small numbers of people at whom they are nominally directed. Gordon (1991) succinctly lists some of these points:

• settled immigrants can only be joined by their families if they can maintain and accommodate them (in other words the new arrivals are explicitly forbidden to have 'recourse to public funds');

• for those who seek naturalization the costs have increased significantly to the extent that it is almost prohibitive for poor families (a proposal to allow a single fee for a family application was rejected by the government in the early 1980s);

• welfare benefits have increasingly been restricted to those with the 'right' immigration status. This, of course, not only affects those without it, but also opens others to increased questioning, making it less likely for people to apply, and more likely for them to be refused through misunderstanding.

Gordon's arguments are substantially supported by the experiences summarized by the National Association of Citizens' Advice Bureaux (NACAB), following a survey of its members. They report that (despite official guidelines to the contrary) it continues to be common practice for requests for passports to be made before benefit applications are considered. Because little emphasis is placed on appropriate training and staff have difficulties with Asian names, it is not uncommon for case files to be misfiled. Unless claimants have English as a first language, there are often difficulties, because offices rarely have interpreters, and forms are always in English (even if some leaflets are now available in other languages). In some cases rules are applied which make the granting of benefit difficult to achieve. One case quoted in the NACAB report is that of a Bangladeshi woman who was defined as not available for work because she did not speak English. In another case officers were doubtful about paying benefit to a wife because her husband was visiting Pakistan — the question posed was 'How did he raise the money?'. Little allowance was made for the fact that contributions for such a trip would come from the wider family and community. Even the attitudes of Social Security Appeals Tribunals are criticized because of the extent to which stereotypes inform their decisions. The report suggests both that black claimants are effectively discouraged from receiving their full benefit entitlement and that many are even deterred from claiming social security benefits at all (NACAB, 1991).

Gordon points to research which suggests that black people have increasingly become 'second class claimants' (Gordon, 1991, pp.80–2) People claiming non-contributory benefits (such as child benefit and disability allowances) have to have been resident in the UK for specified periods (ranging upwards from six months in the case of child benefit). Since the age profile tends to be younger than that of the white population, they have also been hit particularly hard by the decision to pay lower rates of benefit to those under twenty-five. In the longer term their concentration in lower-paid jobs and the higher incidence of unemployment which they experience will also mean that they are unlikely to receive higher rates of pension based on paying greater contributions. So they will lose out at all stages of the life cycle. Although it is important to note the differences between ethnic groups in British society, the ways in which the institutions of the welfare state operate serve to reduce those differences, helping to create a shared experience of poverty for the vulnerable in Britain's black population.

4 LOOKING FOR EXPLANATIONS

It will be clear by now that defining poverty is not easy. Yet it should also be clear that there is widespread agreement about its persistence at the end of the twentieth century. A key issue for social policy, therefore, is to explain this persistence. As we shall discover answering this apparently simple question is by no means easy. It is possible to cluster explanations into three main groups, and this section will consider them in turn. The first starts by assuming that the operation of any market-based (capitalist) system is likely to lead to inequalities of income and wealth, resulting in poverty for those at the bottom. The second blames increasing poverty not on capitalism but on the welfare state, and calls for fundamental changes in its operation. The third moves beyond simple notions of capitalism to suggest that the complex relations between state, market and gender, have worked together to produce poverty and to give it a clearly gendered identity.

4.1   THE NECESSITY OF POVERTY

Perhaps the simplest analysis is the one which concludes that poverty is an unfortunate necessity in a capitalist economy. Marxists have traditionally suggested that it is an inevitable consequence of the capitalist organization of industry. In their evidence to the Royal Commission on the Poor Law at the beginning of the century, for example, representatives of the (Marxist) Social Democratic Federation argued forcefully that:

> ... poverty will be the portion of large numbers of the working class whilst the land and wealth of the country are privately owned and industry is carried on for profit. We assert that only when the land is decreed the common property of the nation, when the wealth created by the people shall belong to the people, and when industry is organized and controlled by the people in their collective capacity, will poverty be banished and the Poor Law or its equivalent be unnecessary.
>
> (Quoted in Clarke et al., 1987, p.78)

Under capitalism, according to this argument, only labour which produces profit for the employers can expect to receive payment and those who are not employed will necessarily suffer poverty. The pressure is always on to keep the costs of labour down. Although more sophisticated arguments have been put forward to take account of the rise of the welfare state, Marxists have tended to argue that there are constant pressures to keep welfare payments down and that one of the reasons for changes introduced in the 1970s and 1980s has been capitalism's inability to meet even the limited costs of the welfare state constructed after 1945.

Marxists would stress the importance of rising unemployment throughout the 1980s as one of the main factors in increasing poverty in the UK, explaining its rise as a consequence of the extensive process of economic restructuring (and deindustrialization) which began in the late 1960s and accelerated in the early 1980s. According to this argument, the particular form taken by poverty in the 1980s was influenced as much by government economic as by its social policies. The process of economic restructuring also encouraged a move away from core full-time employment in manufacturing industry to one of increased 'flexibility' with more casual and part-time employment in service industries (the restructuring of the

UK's economy since the late 1960s is discussed more fully in Allen and Massey, 1989). In practice, it is argued, this restructuring is creating a dual labour market with well-paid jobs at the core, and low-paid jobs in the casualized periphery. The poor will tend to be those dependent on employment in peripheral sectors or not employed at all.

Others — often labelled Fabians, social reformers or reluctant collectivists — have taken a rather different position, accepting — like Marxists — the likelihood of poverty under capitalism, but arguing that the state should intervene to counter the harm caused by the operation of the market. Their argument is that capitalism may be a good way of organizing the production of goods and services, but it is less effective as a system of achieving a fair distribution of what is produced. In a sense this was the argument which underpinned the post-war welfare state, although there were arguments about how far to go and whether it would ever be possible fully to eradicate poverty. The line between allowing capitalism to do what it did best and to intervene where it was least effective proved a difficult one to draw in practice.

In the 1980s it became more acceptable to draw it rather more loosely, stressing the necessity of inequality, and arguing that it helps to provide incentives to individuals as long as it is an expression of the rewards (and by implication punishments) provided through the operation of the market. Thus it is frequently argued that profits are a reward for entrepreneurial risk-taking, reflecting the extent to which investors produce what consumers demand. In orthodox economic models, salaries and wages are largely determined by the scarcity and value of the skills offered by employees. The key underlying principle according to Friedman is 'the incentive of reward' (Friedman, 1962, p. 166).

In principle, following this model, there should be a tendency towards equalization because as one area of investment or employment receives greater rewards, so more investors or workers will move into it. And Friedman argues that capitalism does produce a more equal society than any other available economic system (Friedman, 1962, pp.169-72). As we have seen, however (in Section 2), there is little evidence that it has produced increasing equalization over the last few decades. On the contrary the evidence points in the other direction. So, in practice it is frequently acknowledged that inequality is not likely to disappear, and it may also be acknowledged that those at the bottom of the income distribution pyramid are likely to suffer unduly from poverty. There are particular concerns for those who are excluded from the labour market and it is towards them that any welfare support is likely to be directed.

This understanding of the problem seems to have been the one which underlined policy development in the 1980s. Quoting a series of government White Papers, Barr and Coulter summarize the aims of the UK's social security system in that decade as being to 'meet genuine need', but only in the context of ensuring that the provision of cash benefits did not stop jobs being created or discourage the unemployed from seeking employment:

Two policies are implied by these objectives. First, the replacement rate (i.e. the level of benefit paid to the unemployed) should be reduced, thus giving those out of work a greater incentive to rejoin the labour force. Second, more benefits should be means-tested, the resulting 'targeting' of benefits reducing the cost of the benefit system, thus reducing taxation and improving incentives for those in work.

(Barr and Coulter, 1990, p.277)

In addition to limiting increases in levels of income support, therefore, the 1980s also saw a shift towards the use of repayable loans through the Social Fund and towards means-tested benefits for low-income families through Family Credit.

The social policy assumption here is that it is necessary to provide some sort of basic 'safety net', but not one which stands in the way of the efficient operation of the economy, whose expansion and growth is assumed to provide a growth in real income for the majority. Too much state interference, it is believed, may reduce the possibility of such growth — and may thus also reduce both the opportunities for the poor and their own real incomes.

4.2 THE PRODUCTION OF AN UNDERCLASS?

These arguments have been taken further by those who blame the welfare state itself for causing poverty, and in particular by those who point to the growth of what they call an 'underclass'. This term has been used widely in the social policy literature to highlight the extent to which it is possible to identify a class of 'new' poor separated from other classes in society because of the reliance of its members on casual employment and state benefits (see, e.g. Field, 1989) or to point to the ways in which some sections of society are effectively excluded from access to the full benefits of social citizenship by more powerful groups (see e.g. Rex and Tomlinson, 1979). Here, however, we are concerned with a rather different use of the term, particularly associated with the writings of the US author Charles Murray, according to which the underclass is effectively defined in terms of the behaviour of its members.

Murray distinguishes between two kinds of poor people — drawing on Victorian distinctions between the 'deserving' and 'undeserving' poor or between the 'honest' and 'dishonest' poor. The former may have to live on low incomes, but still seek better employment and have fallen (temporarily or for 'unavoidable' reasons) into poverty; whilst the latter have little interest in finding employment and effectively *choose* to live in poverty. It is, of course, the undeserving poor who constitute the underclass for Murray. He approvingly quotes articles published by Mayhew in the middle of the nineteenth century as a guide to the identification of an underclass at the end of the twentieth. For Mayhew a member of the 'dishonest poor' was:

Supplementary Benefits Office, Bloomsbury, 1986–7

Supplementary Benefits Office 1987

... distinguished from the civilized man by his repugnance to regular
and continuous labour — by his want of providence in laying up a
store for the future — by his inability to perceive consequences ever
so slightly removed from immediate apprehensions — by his passion
for stupefying herbs and roots and, when possible, for intoxicating
fermented liquors.

(Mayhew, 1850, quoted in Murray, 1990c, p.2)

Murray's central argument, both in his writing on the UK and the USA — where he has written more extensively on social policy — is that the failure of these welfare states to distinguish between the 'deserving' and the 'undeserving' has itself been one of the main reasons for the growth of the latter as an identifiable underclass. This failure — according to Murray — has succeeded in undermining the position of the 'deserving' poor, by failing to reward them for their efforts and effectively suggesting that they are not worthwhile. Conversely, of course, this reinforces the position of the 'undeserving' by appearing to reward them for their behaviour, through continuing to provide them with benefits. He argues that even if it is the case that the poor are poor because of the way the system operates (i.e. for structural reasons) it is inappropriate to reinforce this belief, because it makes it less likely that they will seek to get out of their poverty. They will accept that it is not 'their fault' and, therefore, simply expect to be compensated by others for the failures of the system 'People must be held responsible for their actions. Whether they *are* responsible or not in some ultimate philosophical or biochemical sense cannot be the issue if society is to function' (Murray, 1984, p.146).

Murray places great stress on the importance of the family and its breakdown as a key to the growth of the 'emerging British underclass'. His strongest argument seems to relate to illegitimacy — children born outside of marriage. This is taken to be the clearest symptom of the growth of an underclass, because it is 'the purest form of being without two parents' (Murray, 1990c, p.5) and, according to Murray, it is one of the strongest predictors of long-term welfare dependency. Murray argues that the impact of illegitimacy is clear, because it means that boys have no positive male role models to follow: 'You can send in social workers and school teachers and clergy to tell a young male that when he grows up he should be a good father to his children, but he doesn't know what that means unless he's seen it' (Murray, 1990c, p.11). This leads him into the wider argument that the problem spreads through to the surrounding community: gradually whole neighbourhoods are infected, which means that all families and so all children are affected. Murray explains the rise in 'illegitimacy' by arguing that lone parenthood is no longer 'punished' as severely as in the past: since the 1960s it has no longer faced the same social stigma; the benefit system means that it is now possible (if not attractive) to survive financially as a lone parent; it is also possible to get housing (even if it is not the most attractive housing). In other words it is possible for a woman to survive independently with a child or children.

If the notion of an underclass makes a strong popular appeal, building on wider fears of social disorganization, it also builds on the perceived threat to the structures of white America and the UK from their black populations. This is perhaps clearest in Murray's writing on the USA which tends to use statistics for black people as a surrogate for the underclass, despite acknowledging that there are also many white people in that class as he defines it. As Clarke notes, this approach effectively manages to '"ghettoize" poverty and its attendant demoralization within black America' (Clarke, 1991, p.139). It succeeds both in emphasizing the separateness of the underclass from white America and constructing it as a threat to white America. In the UK context the matter is slightly more complicated since, as Murray acknowledges, Britain's black population is too small to justify the fears about a growing underclass which he seeks to develop. Nevertheless the same connections are made in ways which reinforce the definition of black people — particularly African Caribbeans — as the cause as well as victims of poverty. In the case of the UK, however, white working class youths outside the south east of England are expected to play a similar role. The inner cities and declining industrial regions are the homes of the underclass: so, in the prosperous south east it is the 'ghettos' of inner London which represent the problem; outside the south east it is the old white working class ghettos of industrial capitalism without industry which produce the problem. In both cases, of course, the underclass represents a continuing threat to the well-organized lives of those who live outside the inner cities in the south east or its outposts in the other regions and component nations of the UK.

It is easy to see how Murray's analysis succeeds in making links with a wider set of popular concerns while also helping to shape and reinterpret them, giving respectability to arguments which have not been accepted as a central part of welfare policy debate over the past thirty years or so. Indeed Murray himself explicitly recalls the popular notion of the 'ne'er-do-well' as the starting point of his analysis (Murray, 1990c, pp.1-2) and he seeks support for his arguments in the 'popular wisdom' which, he says:

> ... is characterized by hostility towards welfare (it makes people lazy), toward lenient judges (they encourage crime), and toward socially conscious schools (too busy busing kids to teach them how to read). The popular wisdom disapproves of favouritism towards blacks and of too many written in rights for minorities of all sorts. It says that the government is meddling far too much in things that are none of its business.
>
> (Murray, 1984, p.146)

Murray himself denies 'blaming' members of the underclass for the choices they make, suggesting instead that they do so because of the context set by the welfare state. But it is difficult to read his description of the 'undeserving' poor without feeling that they must shoulder most of the blame: the welfare state may have encouraged inappropriate action, but only because there are some people open to such encouragement.

The causal relationships on the basis of which Murray develops his policy recommendations seem to be sustained on the basis of repeated statement rather than the provision of evidence. At best Murray shows that there is a relationship between illegitimacy, crime, unemployment and poverty — but this is not a conclusion which would be challenged by anybody. It is precisely the nature of the causal relationship which would be questioned. It could equally plausibly (indeed more plausibly) be argued for the indicators Murray uses that the relationship is precisely the reverse of the one he identifies: a rise in illegitimacy rates, crime rates and negative attitudes to unemployment among the young might be perfectly reasonable responses to an increased threat of poverty, particularly if it is a result either of structural inequalities arising from gender relations within families, or the restructuring of the economy. It is unclear why social disorganization should be seen as the cause rather than a consequence of poverty. Murray's account is also incapable of acknowledging the significance of the points made by feminists who stress the importance of inequalities within families or the conclusions which suggest that for some women being a lone parent makes it easier to marshal limited resources, not because benefits are high, but because they no longer have to adjust their spending to the demands of male partners (and husbands). Such arguments make it difficult to explain illegitimacy or lone parenthood solely as symptoms of disorganization.

ACTIVITY 5

What sort of policy conclusions would you expect to see drawn from Murray's argument?

Murray's own proposals for policy change are sufficiently 'utopian' to find little support among policy makers. He wants to reconstruct communities like those which he claims to have experienced as a child in the US midwest, by increasing what he calls 'authentic self-government' at the neighbourhood or community level (Murray, 1990b, p.82). Such communities, he suggests, would be able to change the moral framework because their residents would be given responsibility, instead of being dependent on well-meaning welfare professionals and subject to mobilization by ambitious political demagogues. But certainly his broader arguments about welfare dependency were in tune with those of some government ministers in the late 1980s. In one speech to the Institute of Directors, John Moore (then Secretary of State for Social Security) argued that: 'we have sent confusing messages that have undoubtedly contributed to the creation of a dependency culture. In a dependency culture people act in bizarre ways, because they are responding to perverse incentives' (quoted in Deacon, 1991, p.16)

But the attempts in the UK to implement policies drawing on Murray's ideas have produced results which are unconvincing to say the least. One feature of social security changes through the 1980s, accelerating towards the end of the decade, has been to reduce payments to the unemployed. Despite this, unemployment rose inexorably through the decade (remaining at historically high levels even at the height of the 'boom' in

1989). Instead of encouraging more people to stay at home with their parents as was intended, this has effectively resulted in increased numbers of homeless young people (see Chapter 7). Similarly, pressures to encourage families to take greater responsibility for older people have instead resulted in the growth of private sector residential care which is inadequately funded by the state (or families), thus relegating many old people to private rather than public sector squalor (see Chapter 4). At the time of writing, it is unclear how successful the attempt (under the Child Support Act) to make biological fathers responsible for the costs of bringing up their children is likely to be, although doubts have already been expressed.

4.3   THE POSITION OF WOMEN

In Section 3 we looked at the need to move away from discussions which focused on 'the poor' as an undifferentiated 'class'. In particular we emphasized the need to move away from undifferentiated notions of 'poor' households or families. The implications of such a move may also be significant for the explanations we develop for poverty and the policy conclusions we draw from them. Here the key structuring point is the dominant assumption that women are dependent on men within families or households. As we have seen, questioning this has implications which go far beyond what is usually understood as the domestic sphere. The notion of women's dependency on men 'both causes and perpetuates the poverty experienced by women' (Millar and Glendinning, 1987b, p.268). The currently dominant sexual division of labour within the family also has implications outside the home, particularly in the world of paid employment where it helps to confirm a role for women in more low-paid jobs and in part-time employment with fewer rights and fewer 'perks'. The division within the welfare state between social security and social assistance tends to reinforce this position, since social insurance (for those who have been in employment) is provided as a right, while social assistance (for those not in employment) depends on means-tested benefits. And, of course, as we have seen, after retirement occupational pensions are only available to those with continuous employment records.

Not only does the model of dependence assumed within the structure of the UK's welfare state ensure the continued and consistent marginalization of women and ensure that they continue to experience poverty in its sharpest form, but it also bears little relationship to reality. Women's incomes are often crucial to the survival of households, not secondary, and — of course — this is particularly the case with the growing numbers of lone-parent families most of which are headed by women. Payne sharply criticizes the 'model of women as economic dependants, which is not only based on a heterosexual vision of family life, but one which is ethnocentric and takes no account of the different lives women of different races, abilities and sexuality lead' (Payne, 1991, p.83).

The point is, of course, as feminists would argue strongly, that this combination of events is not just accidental — to be changed by well-meaning equal opportunities or equal pay legislation (however welcome that may be as a starting point). It is deeply rooted within the structures of our society. Some would accept that is part of capitalism, but a particular form of capitalism — what Williams (1989) has called a 'patriarchally and racially structured capitalism'. It is argued both that the welfare state has been an essential element in the stability and expansion of post-war capitalism, and also that women — and black women in particular — have played a major role in the maintenance of the welfare state since 1945 as the main providers of low-paid and casual labour. More recently they have been central to the wider flexibilization and casualization of the British economy, with a dramatic expansion of part-time employment through the 1980s in all sections of the economy. The role of the home-based dependant has helped to reinforce the position of women as part-time workers. And dependence has also been reinforced by the operation of the welfare system itself.

This is, perhaps, most apparent in the ways in which the benefit system deals with the lone-parent families. The dependence of lone parents is reinforced by the ways in which income support is provided through means-tested benefits and — increasingly — the requirement that absent parents (usually fathers) contribute to the maintenance of their children (with state benefit being reduced accordingly) (see **Land, 1992**). In effect this guarantees continued poverty for most lone parents both because they rely on basic levels of income support and because access to paid employment is restricted. Any financial gains (e.g. from part-time employment) are clawed back in benefit reductions and there is little access to publicly funded child care which might make it easier to find better paid employment.

In this context it is worth asking whether there are different methods of organizing welfare systems in ways which mean that lone parents are not automatically consigned to poverty. To help with this, it is worth briefly considering two currently existing alternatives to the UK model, which have rather different ideological starting points. The first is the Swedish model, which is based on the expectation that men and women are in paid employment. The state pays compensation if they are not. There is extensive child care provision, as well as legislation providing for parental leave, when children are born, and leave when children are sick. As a result most women (including most lone parents) are in paid employment, although lone parents continue to face a range of additional pressures, and a dual labour market has developed with men tending to be in the better paid and more prestigious jobs, and much less likely to take up the rights to paternal leave (see **Ginsburg, 1992**). Whatever the difficulties, however, few would claim that Swedish lone parents were automatically poor.

In France, emphasis is placed on family policy — rather than a formal recognition of the equality of individuals in the labour market as in the Swedish case. Baker suggests that:

French one-parent families appear to be better off than Britain's as an indirect and probably unintended result of policies aimed at helping women, children and families generally. The main driving force behind those policies appears to be the wish to increase the birth rate, by reducing the difficulties working mothers have in rearing children.

(Baker, 1991, p.122)

Some French lone parents may be worse off than they would be in the UK because the welfare system does not provide universal income support in the same way, but most are substantially better off. At the start of the 1980s the average income of lone-parent households in France was between 68 per cent and 89 per cent of the national average — with the average income for single (i.e. unmarried) mothers (the biggest group) being 89 per cent. If anything it seems likely that matters have improved since then for many lone parents (Baker, 1991, pp.115–16). The contrast with Britain where half of all lone-parent families have incomes of less than 60 per cent of a (lower) national average could hardly be more marked. The benefits available to lone mothers are higher in France than in the UK, with more generous allowances for children, but the main reason for incomes being higher seems again to lie in access to the labour market. In France nearly 80 per cent of lone parents are in paid employment, most in full-time employment, with the help of high levels of nursery and daycare provision for children. Stress is placed on keeping jobs open for mothers for two years and child benefit for young children is around three times that paid in the UK for the first nine months of the baby's life. This benefit may be continued for up to three years for low-income families, thus effectively providing a bridge until it is possible for women to re-enter paid employment (Baker, 1991, pp.119–20).

Of course, none of this is to deny that lone parents face significant problems both in Sweden and in France. The most obvious of these is the need effectively to work a 'double shift' with little support at home. But that is also a problem in many two-parent families in which both parents work, and women are expected to care for their spouses as well as their children. In France — as in Sweden — there is a concentration of women's employment in routine manual and routine non-manual activities, so their access to better-paid jobs is limited. This effectively means that the incomes of lone parents are likely to be lower than the average, but — as Baker points out — at least these are 'normal' jobs rather than the more 'marginal, semi-casualized' forms of employment which seem to be the rule for lone parents in the UK.

ACTIVITY 6

What policy conclusions would you expect to follow from feminist arguments further informed by the experiences of Sweden and France?

The main emphasis is likely to be on identifying ways of removing the dependence implicit within the UK's welfare system, in particular stressing the need to move towards independent benefits for women, and towards a recognition of the cost and value of work undertaken in the domestic sphere. Minimally, there would be support for child benefit to be extended and paid at a higher rate: this would be a step towards paying women for caring, rather than using this role to define them as dependants. More basically, however, it would be important to question the way in which the caring role is in any case always assumed to be that of women, so that the existing domestic division of labour would have to be challenged. One way of doing this might be to open up wider areas of the labour market to women's employment, to ensure that part-time employment does not also mean low pay, and to provide adequate levels and accessible forms of child care. But simply offering this will not necessarily solve all the problems as long as women continue to be given the responsibility for bringing up children or looking after elderly parents.

5   CONCLUSION: DRAWING UP A BALANCE SHEET

There is a danger that focusing on debates about definitions, as we did at the beginning, and on debates between different positions as we did later on, will make it easy to forget the problems which provide the starting point for those debates. There is always a danger that academics feel that a matter is resolved once they have won an argument on their own terms (and often only to their own satisfaction). But, of course, poverty remains, however we define it and whether or not we label some of the poor 'undeserving' or place them in an underclass.

And yet, the debates are important both because they make it possible to move beyond shocked expressions of concern, and because they help to clarify some of the major issues which need to be considered in developing programmes intended to deal with or overcome the problem of poverty. Let me try (in very broad terms) to draw out some of the key points from the arguments which have gone before:

- poverty cannot simply be defined in terms of income or lack of income: it is better viewed as a lack of access to resources without which the poor are effectively excluded from normal society — some would say they are excluded from citizenship;

- whatever form of definition is used, poverty increased substantially through the 1980s;

- poverty is concentrated in particular places and among particular groups: this makes it easier for those in positions of political and economic power to ignore or underplay its significance;

- poverty implies multiple deprivation: that is once you are poor in terms of income, you are also likely to suffer a range of other deprivations;

- it is misleading simply to see the poor as one class: different groups are affected differently, and are in poverty for different reasons (divisions on lines of gender and 'race' are particularly important);
- it is important to understand the significance of differences between members of families and households: both because household poverty affects women differently from men, and because women may be poor even when households are not so defined;
- state policies may affect the incidence of poverty in unpredicted (and sometimes even unpredictable ways): some commentators (from different parts of the political spectrum) would argue that the UK's benefits policies have themselves encouraged the growth of poverty.

It is probably not appropriate to draw out any explicit policy proposals from a survey of the kind undertaken in this chapter. It is, however, perhaps worth concluding by noting that whatever policies are developed, they need to take into account not only the significance of economic changes which have altered the meaning of employment as well as full employment, and the importance of demographic shifts which have already brought significant increases in the population of old people and are likely to continue, but also the implications of changes in attitudes and behaviour which have undermined traditional models of family life. It is increasingly necessary to direct policy not just at, but also within families, to take account of internal inequalities. Finally, it is necessary to take account of the ways that these changes have affected different groups differently: the poor are not an undifferentiated whole — not only do they often have to cope as individuals, but their ability to do so will vary significantly according to where they live and according to the ways in which they are defined by state and society.

REFERENCES

Allen, J. and Massey, D (eds.) (1989) *The Economy in Question,* London, Sage.

Baker, J. (1991) 'Family policy as an anti-poverty measure' in Hardy, M. and Crow, G. (eds.) *Lone Parenthood. Coping with Constraints and Making Opportunities,* London, Harvester Wheatsheaf.

Barr, N. and Coulter, F. (1990) 'Social security: solution or problem?' in Hills, J. (ed) *The State of Welfare. The Welfare State in Britain Since 1974,* Oxford, Clarendon Press.

Becker, S. (ed) (1991) *Windows of Opportunity: Public Policy and the Poor,* London, Child Poverty Action Group.

Beechey, V. and Perkins, R. (1987) *A Matter of Hours. Women, Part-time Work and the Labour Market,* Cambridge, Polity.

Beveridge, W. (1942) *Social Insurance and Allied Services,* Cmnd. 6404, London, HMSO.

Bhachu, P. (1988) 'April Marzi Kardhi: home and work: Sikh Women in Britain' in Westwood, S. and Bhachu, P. (eds.) *Enterprising Women: Ethnicity, Economy and Gender Relations,* London, Routledge & Kegan Paul.

Brah, A. (1986) 'Unemployment and racism: Asian youth on the dole' in Allen, S., Waton, A., Purcell, K. and Wood, S. (eds.) *The Experience of Unemployment,* London, Macmillan.

Clarke, J. (1991) *New Times and Old Enemies. Essays on Cultural Studies and America,* London, Harper Collins.

Clarke, J., Cochrane, A. and Smart, C. (1987) *Ideologies of Welfare. From Dreams to Disillusion,* London, Hutchinson.

Cochrane, A. and Muncie, J. (eds.) (1992) *Politics, Policy and the Law,* Book 1 of D311 *Family Life and Social Policy,* Milton Keynes, The Open University.

Coote, A., Harman, H. and Hewitt, P. (1990) *The Family Way. A New Approach to Policy-making*, Social Policy Paper No. 1, London, Institute for Public Policy Research.

Deacon, A. (1991) 'The retreat from state Welfare' in Becker, S. (ed.).

Economic and Social Research Council (1986) *Unequal Jobs, Unequal Pay,* 'The Changing Social and Economic Life Initiative', Working Paper 6, ESRC.

Field, F. (1989) *Losing Out. The Emergence of Britain's Underclass,* Oxford, Blackwell.

Friedman, M. (1962) *Capitalism and Freedom,* Chicago, University of Chicago Press.

Ginsburg, N. (1993) 'The social-democratic case: Sweden' in Cochrane, A. and Clarke, J. (eds.) *Comparing Welfare States: the UK in International Context,* London, Sage.

Glendinning, C. and Millar, J. (eds.) (1987) *Women and Poverty in Britain,* Brighton, Wheatsheaf.

Gordon, P. (1991) 'Forms of exclusion: citizenship, race and poverty' in Becker, S. (ed.).

Graham, H. (1987a) 'Women's poverty and caring' in Glendinning and Millar (eds.).

Graham, H. (1987b) 'Being poor, perceptions and coping strategies of lone mothers', in Brannen, J. and Wilson, G. (eds.) *Give and Take in Families: Studies in Resource Distribution,* London, Allen and Unwin.

Hadjipateras, A. and Slipman, S. (1988) *Helping One Parent Families to Work,* London, National Council for One Parent Families.

Land, H. (1992) 'The family and law' in Cochrane, A. and Muncie, J. (eds.).

Mack, J. and Lansley, S. (1985) *Poor Britain,* London, Allen and Unwin.

Millar, J. (1991) 'Bearing the cost', in Becker, S. (ed.).

Millar, J. and Glendinning, C. (1987a) 'Invisible women, invisible poverty' in Glendinning and Millar (eds.).

Millar, J. and Glendinning, C. (1987b) 'Towards the femininization of poverty' in Glendinning and Millar (eds.).

Millar, J. and Glendinning, C. (1989) 'Gender and poverty', *Journal of Social Policy*, 18, p.3.

Muncie, J. and Sapsford, R., (1992) 'Issues in the study of the family', in Cochrane, A. and Muncie, J. (eds.).

Murray, C. (1984) *Losing Ground. American Social Policy 1950–1980*, New York, Basic Books.

Murray, C. (1990a) *The Emerging British Underclass*, London, The IEA Health and Welfare Unit.

Murray, C. (1990b) 'Rejoinder' in Murray, C. (ed.) (1990a).

Murray, C. (1990c) 'Underclass' in Murray, C. (ed.) (1990a) (article first published in *The Sunday Times Magazine*, 26 November 1989).

National Association of Citizens' Advice Bureaux (1991) *Barriers to Benefit: Black Claimants and Social Security*, London, NACAB.

Oppenheim, C. (1990) *Poverty: The Facts*, London, Child Poverty Action Group.

Pahl, J. (1989) *Money and Marriage*, London, Macmillan.

Payne, S. (1991) *Women, Health and Poverty. An Introduction*, Hemel Hempstead, Harvester Wheatsheaf.

Piachaud, D. (1988) 'Poverty in Britain', *Journal of Social Policy*, 17, 3, pp.335–49.

Rex, J. and Tomlinson, S. (1979) *Colonial Immigrants in a British City*, London, Routledge and Kegan Paul.

Rowntree, S., (1922) *Poverty: a Study of Town Life*, London, Thomas Nelson.

Rowntree, S., (1941) *Poverty and Progress: a Second Social Survey of York*, London, Longman.

Sarre, P., (1989) 'Race and the class structure' in Hamnett, C., McDowell, L., and Sarre, P., (eds) *The Changing Social Structure*, London, Sage.

Stone, K. (1983) 'Motherhood and waged work: West Indian, Asian and white mothers compared' in Phizacklea, A. (ed.) *One Way Ticket: Migration and Female Labour*, London, Routledge and Kegan Paul.

Taylor-Gooby, P. (1990) 'Social welfare: the unkindest cuts' in Jowell, R. et al. (eds.) *British Social Attitudes. The Seventh Report*, Social and Community Planning Research, Aldershot, Gower.

Townsend, P. (1979) *Poverty in the UK*, Harmondsworth, Penguin.

Townsend, P. (1991) *The Poor are Poorer: A Statistical Report on Changes in the Living Standards of Rich and Poor in the United Kingdom 1979–1989*, Bristol, Department of Social Policy and Social Planning, University of Bristol.

Townsend, P., Corrigan, P. and Kowarzik, U. (1987) *Poverty and the London Labour Market*, London, Low Pay Unit.

Wetherell, M. (1992) 'The social construction of family life' in Wetherell, M. et al. (eds.) *Interaction and Identities*, Book 2 of D311 *Family Life and Social Policy*, Milton Keynes, The Open University.

Williams, F., (1989) *Social Policy: a Critical Introduction*, Cambridge, Polity.

Wilson, G. (1987) *Money in the Family*, Aldershot, Avebury.

CHAPTER 7
HOMELESSNESS

RICHARD SKELLINGTON

I   INTRODUCTION

In 1966, when *Cathy Come Home* was first transmitted on British television a minimum of 2,558 homeless households lived in temporary accommodation in England. By March 1992, this figure had reached a record of 61,920, itself an increase of 25 per cent over the previous year. At the beginning of the 1990s homelessness affected over half a million people in Britain (Department of the Environment, 1991a; Shelter 1991; *Social Trends 22*, 1992). In December 1991, Sheila McKechnie, in a report published to mark Shelter's twenty-fifth anniversary, argued that levels of homelessness were at an all time high and would more than *double* in the next ten years unless tens of thousands of affordable homes were built. She predicted that more than a million families would become homeless in Britain by 1996 (Shelter, 1991).

Since *Cathy Come Home* was first broadcast and Shelter formed, the percentage of government expenditure on housing has fallen from 5.3 to 2.6 per cent (Shelter, 1991). In December 1991 John Greve, the social scientist who helped launch Shelter through his report on housing and homelessness in 1965, announced that homelessness was a far greater

Queue for lunch, Crisis at Christmas — Christmas Day

227

social problem than it had been in 1966 (*The Guardian,* 4 December 1991). A BBC 'Panorama' programme transmitted at Christmas 1991, poignantly entitled *Has Cathy Come Back?*, reported that the Institute of Housing had urged the government to construct 100,000 new dwellings each year between 1991 and the end of the century in order to tackle the rising scale of homelessness. In February 1992, the Royal Institute of Chartered Surveyors echoed the Institute's demands, and recommended that the government allow local authorities to spend more of their £8 billion receipts from council house sales to provide dwellings for homeless people and families, and to phase out mortgage tax relief.

Homelessness remains a deeply emotive issue which drifts on and off the British political agenda. Each Christmas the media pricks our consciences with seasonal reports from soup kitchens or underneath railway arches, while every decade or so the homeless are 'rediscovered' by politicians and social scientists. Occasionally the homelessness scandal becomes the *cause célèbre* of British politics only to disappear once more from the agenda, like the homeless themselves. Pledges are made, resources are not allocated to deal with the root causes, promises are broken. The cycle is complete.

Homeless woman, Crisis at Christmas, London

Homelessness. Say it ten times and the word will mean nothing to you. Use it in a television report or a party political broadcast and you're dealing with emotional dynamite. Like abortion, or cancer, homelessness has a peculiar ability to provoke an immediate mental response. That response, typically an image of a young person huddled in a cardboard box, is a powerful one for a word to subconsciously transmit to your mind's eye. Yet it doesn't come unprompted … the very little most people know about the subject is almost entirely shaped by popular images … the public knows it is a real problem, but it thinks it's happening somewhere else … the government says there is 'no evidence of substantive changes in the nature of the "homeless" population over the last few years'. Not only are those who happen to have nowhere to live being attributed a 'nature' (poor, financially incapable, black, beaten up, undeserving?), they are now a 'population', citizens presumably of another country.

(*Roof*, 1990)

By studying homelessness, its definition and scale, its aetiology, its impact, the housing policies and social interventions directed at reducing it, and the unintended effects of *other* state interventions, this chapter examines people living in the margins of society at the bottom end of 'the underclass'. A focus on homelessness enables us to examine levels of intervention which are aimed at regulating individual lives and at the same time permits an exploration of the tensions between strategies of control and family life. It illustrates how wider social policies, such as housing and welfare, have intended and unintended consequences on families, especially on women and children. The focus is upon that front line where family life and social policy articulate and intersect. It crucially explores issues where the family and social policy, as systems of support, have broken down; where family and community care have failed to deliver; and where state policies have struggled to cope in a context of crisis management, often squeezed through lack of resource and political will. A study of homelessness clarifies the relationships between ideology, state intervention, regulation and family life. It also demonstrates the ways in which power affects diversity of experience and its impact on societal inequalities, and highlights the necessity to empower disadvantaged people to help tackle the root causes of one of Britain's most contentious social problems.

The chapter has six interrelated aims:

1   to trace the historical roots of homelessness, especially in relation to housing and welfare policy;

2   to examine how the category of homelessness has been constructed, and to explore the links between homelessness and pathological stereotypes (e.g. about the deserving and undeserving poor);

3   to identify the immediate and underlying causes of homelessness;

4   to examine the increasing scale of the problem of homelessness;

5   to evaluate how changes in welfare provision (e.g. restrictive social security policies, benefit allocation rules), and changes in state policy on housing (e.g. the introduction of the tenants' 'right to buy' council housing) can generate and exacerbate levels of homelessness;

6   to analyse the impact of homelessness and the interconnections between homelessness and other concerns of this book (e.g. child abuse and mental ill-health), and issues surrounding 'race' and gender.

2   HOUSING POLICY AND HOMELESSNESS: THE HISTORICAL CONTEXT

Homelessness is not a new 'problem' in the UK. One of the earliest studies was conducted over a century ago when the first volume of Charles Booth's *Life and Labour of the People of London* was published. Booth's analysis of housing and poverty was the first fully comprehensive study of Britain's poor which focused on the way people lived. He examined the plight of 30,000 people living in common lodging houses and on the streets and identified a twilight world where homeless people drifted between sleeping rough and dossing in appalling East End lodging houses. Booth revealed a London where poverty was much more prevalent than expected by the authorities — nearly a third of the city's population was, by his analysis, poor (Wolmuth, 1989). Booth was not alone in exposing

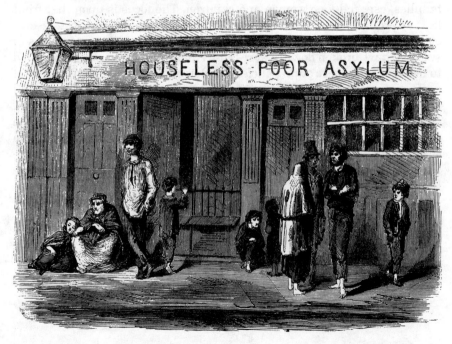

Source: Mary Evans Picture Library

the link between poverty and homelessness. In the 1880s, Flora Tristan wrote in her *London Journal* of a Spitalfields where the homeless and destitute lived in dreadful squalor next to burgeoning City financial houses: 'Oh, the sight of thousands of old worn out shoes, the rags and the rubbish ... gives a truer idea of the monster city than all the findings and reports that could be published. It makes one shudder' (Tristan, 1880).

A century later homelessness has survived, still cheek by jowl with some of the richest financial houses on earth. David Widgery's 'asylum without walls' is an image which Tristan would recognize, except that for Widgery the situation in Spitalfields in 1991 may have deteriorated since Tristan's day:

> And here a change still more ugly than the triumphalism of the City, although not unconnected to it, is noticeable ... the relative impoverishment of the people of the East End over the last decade, the rise of homelessness, its most extreme form, and the return of the scourges of malnutrition, tuberculosis, alcoholism and psychotic illness ... The East End has always been London's Skid Row and had high levels of mental illness, much of it in-coming as the mentally ill person remorselessly slides down the social ladder to the East End asylum without walls ... I estimate there are more people openly demented on our streets today then at any other point in London's history.
>
> (Widgery, 1991, p.13)

The homeless have so often, it appears, been seen as 'somebody else's problem'. Authorities invariably have moved the 'problem' on — out of sight, out of mind. Cardboard boxes can so easily be demolished and their inhabitants displaced, even more so in our property-owning democracy. It is a telling paradox that the escalation in homelessness, especially among families living in inadequate bed and breakfast temporary accommodation which occurred during the long period of Conservative political hegemony since 1979, happened during a time when government placed family values high on the political agenda.

The homeless have indeed always been with us but unlike some of the other social problems discussed in this book, homelessness has received far less systematic attention from social scientists. Nevertheless, enough work has been done to demonstrate the complexity of the issue — transcending as it does welfare and housing boundaries.

ACTIVITY 1

But what is homelessness? It might be useful here to pause and compile your own 'common-sense' definition of homelessness. You will soon see how complex a task this is. It is useful to begin by thinking about those persons who are most visibly homeless (i.e. the street homeless) and move to broader categories of people, especially in families, who might be more hidden but who, to a greater or lesser degree, are at risk and vulnerable to homelessness. What kinds of criterion do you think are most important?

DISCUSSION

How did you do? Your list might have included victims of mortgage repossessions, families with or without children living in temporary accommodation, disabled people with special needs, people with mental health problems, and people forced out of their homes by physical or sexual abuse. You might like to compare your list with Bramley's below. For Bramley being homeless means lacking the right of access to your own secure and minimally adequate housing space and he identifies seven common-sense categories:

1   People literally without a roof over their head, including those regularly sleeping rough, newly arrived migrants, victims of fire, flood, severe harassment or violence, and others.

2   People in accommodation specifically provided on a temporary basis to the homeless (hostels, bed and breakfast accommodation etc.).

3   People with insecure or impermanent tenures: this includes other ('self-referred') hotel or bed and breakfast residents, licensees and those in holiday lets, those in tied occupation who change job, tenants under notice to quit, squatters and licensed occupiers of short-life housing, and owner-occupiers experiencing mortgage foreclosure.

4   People shortly to be released from institutionalized accommodation, including prisons, detention centres, psychiatric hospitals, community or foster homes, and other hostels, who have no existing alternative accommodation or household to join.

5   Households which are sharing accommodation involuntarily.

6   Individuals or groups living within existing households where either (i) relationships with the rest of the household, or (ii) living conditions, are highly unsatisfactory and intolerable for any extended period.

7   Individuals or groups living within existing households whose relationships and conditions are tolerable but where the individuals/ groups concerned have a clear preference to live separately, including cases where the 'potential' household is currently split but would like to live together.

(adapted from Bramley, 1988, p.26)

'Who are the homeless?' is clearly a complex question of definition and, as this chapter will amplify, how we define homelessness can crucially distort the scale of the problem, constrain the scope for intervention, and affect its impact. First we must trace the historical context of the relationship between housing policy and homelessness. A brief analysis of these roots will help us understand the nature of homelessness and the reasons for its recent escalation.

2.1 HOUSING POLICY 1919–90: AN OVERVIEW

The history of housing policy in Britain since the 'homes fit for heroes' campaign after the First World War until the late 1980s, can be divided into four distinct phases. The first phase, from 1919 to 1953, is very much characterized by a broad, if uneven, political consensus about the role of state-subsidized public housing. Between 1939 and 1945, 3.7 million dwellings were either lost or required rehabilitation following war damage. The second phase, from 1953 to 1972, saw this consensus shift gradually towards a more dominant role for owner occupation with tax relief on mortgage interest and grants for home improvement and rehabilitation, and crucially away from a state-subsidized public sector of housing construction which played a subsidiary role, once slum clearance programmes had been completed. Both phases were typified by a decline in private renting. During these two phases governments were willing to tolerate the growth of state housing as a 'necessary evil' — but it was housing which was carefully *rationed* by access criteria including national and local residential qualifications and means tested social need, in which the homeless were marginalized or removed altogether from priorities. The owner-occupied tenure, as the 1953 Conservative White Paper on housing, *Houses: the Next Step* stressed, was now 'the most satisfying to the individual and the most beneficial to the nation' (HMSO, 1953). This was a view shared by the Labour Party and is best expressed in their 1965 White Paper on Housing: 'The programme of subsidized council housing should decrease. The expansion of building for owner occupation is *normal*; it reflects a long term social advance which should gradually pervade every region' [my emphasis (HMSO, 1965)]. Not to aspire to belong to the new property-owning democracy was deemed to be not 'normal' and not 'beneficial' to the nation. In these first two phases the homeless were not seen as legitimate nor deserving for public housing. Housing had to be *earned* (Merrett, 1979). It is worth emphasizing that moves away from a state-subsidized public sector are not a move from either state subsidy or the public sector but a re-routing of resources to subsidize owner-occupation; the subsidies are like those available under 'right to buy' schemes and mortgage tax relief, public sector activities funded from the public purse.

During the early 1970s, Conservative opposition to the cost of state housing hardened, ushering in a third and crucial phase before the radical shift in housing policy of the Thatcher years. The 1971 Conservative White Paper, *Fair Deal for Housing*, announced substantial reductions in state subsidy for council housing. The Housing Finance Act of 1972 strengthened central control of housing expenditure and further stimulated owner occupation. It was the first Act to move towards market rents and away from universal to targeted housing subsidies, favouring mortgage tax relief. The reduction of the housing subsidies total to the poor in the 1970s was intended to rationalize Exchequer revenue, while at the same time, 'to raise sharply the rents of the higher wage strata of the working class so that they were more likely to become owner occupiers' (Merrett, 1979, p.261).

The return of the Conservatives to power in 1979 marked a watershed in housing policy and saw an end to consensus. Housing policy became much more centralized with a dramatic switch from local control. For sixty years, from 1919 to 1979, it had been assumed that council housing required central government subsidy. The 1980 Housing Act dispelled that assumption. By enabling local authorities to operate at a surplus (but not at a loss), central government effectively announced that council housing could function at a profit without state subsidy. During Mrs Thatcher's first prime ministerial term of office council rents rose by 119 per cent compared with a rise of 55 per cent in the Retail Price Index. In cash terms subsidies fell rapidly — from £1,274 million in 1979 to £280 million in 1983–4. In real terms (taking inflation into account) the decline in subsidy was even greater (Hamnett, 1992). The introduction of the 'right to buy' council dwellings, the constraints imposed on local authorities to spend sale income on other areas of housing need, the large cuts in council housing subsidies and the building programme, and the introduction of housing benefit were part of a policy to sharply reduce and replace council housing in Britain with a fundamentally more market-oriented system. The system now enabled home ownership to expand further (mortgage tax relief was increased in 1983) and attempts were made to revitalize private renting through the growth of alternative landlords, such as housing associations. This was not so much a housing policy based on social need, but a *tenure policy* based on a reassertion of the role of market forces backed by a minimal poor law service in which certain categories of people, such as the homeless, would become an extremely low priority. You will find Figure 7.1 a useful backdrop to this and subsequent discussions.

2.2 HOMELESSNESS: A 'PROBLEM' REDISCOVERED

During the 1950s and 60s the issue of homelessness received increased publicity and was the subject of political debate. Christian concern over homelessness led to the formation of voluntary pressure groups offering advice and accommodation (for example Christian Action in 1963). In 1966 a Ministry of Housing Circular broke new ground by emphasizing that losing one's home was a potentially damaging social and personal experience. The circular represented the first government initiative to lay down minimum standards for hostels and was the first to require local authorities to monitor the scale of homelessness and to evaluate local practice (Richards, 1981).

Focus: Housing

Housebuilding completions: by sector
thousands

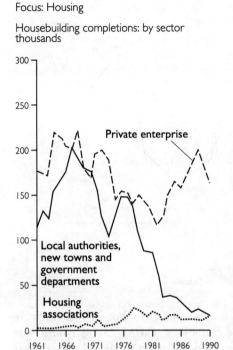

Figure 7.1 (a)

Allocation of local authority housing to
new tenants, %

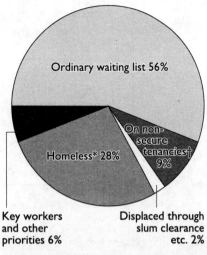

Key workers
and other
priorities 6%

Displaced through
slum clearance
etc. 2%

* Households housed under the homelessness
provisions of the Housing (Homeless
Persons) Act 1977 and the Housing Act 1985.

† As defined in schedule 1, Housing Act 1985.
n Non-secure tenancies in Wales are
included under the other categories listed.

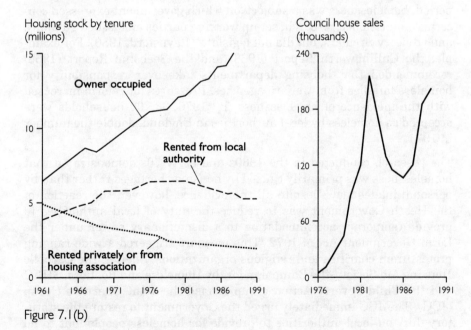

Figure 7.1 (b)

What really raised the issue of homelessness fully into the public domain
was Jeremy Sandford's documentary-style television play *Cathy Come*

...and affordability

Initial repayment as % of average earnings

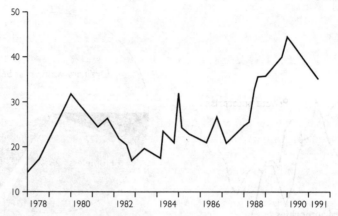

Figure 7.1(c)

Source: *The Independent On Sunday*, Business Review.

Home (BBC, 1966), about a young London couple whose children were taken into care when they became homeless. *Cathy Come Home* was watched by 12 million people, and earned an unprecedented repeat four months later in response to public demand and growing all-party political concern. Shelter, the National Campaign for the Homeless, was officially launched two weeks after the first transmission. However, during this period, homelessness was a subject 'on which government expressed concern, commissioned research, set up working parties and issued guidance and advisory circulars, but did not legislate' (Raynsford, 1986). For example, the Cullingworth Report (1968) and the Seebohm Report (1968) recommended that housing departments take over responsibility for homeless families from welfare agencies. Pressures for reform increased with the incidence of homelessness. By 1976, 33,700 households were accepted as homeless by local authorities in England, double the number in 1971.

The research conducted in the 1960s and early 70s demonstrated that homelessness was primarily caused by housing shortages rather than by personal inadequacy. Despite all the evidence, however, the reaction of the Heath Government was to reduce the duty of local authorities to provide temporary accommodation to a discretionary power under the Local Government Act of 1972. This measure triggered a wide-ranging protest from charities and religious organizations. Shelter, the Catholic Housing Aid Society, the Campaign for the Homeless and Rootless, SHAC and the Child Poverty Action group formed the Joint Charities Group (JCG). The JCG immediately urged the Government to restore the statutory duty on local authorities to provide for homeless people, but to no avail (Richards, 1991, p.35). This typifies much of the early Government response. Albert Booth explains:

Homelessness thinking seldom extends beyond the latest survey exposing the shocking consequences of homelessness or the ritual demand for more decent, affordable, rented homes. As each new study reinforces the view that things are getting worse, they have, ironically, fuelled complacency about the need to critically examine failed campaigns.

(Booth, 1989a)

One of the problems local authorities experienced in responding to the needs of homeless people was that, until 1977, as Cathy discovered, homelessness was primarily treated by central Government as a *welfare* issue. Under the Poor Law, for example, homeless people were eligible for workhouse accommodation only — provided they had a right to settle in the district. The Poor Law had established the perception of the homeless as typically undeserving, and feckless, and the often punitive surroundings of the workhouse were seen as the limit to which society should sanction the shelter of homeless persons. Although the National Assistance Act 1948 abolished the Poor Law and compelled county authorities to provide temporary accommodation for persons in urgent or unforeseen need, a Ministry of Health Circular stressed that the purpose was to assist not those persons inadequately housed in society, but those made homeless through fire or flood. Welfare and social service departments interpreted their role under the 1948 Act as providing a hostel service with the result that the punitive, deterrent Poor Law service practices, such as sex segregated communal facilities with time limits on length of stay, lived on. Housing departments were unwilling to house homeless people because the homeless were perceived as irresponsible. It was either their own fault they were homeless or they chose to be homeless. The link between alcoholism and homelessness was often cited as a justification for non-intervention. To house such people was considered contrary to waiting list priorities and would only serve to alienate the more deserving sections of the working class in housing need, such as those who had not fallen behind with their rent payments to private landlords. Many authorities applied eligibility constraints, for example, by imposing residential criteria. This often resulted in the homeless being shuttled from one local authority area to another with neither area ultimately accepting responsibility for providing accommodation. Other authorities arbitrarily refused to help pregnant women until after the birth of their children. This had the effect of splitting up homeless families and placing children into care, as dramatically revealed in *Cathy Come Home*. In 1974–75, for example, 2,800 children in England and Wales were placed in care simply because of homelessness (Richards, 1991, p.34).

The homeless were thus caught in a *policy vacuum* for over thirty years. It was a vacuum in which neither the Ministry of Health nor the Ministry of Housing took any decisive action until the Homeless Persons Act of 1977. Prior to the 1977 Act increasing numbers of homeless people were victims of housing shortages, not emergencies: 'they needed permanent homes, *which welfare departments, with no housing stock*, were unable to provide'

(Richards, 1991, p.34). The primary concern of intervention policy before 1977 was with people living in substandard accommodation (e.g. slum clearance), not those who were homeless.

The Housing (Homeless Persons) Act of 1977 marked a landmark in British housing policy since it established homelessness as an integral part of the housing system, and ensured that housing authorities had a statutory responsibility for homelessness. But the legacy of those negative attitudes to the homeless which were apparent in our brief analysis of the historical context had a great impact on the 1977 Act. Local authorities still believed that a duty to house homeless people would interfere with the 'everyday' provision and management of public housing. In addition, authorities did not have sufficient resources to cope with the rise in homelessness. Thompson (1988) saw the 1977 Act not as a piece of legislation primarily directed at homeless persons, but one which sought to resolve tensions between *competing* groups, the deserving and undeserving poor, in a context of diminishing housing resource allocation. The Act also represented a *compromise* between those who questioned the legitimacy of local authorities to house the homeless and those whose ultimate aim was that all homeless persons should have statutory rights to accommodation. One local authority officer justified his reluctance to house homeless people under the Act to Thompson: 'I have to pay attention to the ordinary standards of decent people. We don't want these deadlegs. They muck up the books and make life a misery for ordinary folk' (Thompson, 1988, p.2).

As the Act passed through Parliament the homeless were vilified by opponents as 'queue jumpers', 'rent dodgers' and 'scroungers and scrimshankers' (Richards, 1991). Hostility towards the homeless increased because the homeless were perceived to be disreputable and irresponsible. To allocate them to permanent stock in good condition ahead of other categories of households on local waiting lists penalized others who waited their turn or who were perceived to be more responsible (see Murie, 1988a). These perceptions influenced the ways in which definitions were formulated, legislation framed and intervention structured.

3 HOMELESSNESS: THE CONSTRUCTION OF A CATEGORY

'Homeless people are the sort you tread on when you come out of the opera' (Sir George Young, Housing Minister, quoted in *The Mail on Sunday, You Magazine,* 1991).

HOMELESSNESS

You passed me by on your way to the theatre the other day,
Head up, shoulders stiff, eyes looking straight ahead
at some imaginary destination deep in the distance.
What did you think I was going to do?
Mug you with my cardboard begging box?

You pretended not to see me on your way to the play,
Though your friend cast me a coin to scrub my unwanted
image from his eyes.
What was the play about I wonder?
Did it give you good conversation on your way home past my
bed?

Don't get me wrong.
I wouldn't dream to trespass on your time,
Or deny your pleasure in your hard-earned recreation.
All I ask is that your eyes acknowledge my existence
next time you pass this way,
So if you step on my toes again beneath my grubby blanket
You'll realize that you've done it,
Instead of simply passing by.

Laveric John (homeless man)

(*New Statesman and Society*, November, 1989, p.21)

The real incidence of homelessness can be disguised by official definitions and categorizations, much of them embedded in complex legislation; it can also be distorted through the failure of some local authorities to collate and monitor homeless statistics. Statistical data on homelessness is problematic and may only measure the tip of an iceberg.

The official definition of homelessness is enshrined in the Housing (Homeless Persons) Act 1977. Although this has subsequently been consolidated by Part III of the Housing Act 1985, the 1977 legislation still informs the operational definition of homelessness. *Homelessness is essentially defined as the lack of secure accommodation free from violence or the threat of violence.* Under the 1977 Act people could present themselves to local authorities as homeless if they fell into one of four categories:

1   Whether they were homeless as defined in the Act (or threatened with homelessness within 28 days).

2   Whether they fell into a priority need group listed in the legislation. Priority cases basically comprise families with children, pregnant women, emergency cases (e.g. ex-psychiatric patients, young people leaving care) and people who may be at risk because of disablement or old age.

3   Whether they were classified as intentionally homeless within the meaning of the Act.

4   Whether they had a local connection with the district.

Richards identified crucial flaws in the 1977 Act. The duty to secure accommodation did not extend to non-vulnerable single adults and young people. The definition of homelessness did not encompass violence from persons outside the home, nor racial and sexual harassment. Applicants, whether single or in families, had no right of appeal. The main failure of the Act, however, was that it did not achieve uniform and consistent practice throughout Great Britain. Some observers felt that local authorities were given wider powers of discretion than was originally intended as a result of the ambiguity of some of the key terms, such as 'intentionally homeless', 'vulnerable', and 'inappropriate advice and assistance' (Richards, 1991, p.37). Outcomes were determined by political and professional considerations in the context of limited available resources (Bramley, 1988, p.29). Bramley's research clarifies just how 'the definitions provided by the legislation may not be alone sufficient to comprehend ... homelessness' (ibid., p.26). He also argues that the definitions *themselves* are part of the homelessness 'problem'.

A first difficulty is that housing legislation defines homelessness to mean lack of 'accommodation' rather than lack of a 'home', and this narrow definition can result in the housing needs of a number of different groups of people being *concealed* from official statistics and help: for example, single people in shared accommodation, persons remaining in their parents' household, disabled people in residential establishments, and women wanting to leave a failed marriage. Each of these examples represents groups which may need accommodation which they regard as their own home, rather than merely a roof over their heads (Morris and Winn, 1990, pp.183–5).

Even more important, however, is the role pathologizing people into deserving and undeserving cases plays in the allocation of scarce housing resources. It is a distinction which, as our historical overview revealed, framed much state housing practice in Great Britain (Merrett, 1979). The Homeless Persons Act distinguishes between those persons who are 'deserving' of local authority intervention and those who are not. This serves to undermine the legitimacy of the genuine housing needs of those groups that do not qualify because they are not in priority need, have a local connection or are intentionally homeless. Because of its failure to develop a more comprehensive concept of homelessness, housing policy generally does not address the needs of those whose homelessness is concealed.

A second difficulty is that official homelessness figures do not provide an *accurate* count of those applications actually made to local authorities. Local authority records are often incomplete rendering trend analysis impossible. Of the three principle sources of official data on homelessness, only the Housing Investment Programme return (HIP) is compulsory on local authorities, but even this data, although collected, are often not analysed at local authority level.

There are two other data sources on the homeless. The first are quarterly statistics for the Department of the Environment (DoE). These record the numbers of households applying for and being accepted as homeless. The DoE also collects quarterly returns on people living in temporary accommodation (short-life dwellings including properties leased from private landlords, bed and breakfast accommodation, hostels and refuges). Much of this temporary accommodation is in poor repair. In 1991 the Audit Commission estimated that more than one half of all bed and breakfast hotels and hostels, fell below health and safety standards (The Audit Commission, 1992). The DoE also collects special data on the numbers of intentionally homeless. A third data source, collected by the Chartered Institute of Public Finance and Accountancy (CIPFA), only deals with identifiable local authority expenditure under the 1977 Act.

Statistics on homelessness are affected by the ways in which local authorities interpret their statutory responsibilities and exercise their discretionary powers. The DoE and CIPFA measures are not compulsory. Some authorities, particularly London boroughs and Metropolitan districts, do not complete either return. For example, nearly a fifth of local housing authorities did not complete the DoE homelessness returns for the second quarter of 1989. Research in the 1980s has highlighted the considerable variation between local authorities in dealing with homelessness. For example, Niner's study in nine local authorities assessed their response to homelessness on a continuum ranging from providing maximum to minimum support. Whereas in Nottingham and Newcastle upon Tyne nobody intentionally homeless was found between 1980 and 1988, some local authorities — for example, the London Borough of Westminster, pursued a far tougher line with applicants (see Niner, 1989, p.32 and p.95). In April 1991, for example, Westminster City Council's attempt to pass its homeless families on to authorities outside London was rejected by the fifty-seven councils it contacted.

Non-response remains a problem for those researchers working in the field of homelessness who need reliable data, and data which can be subjected to trend analysis. It is worth emphasizing that the problems associated with data collection and access have made the production of this chapter problematic (for example, data analysing homelessness by gender, and data identifying the long-term homeless is difficult to obtain, and time series data is only possible through locality studies).

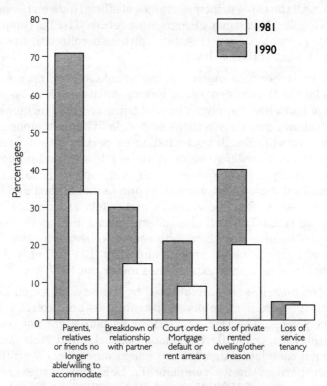

1 Households for whom local authorities accepted responsibility to secure accommodation under the Housing (Homeless Persons) Act 1977 and the Housing Act 1985, which defines 'priority need'.

2 Categories in Wales differ slightly from those in England so cases have been allocated to the closest English category. Data for Wales include cases given advice and assistance.

Figure 7.2   Homeless households found accommodation by local authorities:

Source: *Social Trends 22*, 1992

4   WHY PEOPLE BECOME HOMELESS

In looking at homelessness aetiology researchers have often adopted a dual approach focusing on the characteristics of homeless households. First, we will explore some of the *immediate reasons* for homelessness. This will involve focusing on some of the major characteristics of homeless households and looking at the level of individual and family behaviour (changes in attitudes and values). Second, we will look at the *underlying causes* of homelessness: factors emanating from latent influences operating at the level of policy (housing and welfare interventions).

4.1   IMMEDIATE REASONS

The biggest contributing factor to statutory homelessness, according to the 1992 edition of *Social Trends*, is that parents, friends or relatives were no longer able or willing to accommodate people (see Figure 7.2). In 1990 this reason accounted for 42 per cent of all cases. Other significant reasons for homelessness include relationships with a partner breaking down (17 per cent) — in over one half of these the relationship had broken down violently; the loss of owner occupied homes (12 per cent); and privately rented evictions (10 per cent).

In 1988, it was estimated that women and children make up 80 per cent of the homeless (*New Statesman and Society*, 1989). In June, 1991, DoE data for England only showed that in the second quarter of 1991, 63 per cent of those households accepted into temporary accommodation were families with young children, a further 20 per cent were accepted because a woman in the household was pregnant, the remainder were accounted for by a member of a household becoming homeless because of physical handicap, mental illness, and old age (DoE, September, 1991a).

The DoE evidence emphasizes the way in which changing environments (in family values and behaviour, and in government strategies) can generate new elements in homelessness. Compared to the 1960s, for example, homeless households are less likely to result from landlord eviction but more likely to be the result of mortgage repossession. Between 1981 and 1990, statutory homelessness as a result of a court order following mortgage default doubled.

Violent and non-violent disputes with spouses or the inability of parents, relatives or friends to provide accommodation has also risen in importance since the 1960s. These factors accounted for up to six out of ten homeless households in 1991, whereas in 1959–61, for example, they represented only two to three out of ten homeless households (Greve, 1964). Though these differences are undoubtedly influenced by the types of definition used, the growth of marital and family disputes as a cause of homelessness is undeniable. Austerberry and Watson's study of women in hostels found domestic violence and/or relationship breakdown to be the biggest reason for single women's homelessness (Austerberry and Watson, 1983). Mama (1989) too testifies to its importance. She concluded that for many black women, leaving a violent home may well mean embarking on a long ordeal of racism, homelessness and destitution. The important point to make about the role domestic violence plays in generating homelessness is that it *disproportionately affects women*:

> Women's generally low income levels mean that the majority cannot afford to rent or buy decent private accommodation, so that as a group, low income families (a significant proportion of whom are black and/or female headed) are at the mercy of the public housing establishment. This is particularly true of abused women who often have to abandon their jobs in order to move away from violence, as well as having to become single parents.
>
> (Mama, 1989, p.104)

Child abuse is also a significant factor in homelessness. Among young people, 'runaways' leave their homes to escape from family situations they do not like, such as physical or sexual abuse, others run away from local authority care (Hardwick, 1991, p.10). A *You and Yours* BBC Radio 4 report claimed that the relationship between child abuse and young people leaving home was a significant factor in the rise in homelessness among young women (BBC, 1992) — especially important was the effects of step-parent sexual abuse. Hardwick points out that older people too 'run away', and for less dramatic reasons: 'pressures at work or home get too much and they simply disappear into the anonymity of London's streets', others leave because their parents want them out of the home and they respond to that pressure.

People leave institutional life and drift into homelessness. Hardwick's research revealed that two out of five young homeless people spend most of their lives in and out of care; a significant number of others become homeless after leaving prison, asylums or mental hospitals without any family to return to or without any house to live in.

Certain categories of the homeless often spend long periods in mental hospitals and, though they would normally be allocated a place to stay and receive social work support, might find that support withdrawn too quickly, and this places them at greater risk. In 1989, a Fulham homeless refuge, St Mungo's Community, reported that 75 per cent of the men in its hostel were mentally ill: worse, none of its staff had received any psychiatric training. In 1992 the mental health charity Concern estimated that 40 per cent of homeless people have suffered from some form of mental illness.

ACTIVITY 2

Now read 'Norman, a tragedy that slipped through the net'. What conclusions do you draw from Norman's experience? His plight graphically illustrates how homelessness cannot be fully understood without reference to state policy in areas other than housing. It shows how persons in priority need can slip through the net, and confirms the vital importance of analysing underlying causes. To what extent are resources a factor?

■ NORMAN, A TRAGEDY THAT SLIPPED THROUGH THE NET
COMMUNITY CARE WAS A BRILLIANT IDEA THAT FAILED FOR 75,000 HOMELESS WHO NEED MENTAL SUPPORT
BY TIM RAYMENT AND REBECCA FOWLER

His name was Norman. He should be in sheltered housing, but they found him in a shed.

He has witnessed many of the developments in Britain's 30-year drive towards community care. But he cannot remember them: 'I've been sick' he said.

Norman is one of thousands of people who are homeless and mentally ill. Last week he was at a day centre in Worcester, another vulnerable person failed by the system. Nobody knows much about him, or if he will ever be offered a home. All he could say was that he had been a labourer, diagnosed as schizophrenic 'when Fred died' 20 years ago. Asked who Fred was, he did not know.

Norman, who has had electric-shock treatment, is part of a trend. Hostels and day centres throughout Britain are being filled by homeless people with psychiatric needs, including many who were once in hospital. According to one estimate, 75,000 single homeless people require some kind of mental care.

At the Maggs day centre in Worcester, more than half the users are significantly ill and many have slipped through every net. Sue Smyth, a child-like 34, was found by police on a motorway. She has no link with Worcester: she simply wanted to get away from Birmingham, where a boyfriend was beating her up.

'At the beginning a few old boys who had nowhere to go would come and play cribbage' Alan Higgins, who chairs the Maggs centre management committee, said yesterday. 'Now it is full of deeply disturbed people.'

The trend is particularly alarming in a city that thought it led the country in developing community services. What is going wrong?

It was Enoch Powell, then minister of health, who first suggested shutting the big old mental hospitals — as long ago as 1961. Inspired by better drugs and a belief that long periods in institutions were damaging, he declared: 'For the great majority of these establishments there is no appropriate use.'

245

Hospital in-patients fell from about 150,000 in England and Wales in the mid-1950s to less than half that figure in the mid-1980s. But the hospitals did not close. For some patients the new treatments for schizophrenia had come too late: others still needed the shelter of hospital: the numbers of confused elderly people grew. The closures were being postponed.

By 1988, when Sir Roy Griffiths delivered his report on community care only a handful of hospitals had shut. Closing others, he said, was a matter of national importance. But as individual wards were shut, the programme was provoking a crisis: hospital beds were being taken away faster than anything was created to replace them.

Homelessness was already rising because of a shortage of affordable homes. When people such as Norman joined the competition, they had no hope. By 1989, St. Mungo's Community in Fulham, London, was reporting that 75 per cent of the men in its hostel were mentally ill — and none of its staff had psychiatric training. Other homeless people were being turned away, in central London between 500 and 1,500 people with mental problems sleep rough.

More homeless mentally ill people began appearing in courts and therefore in prisons. The problem became so serious that a medical journal claimed it was an abuse to compare with the Soviet Union, and that it would attract international action. 'For how long is it ethical to preside over mindless incarceration under conditions of secrecy, squalor and neglect?' the *Lancet* asked. 'There is a risk that if British doctors do not act, European colleagues may eventually act for them.'

Conservatives began to be alarmed. 'What bothers me is that as a human being, as well as a Conservative, I see more and more of the mentally ill being released from hospitals — sometimes prematurely — onto a society that neither wants them or is adequately prepared' the manager of a private hostel in Plymouth wrote to his MP. 'Cost-cutting is one thing; inhumanity another.'

Health authorities, however, were caught in a trap. To close their big hospitals humanely, they needed to invest in community services. To get the money to develop these services, they needed to shut the hospitals first.

The government introduced grants and loans, but they are small compared with the task. Further measures were expected, but they have been postponed until 1993.

Even when a mental hospital closes, the savings do not have to be spent on psychiatric care. After Banstead hospital was shut in 1986, much of the money went into services for the *physically* ill. Mind, the mental health charity, has tried for eighteen months to find out what has happened to about £60m from two hospital closures in Exeter. 'There's a lot of anxiety about asset-stripping' Liz Sayce, Mind's policy director, says.

Taxpayers' spending on mental health care is £1,437m a year, a real rise of 34 per cent in a decade. But most of it continues to be swallowed by hospitals, despite the exodus of patients. Other targets are not being met. There are fewer than 3,000 community psychiatric nurses: some authorities have none.

Norman is one of the lucky ones. He might have no prospect of a home, but Worcester has a day centre and night shelter — funded with the help of *The Sunday Times* Crisis at Christmas appeal.

The centres offer a bed and somewhere warm to conduct his one-way correspondence with Samantha Fox, the former page three model. Norman is popular there, because he is gentle and generous. Perhaps too gentle: he must be accompanied to collect his giro, because he will hand it over to anyone who asks.

Last week *Sunday Times* readers gave £25,806 to the appeal, which aims to raise £250,000 as Christmas approaches. Stuart Craig, director of the charity Crisis said: 'It's a tremendous start.'

At his home in Belgravia, London, Enoch Powell was pondering the outcome of the great experiment he began a generation ago. 'I hear the voice of the Treasury declaring no net increase in expenditure by central government. Can that really be right? Community care is not a cheap option.'

(*Sunday Times*, 12 March 1991) ∎

4.2 UNDERLYING CAUSES

Why people like Norman become homeless is clearly a complex issue. Doogan (1988) has argued that we need to seek underlying causes in the economic, political and social fabric of society:

> Homelessness is as much a housing problem as famine is a 'food problem'. Just as with the latter we have to seek out the structural reasons which explain the continual vulnerability of certain countries to famine, so too with homelessness must we locate the same economic, political and social determinants that explain the continual vulnerability of social groups.
>
> (Doogan, 1988, p.87)

Doogan thus locates the underlying causes of homelessness in the social and economic context of Britain in the 1980s: 'The rise in youth homelessness is but one symptom of the deteriorating economic position of young people that has its roots in the dramatic restructuring of the world of work' (ibid., p.91). The search for underlying causes in the structure of society applies whether the victim is young or old, or a family living in poor temporary accommodation. This involves investigating links between unemployment, poverty, housing and welfare, especially in relation to public policy.

The 1980s and early 1990s saw dramatic rises in youth unemployment, especially in long-term unemployment. The period also witnessed a reduction in income for young people and in benefit entitlement. It also saw an increase in the levels of poverty. In the autumn of 1990, the Child Poverty Action Group (CPAG) estimated that 10.5 million people — 18.5 per cent of the UK population (including three million children) lived in poverty (Oppenheim, 1990). In May 1991, a House of Commons committee estimated that in the decade 1979 to 1988, the number of people with incomes below half the average grew by 3.7 million (Department of Social Security, 1991).

The 1980s saw widespread erosion in the value of state benefits for *all* people, not just the young. Unemployment benefit dropped substantially as a proportion of average male earnings. In 1979 the figure stood at 16.2 per cent. By 1989 it had fallen to 12.9 per cent (DSS, 1989). Between 1987 and 1991 child benefit was frozen. The CPAG have argued that the *real* value of child support for a standard rate tax-paying family (compared with the old family allowances and child tax allowances) was worth much less in 1990 than it was in 1960 (Oppenheim, 1990, p.71).

The combined effects of job loss and insecurity, reduced entitlements to welfare and housing benefit, higher rents, and poverty has influenced homeless vulnerability. According to the Association of Metropolitan Authorities (AMA) rent arrears rose by 38 per cent in the six months immediately following benefit changes introduced in April, 1988. The shift to income support also exacerbated the problem. The 1986 Social Security Act introduced substantial cuts in benefit for young unemployed people. People aged sixteen to seventeen years old could only receive income support if they had a youth training place or if they fell into one of the strictly defined categories of hardship.

The appearance of youngsters begging on the streets in growing numbers can be dated to late 1988 when conditions for benefit entitlement were fundamentally altered. Many homeless sixteen and seventeen year olds found they had no legal source of income at all. In November, 1991, the Unemployment Unit (UU) estimated that Britain's 'invisible army' of penniless school-leavers without jobs or government allowances had grown to record levels. The UU claimed that 114,300, more than one in six of the sixteen to eighteen year olds outside full-time education, were unemployed — and that 94,000 of these received *no* state benefits at all (Unemployment Unit, 1991).

These changes signalled a rise in the visibility of begging and homelessness. The CPAG estimated that between April 1987–88 and April 1990–91 income support for a single person aged between eighteen and twenty-four fell by 27 per cent in *real* terms (Oppenheim, 1990, p.66). The full adult rate paid to over twenty-five year olds was just over £2,000 a year, barely enough on which to survive, placing more people at risk of homelessness (*The Big Issue*, 1991, p.11).

Housing provision is a crucial factor explaining homelessness. The shortage of owner-occupied and rented housing at costs and rents which the poorer sections of the population could afford is of vital importance. In 1989 government research revealed that only in two locations in England could a couple with two children on housing benefit afford the average market rent for a two-bedroom house — Leicester and Newcastle upon Tyne (Joint Charities Group on Homelessness, 1989).

The years since 1979 witnessed three significant and related shifts in housing tenure policy: a rapid rise in the level of owner occupation, a sharp fall in local authority tenancies, and a further decline in private rented housing. For example, between December 1980 and June 1990 the number of owner-occupied dwellings in England rose from 10.2 to 13.3 million (from 57 to 69 per cent of all dwellings). Between 1979 and 1989 over 1.4 million public sector dwellings were sold, while the decline in private renting left the remaining supply very expensive to obtain. Insecurity of private renting continued to be a major factor affecting homelessness as Rent Acts failed to provide tenant protection, thus diminishing access for homeless families (Murie, 1988b).

On 13 February 1991, the Chancellor of the Exchequer, Mr Norman Lamont, revealed the extent of cuts in housing resource allocation during the 1980s. Replying to a House of Commons question from Mr Nicholas Ridley (Conservative) he announced that Government spending on housing had fallen by more than one-half in *real* terms since 1979. Government spending on all public housing dropped by 75 per cent between 1979 and 1990, while subsidies to owner occupiers increased. During this

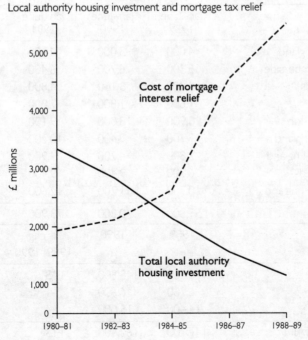

Figure 7.3
Source: Platt (1989) p.14

period Britain recorded one of the lowest housing investment programmes in Europe. Figure 7.3 starkly illustrates the relationship between UK local authority housing investment and mortgage tax relief subsidies during the 1980s. This neglect of the housing infrastructure meant there was increasingly no place for the homeless, who were squeezed out into expensive temporary accommodation (see Section 5.1).

The emphasis of Conservative housing ideology in which owner-occupation was paramount, relegated social need housing to an extremely low priority. The tenure policies adopted saw tax relief on mortgages as sacrosanct [this doubled between 1979 and 1986 and was projected to cost the Exchequer £6,750 million in 1990 — five times the level of 1979 (Platt, 1989)]. Substantial reductions in housing investment and housing construction were made. Between 1978 and 1989 housing built by local authorities and housing associations fell from 104,000 to 22,000. This decline applied across most regions of the UK: the biggest fall was in North West England where, in 1988, 48 per cent fewer dwellings were built. Interestingly this was also the area where homelessness increased the most — up 150 per cent between 1983 and 1989, compared to a UK average of 61 per cent. Greater London's increase was only 38 per cent, illustrating the extent to which homelessness is a national problem, not one simply confined to the capital (Department of the Environment, 1990). While in absolute terms London remains the area with by far the worst problems it is important to recognize that other urban centres have

Table 7.1 Households accepted as homeless, 1989–1991

N=households	Jan–June 1989	Jan–June 1990	Jan–June 1991	% chg 1990–1991
Northern England	4,000	5,000	4,600	–7
Yorks & Humberside	5,300	6,700	6,400	–5
East Midlands	4,000	5,100	4,800	–6
East Anglia	1,600	1,800	2,000	+9
Greater London	15,900	18,000	19,100	+6
Rest of SE England	7,700	9,400	10,200	+9
South West England	3,800	4,200	4,900	+17
West Midlands	6,900	9,400	9,400	0
North West England	10,300	11,200	12,600	+12
ENGLAND	59,600	70,800	73,900	+4

N=people	1989	1990	% chg 1989–1990
ENGLAND	126,700	145,800	+15
WALES	6,700	6,600	–1
SCOTLAND	14,400	15,000	+4
GREAT BRITAIN	147,700	167,400	+13

Sources: DoE *Homelessness Statistics* (1991a), Scottish Office, Welsh Office

seen greater percentage increases (for example, Manchester recorded a 325 per cent increase in homelessness between 1979 and 1988 (Platt, 1989)). Nor was homelessness confined to the big cities. In 1988, 43 per cent of homeless households were found in small towns and rural areas. While, between 1988 and 1992, homelessness grew faster in rural areas than in towns and cities; tripling in sparsely populated areas of Britain (Rural Development Commission, 1992). Table 7.1 provides an analysis of accepted homeless households between 1989 and 1991 — note the huge increases across most regions during 1990.

The 'Right to Buy' council housing was one of the most significant factors in the decline of affordable renting which would otherwise have provided accommodation for the homeless. Government housing policy directives prevented the resources gained by local authorities under right to buy sales from being used to construct new dwellings for those in greatest housing need or from refurbishing and improving existing stock thus exacerbating the housing shortages for those who could afford only the cheapest dwelling. According to Morris and Winn (1990) it was this single plank of Government policy which more than any other generated the rise in homelessness during the late 1980s. The Housing Act 1988 left the voluntary sector to bridge the gap in housing provision for the homeless. Housing Associations however have had only a marginal impact on housing the statutory homeless. Only 11.5 per cent of the lettings of the twenty biggest housing associations were let to homeless households between March 1990 and March 1991. Moreover, since 1988, the privatizing of entire council estates to new consortia has done little to ease the plight of homeless people.

The late 1980s and early 1990s witnessed a big increase in mortgage repossessions, as unemployment increased and the 1990–92 recession hit home harder (Shelter, 1991). By the middle of 1991, the number of mortgages with payments behind by between six months and a year had risen to over 150,000 — 84 per cent more than the figure for 1990 (*The Indepen-*

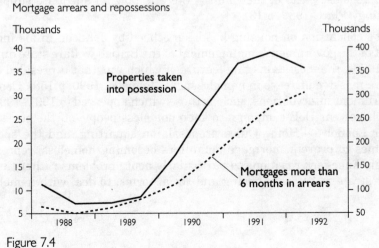

Figure 7.4

Source: *The Independent*, 14 February 1992

dent, 14 February 1992). Data from the Council of Mortgage Lenders revealed that the number of homes repossessed in 1991 was 75,540, a 72 per cent increase on 1990. In 1991, 12 per cent of homeless families were found temporary accommodation because of mortgage repossessions, a substantial increase on previous years.

Steve Platt, reviewing the 1980s for a *New Statesman and Society* special issue on homelessness, argued that the decade's social history was littered with reports warning of the consequences of cuts in housing on the scale carried out by the Conservatives. Indeed one of the most remarkable features of the housing debate was the degree of consensus, almost unanimity, among non-government organizations about the extent of the problem and the nature of the solution. From the churches to the building societies, from charities to big business, the conclusions fly in the face of the government's bald assertion, made in an expenditure white paper, that: 'In most parts of the country there is now an adequate supply of housing' (Platt, 1989, p.13).

Platt's conclusion on housing has been echoed by Johnson in his indictment of the government's management of the British welfare state during the 1980s, the most damaging feature of which was that it presided over such a massive increase in homelessness (Johnson, 1990, p.158). Central government interventions, such as those which appeared in 1991–1992 — the three-year DoE campaign to keep homeless people off the streets of inner London — Home Office proposals on squatting, and the special schemes to prevent mortgage defaulters becoming homeless, represent merely knee-jerk reactions to particularly acute problems rather than a clear strategy, both in housing and social terms, to deal with homelessness.

5 THE 1990s: THE ESCALATING SCALE OF HOMELESSNESS

Government strategies, or the lack of them, resulted in a dramatic rise in homelessness at the beginning of this decade — for example, homelessness rose by 30 per cent in 1990–91. This section evaluates this rise across four areas: the use of temporary accommodation; the intentionally homeless and hidden homeless — here we look at the role played by positive and negative stereotypes; at one government intervention to ameliorate it; and at evidence which suggests that black and minority ethnic groups may be more at risk.

5.1 HOUSEHOLDS SEEKING TEMPORARY ACCOMMODATION

Margaret Moran, the chair of the London Housing Unit, reflecting on the 'human catastrophe' of homelessness, estimated that unless substantially greater government action was forthcoming, in London alone, 80,000 families — a quarter of a million people — 'would be living this life of hell by 1995' (*The Guardian*, 11 September, 1991). During 1991, 36,000 families each quarter were being *newly* defined as homeless. In London an extra 1,000 families were moving each month into temporary accommodation. The DoE response was to call for some of the 100,000 empty local authority properties in London and the South East to be put into use. The government could produce only 16,000 permanent new homes for families during the two years 1991 and 1992. To meet the shortfall expensive emergency bed and breakfast facilities were the only alternative — at a time when the reliance on temporary accommodation itself was rising by 25 per cent a year (*The Guardian*, 11 January 1991). By 1994, the number of people accepted as homeless and living in temporary accommodation was expected to exceed 250,000 in London. The immense financial burden of this provision should not be underestimated, especially that on local authorities struggling to set council tax rates in the face of competing claims on limited capital budgets. The cost to English local authorities of providing bed and breakfast accommodation for the homeless in 1988–89 totalled £137 million with the brunt of this bill borne by the London boroughs — where 62 per cent of all households in temporary accommodation in England were found. As long ago as 1985, the burden of providing temporary hotel accommodation was estimated to be £11,600 a year, while the cost to finance the first year of building a flat was only £7,700. Building the flat would permanently solve the family's housing need, putting them in temporary accommodation would not (Drake, 1989, p.20).

The costs of meeting the barest minimal needs of the U.K.'s homeless is enormous, and would escalate further if one added the *real* financial costs of coping with the impact of homelessness itself, of levels of crime, of health (physical and mental), of employment, of care provision and welfare benefits. As Nick Hardwick has observed: 'the cost of keeping people homeless is far greater than the cost of housing them' (Hardwick, 1991, p.11).

5.2   THE INTENTIONALLY HOMELESS AND THE HIDDEN HOMELESS

Local authorities have fiercely defended the primacy of the local waiting list against the claims of the homeless. Councils built council dwellings for *respectable* local residents. Intentionality has often nothing to do with the actual intentions of homeless people, but rather with how their actions can be interpreted by local authorities reluctant to rehouse them.

The escalation in homelessness of the early 1990s is all the more significant because local authorities have been increasingly taking a tougher line (for example, through the 1824 Vagrancy Act). Home Office figures for 1990, (the last year for which data was available, and prior to the new 'tougher line' initiatives of 1991 and deepening recession), show 1,445 prosecutions in London under the 1824 Vagrancy Act for begging in London alone, a rise of 194 on 1989. Mr Matt Kelly, co-ordinator of the End the Vagrancy Act Campaign (EVA) commented: 'These figures are the highest we have seen for years, definitely much higher than in the 1980s, and are a reflection of the numbers being forced on to the streets ... We want begging decriminalized because at the moment people are being penalized for being homeless and poor' (*The Independent*, 28 December 1991).

A Government discussion paper in the autumn of 1991 illustrated the trend towards more punitive forms of intervention. It spoke of the need to deal effectively with those homeless persons 'resistant to persuasion' to move into temporary accommodation, and went on to cite public opinion as a reason for the application of tighter criteria and tougher action (*The*

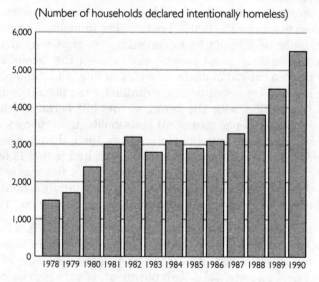

(Number of households declared intentionally homeless)

Figure 7.5   Intentional homelessness: England only: 1978–90

Source: DoE Homelessness Statistics, 1991: reproduced from *Roof*, 7 May 1991

Guardian, 17 September 1991). Evidence for this tougher line can be found in the number of households who, according to local authorities, were declared to have made themselves 'intentionally homeless' (see Figure 7.5). In 1990, twenty-nine of the thirty-two London boroughs made declarations of intentional homelessness in England. This represented a rise of nearly 70 per cent over the previous three years and partly explains the rise in the use of temporary accommodation by local authorities noted in Section 5.1.

The hidden homeless, the roofless, those without temporary accommodation, often fall outside legislative definitions. Here our focus is not on families as victims, but on single persons. Randall's (1989) survey of young people who came to stay at Centrepoint's night shelter in London revealed:

+ 41 per cent had been living in care at some point in the past
+ 77 per cent were unemployed
+ 50 per cent had no money at all
+ 33 per cent were begging
+ 50 per cent did not have enough money for food
+ 33 per cent had been approached to become involved in prostitution.

(Randall, 1989)

The Salvation Army claimed 'Cardboard City' was only a 1 per cent tip of the London homeless iceberg. It found 753 people living openly out on the streets and in bus, tube and rail stations in April 1989, and estimated the numbers of single homeless people in London hostels, bed and breakfast

'If you haven't got a home, you can't get a job — and if you haven't got a job, you can't get a flat. What are we supposed to do — disappear?'

hotels, and squats, to be 75,000, 'a shanty town as large as might be expected in any Latin American City, but it is hidden' (Canter, 1990). The National Foundation of Housing Associations estimated the number of single homeless people in London was 125,000 (NFHA, 1990). Many of these young homeless people are caught in a double constraint: 'If you haven't got a home, you can't get a job, and if you haven't got a job, you can't get a flat. What are we supposed to do — disappear?' (Platt, 1988, p.51).

5.3   THE 1991 'HOMELESSNESS REVIEW': AN INTERVENTION EXPLORED

Let us now briefly examine one type of intervention targeted, though not exclusively, at the single homeless. In January 1991, the Conservative Government announced a three-year 'Homelessness Review', a £96 million scheme to 'achieve a substantial and visible reduction in the numbers of rough sleepers in central London'. The scheme aimed to provide sufficient hostel accommodation to remove the necessity for people, especially young people, from sleeping out. 'Cardboard City' was cleared 'to allow for road repairs' (*The Guardian*, 18 September 1991). On 2 June 1991, the then Housing Minister, Sir George Young declared 'the problem had been successfully tackled'. The following day the page one headline of *The Independent* read: 'It's official: no more homelessness' (*The Independent*, 3 June 1991).

Two months later, on 9 September *The Big Issue,* Britain's first 'street newspaper' produced by the homeless for the benefit of the homeless with a circulation of 60,000 was launched. If in June 1991 there were 'no more homeless' people, how could a carefully constructed media launch a few weeks later be devoted to the needs of the homeless? How could homelessness have moved so quickly from being a non-issue to being the *big* issue? How can we explain homelessness's Jekyll and Hyde existence? The principle of 'out of sight, out of mind' had prevailed. Temporarily, the rough sleepers had been moved on (in London only). Meanwhile the bulk of the homeless iceberg, with its huge number of families with children still awaited a permanent solution, trapped in hotels, hostels, bed and breakfast accommodation and refuges.

Critics of government policy argued that the 'Homelessness Review' was not an attempt to tackle underlying causes of homelessness nor to deal with the roots of the problem but was yet another superficial local response in tourist London which dealt merely with the visible tip of the iceberg. The problem however was not simply one of resource allocation, but stemmed from prevailing attitudes towards homeless people in British politics. Sir Bernard Ingham, former press secretary to Mrs Thatcher, described the homeless as a 'blot on the ... tourist landscape'; they were 'moral blackmailers'; they were 'incapable'; or they chose homelessness as a 'deliberate way of life' (Ingham, 1991). As the *Roof* editorial indicates (see Section 1) the prevailing mood was one in which the homeless were 'citizens of another country'. The Steve Bell cartoon of the time, on page 257, illustrates this perfectly.

One effect of the 'Homelessness Review' was to divert attention away from the scale of homelessness among families living in temporary accommodation or who were squatting (Gosling, 1991, p.19). Julia Unwin, director of 'Homeless Network', welcomed the targeted initiative on street homelessness, but with a crucial reservation. The review didn't do anything to stop people *becoming* homeless. The responsibility for that didn't rest with the DoE but, claimed Unwin, it lay with the Department of Social Security because of punitive social security regulations, the Department of Health because of deficiencies in community care, and the Home Office because of the issue of release from prison (Gosling, 1991, p.19). The 'Homelessness Review' did provide some of the street homeless in central London with accommodation through the creation of more emergency hostels, greater permanent place provision, and by increasing grants to voluntary organizations. But it was only allocated £96 million over three years, *half the cost of providing temporary accommodation for the homeless in London in 1989 alone,* barely enough to cope with the tip of the iceberg itself.

5.4   THE VULNERABILITY OF BLACK AND MINORITY ETHNIC GROUPS

Homelessness is hidden in all communities. but the problem may be particularly acute among minority ethnic groups. In 1990 the CPAG concluded that every indicator of poverty showed black people to be more at risk than white people to homelessness because of high unemployment, low pay, shift work, poor social security rights, and because they were more likely to be imprisoned and treated for schizophrenia (Oppenheim, 1990, pp.85–8). Research in London has revealed black and minority ethnic households to be *four* times more likely to become homeless as white households (Sexty, 1990, pp.45–6). In 1988, a survey by the National Association of Citizens' Advice Bureaux revealed that 26 per cent of its homeless clients were black (NACAB, 1988). In Newham black homeless single people made up 56 per cent of referrals to homeless hostels: of these 40 per cent were under eighteen. The survey also revealed that an increasing proportion of the single black homeless were women — 45 per cent in Sutton, 46 per cent in Southwark, 55 per cent in

The 1990s: the escalating scale of homelessness

(Top) 350 homeless sleeping in a London church

(Left) Bengali homeless protesting outside Tower Hamlets Town Hall

Greenwich, and 60 per cent in Bromley. Cultural as well as economic factors were contributing to the rise, especially in the number of Asian homeless (Single Homeless in London, 1989). Mama's study of black women found they tolerate violence in the home because of the fear of racism outside it (only 5 per cent of the 200 refuges in Britain cater specifically for black needs). Black women, who were the victims of domestic violence and became homeless, reported disturbing levels of racism in white refuges (Mama, 1989). This often led black women into a double constraint. They remained in violent environments for fear of the racism they might experience in white managed refuges.

A whole range of research has shown that black and ethnic minorities face direct and indirect discrimination in their search for permanent accommodation. Ginsburg (1992) provides a valuable overview of the ways in which black people have been discriminated against in the housing market through structured and institutional racism. Other research has pointed to the homelessness caused by the racism of white tenants leading to the flight of blacks from council tenancies (Commission for Racial Equality, 1988; Gordon, 1990). The vulnerability of homelessness for minority ethnic groups may be concealed simply because many local authorities do not maintain accurate and complete records of homelessness, nor do they monitor ethnic homelessness.

Immigration legislation is also a factor. Following the Immigration Act 1988, immigrants seeking admission to Britain have to prove that they can maintain and accommodate themselves without having 'recourse to public funds' (e.g. income support, family credit and housing benefit). Insecure immigration status may also make someone from a minority group more reluctant to register to seek accommodation. Demographic factors are also important. For example, young black people may also be potentially more vulnerable to homelessness due to their younger age profile compared to the rest of the British population (*Population Trends 64*, 1990). Family patterns are also likely to be a significant factor. Afro-Caribbeans, for example, are four times more likely than whites to belong to lone-parent households.

6 THE IMPACT OF HOMELESSNESS

The impact of homelessness can be potentially devastating on its victims, a vicious circle of deprivation can result — unemployment, physical and mental ill health, poverty, delinquency, drug addiction, prostitution, new risks and vulnerabilities. Homelessness creates its own unique pressures and stress related effects, loneliness, frustration and despairs: 'Homeless people do not declare their existence; they make do with temporary solutions; stay trapped in disastrous, often violent relationships; bed down in empty buildings; sleep outside; and live a life of poverty and loneliness' (Booth, 1989b, p.45).

It is important to recognize that vulnerable groups are often unaware of their rights under legislation. Homeless people are sometimes the *last* people to realize the full extent of state provision, and may also be most reluctant to seek help from authorities if practices are perceived as punitive. A study of single homeless women found only one woman out of 102 sampled who knew she had rights under the 1977 Housing (Homeless Persons) Act (Austerberry and Watson, 1983), while a Centrepoint Soho study found that 90 per cent had not contacted any local authority since becoming homeless (Randall, 1989).

It is an often taken for granted that the security of a home is one of the essential prerequisites for health, along with a sense of well-being, and access to services and employment (Oppenheim, 1990, p.53). For families with children the conditions of living in bed and breakfast and hotel accommodation take their own human toll upon welfare and self-esteem (Crane, 1990). In 1992, the London Research Centre reported that the average time households in London spend in temporary accommodation is 47 weeks, while 35 per cent remain for over a year (*The Independent*, 28 May 1992).

ACTIVITY 3

You should now read the account (below) of Helen Morris and her three children's experiences of the snakes and ladders world of homelessness among the guest houses of Margate, which in 1992, instead of housing thousands of tourists, provided temporary accommodation for 3,000 people from all over Britain — a dead end for the displaced. How typical do you think are Helen's experiences? What effects do you think such experiences would have on her and her family?

■ THE HOTELS WITH GUESTS WHO CAN'T GO HOME

A ONCE-THRIVING HOLIDAY TOWN HAS BECOME A DEAD END FOR THE DISPLACED. JUDY JONES REPORTS

Helen Morris and her three young children hitched a lift from the Midlands to Margate, Kent, five months ago, with nothing other than the clothes they were wearing and in fear of their lives.

Helen (not her real name) could no longer tolerate the beatings from her drug-dealer boyfriend and had fled from their home in Manchester, initially to a battered-women's refuge in Chesterfield. Intimidated by other women there, she left after the husband of one stabbed his wife. Since arriving in Margate penniless and friendless, Helen and her children have moved eight times from one dingy bed-and-breakfast to the next. Rats and cockroaches prompted one move, unwelcome sexual advances from the proprietor another. Thanet council, which serves one of the most socially deprived parts of south-east England, told Helen that it did not regard her as a housing priority since she 'left secure accommodation' in Chesterfield and made herself 'intentionally homeless'.

Thanet has taken a hard line on intentional homelessness. Four generations of the Guess family lived in B&Bs for six years. They were declared 'intentionally homeless' after the bread-winner lost his job, fell into mortgage arrears and the family home was repossessed.

Margate, once a thriving holiday resort, is the largest town in Thanet and the centre of a growing B&B population. The Children's Society, one of the largest charities working with young people, estimates that

3,000 people are living behind the peeling facades of hotels that no longer attract holidaymakers.

Helen Morris, now living in a gloomy hotel near the seafront, sharing kitchen and shower with eight others, has learned that it could be four years before she gets a council home. She said:

> It's tough to have to wait that long. This place is all right, I've been in worse. We live in this room, me and my little girl sleep in here and the two boys share a bedroom.
>
> If I'd stayed in Manchester, I'd be dead by now. I have no family of my own. I came to Margate because I used to do waitressing here in my teens, silver service. Most of the time I'm just trying to make ends meet. The kids' clothes are all second-hand. We don't go hungry, although it's hard sometimes when the kids are off school and I have to give them a dinner.
>
> Lots of places have closed down since I was here. People have to go miles to the nearest picture house. The Lido and the aquarium have closed. The arcades are too expensive. If it's nice, we just go down to the beach.

Margate has suffered in the recession. In the last two years, several large employers including the east Kent coal mines, British Oxygen, Astra Fireworks and Volkswagen have shut or pulled out of the area. About 1 in 10 people is on housing benefit, and those in work tend to be in low-paid jobs. Adverts for portering and cleaning at £2 an hour are not unusual. Nor is the sight of people clutching lists of bed-and-breakfast establishments, lugging their possessions in black rubbish sacks, looking for somewhere to stay.

'It's like a game of snakes and ladders. If you stick it out somewhere that's really bad, eventually you will get a council house. But if you move to a B&B that's even slightly better, you risk losing housing points, and having to wait longer.'

The four generations of the Guess family, all born and bred in Thanet, have recently been given council homes. Vanessa Guess, her five children, their father and her mother shared cramped accommodation for two years. Heather, one of her daughters, had her first child in 1987.

'We lived off sandwiches and takeaway chips a lot of the time because there wasn't anywhere to cook,' Mrs Guess said, 'I have known my children going round the block until their schoolfriends were out of sight because they didn't want them to see where they were living. It made the children very bitter.'

Thanet's policy at the time was to defer all applications for council housing from people with outstanding housing debts until these were cleared. This was relaxed last year. Tony Unwin, the chief housing officer, said that another reason the Guesses had had to wait so long was the shortage of properties for large families. 'Mrs Guess wanted a four-bedroomed property, and the main problem there was the lack of this type of accommodation.'

In the case of Helen Morris, he said her application had not mentioned her fears for her safety at the Chesterfield refuge. 'She told us she left because of a dispute with other clients. The council takes a fairly robust view of people who come to Margate seeking council accommodation, and that is why we have a two-year residency rule. She has to take her place in the queue.'

Most of the 2,600 current applications for housing by Conservative-controlled Thanet council are from families. The waiting list has grown by 200 in a year, and the figures have been rising more steeply in 1992. The council housing stock has fallen by 800 properties since the right-to-buy legislation came into force.

'Our shortage of accommodation has been compounded by Government policy that has prevented councils building new accommodation.' Mr Unwin said, 'Housing associations cannot make up the shortfall, they don't have sufficient funds. Unless we are able to invest more in housing, I cannot see much prospect of change.'

(*The Independent on Sunday*, 22 March 1992) ■

The article vividly portrays how children like Helen's are particularly vulnerable in the shifting environment of the homeless. Let us briefly focus on the broader implications of some of these impacts.

The lack of space for play, cooking, personal leisure and for hygiene are inimical to happy, healthy families. In 1988 health visitors reported that 'because of their generally poor nutrition and poor standards of health, homeless women are more inclined to postpartum haemorrhage and severe anaemia' (Drake, 1989, p.20). Children were likely to suffer from infections and sickness; babies born to mothers living in bed and break-fast accommodation were likely to have a lower than average birth weight (Shelter, 1988)

Homelessness has educational effects. A survey by HMIs found that homeless children did not enrol at school, or were frequently absent. Children also performed relatively poorly in class, and suffered from low self-esteem and expectations. Further studies have shown that children born to hotel and bed and breakfast mothers are multiply deprived, suffer from slow development and are at a greater risk of accident.

In 1988, *Prescription for Poor Health,* a Shelter report on homeless house-holds living in temporary accommodation, revealed a high level of stress among the women (44 per cent said they were unhappy; 41 per cent said they were tired; 35 per cent lost their temper; 34 per cent couldn't sleep at night; 33 per cent said their children got on top of them; and 24 per cent burst into tears for no reason).

The homeless outside temporary accommodation face other difficulties. Those who sleep rough are especially vulnerable to diabetes and epilepsy

(Shelter, 1988; Drake, 1989, p.20). A combination of bad diet and living in poor environments has meant that homeless people become particularly susceptible to chest infections. The homeless also suffer from a kind of First World War 'trench foot' — a condition which rots the feet. Tuberculosis, the 'disease of the poor', which doctors thought had been largely stamped out in the UK in the 1980s, reappeared among the homeless late in the decade. A 1991 report undertaken by Dr Simon Ramsden of the Great Chapel Street Medical Centre, a clinic for the homeless in central London, showed a sudden increase in the incidence of tuberculosis among the homeless — an increase which official data could only superficially represent since tuberculosis often remained undiagnosed. Dr Ramsden's research suggested that one in ten homeless people attending Great Chapel Street suffered, or had suffered from tuberculosis. Only one-third of his patients were cleared of the disease after a year. Evidence that the incidence of AIDS among the homeless is disproportionately distributed is so far inconclusive, although it was not insignificant that the first issue of *The Big Issue* included an article on 'the dangers of safe sex' which critically examined some of the values of the new 'condom culture', especially in relation to the vulnerability of homeless people to rape and sexual exploitation (De La Rue, 1991, pp.18–19).

The homeless are often placed at the risk of injury and attack. Voluntary organizations believe that many incidents of rape on homeless women go unreported. In the early months of the launch of *The Big Issue* in London two of its vendors were murdered. Homelessness can lead to alcoholism, and worst of all to despair and a real sense of hopelessness.

The worst thing homelessness does is the damage to self-respect and confidence, whether living in temporary accommodation or not: 'You're likely to spend most of the time cold, hungry and frightened. It's difficult to keep clean and you rely on hand-outs. It's not surprising that, in these circumstances, some people find escape from these troubles through drink, or get so used to failure that they stop accepting offers of help' (Hardwick, 1991, p.11).

7   CONCLUSION: A WAY FORWARD?

How to tackle homelessness is going to be of continuing concern in the 1990s. Shelter has proposed a massive investment across the housing market, coupled with more flexible approaches to housing provision and welfare access. Their 1991 annual report called for a £25 billion emergency programme which would include constructing 365,000 low-cost homes.

Murie (1988b) argues that nothing can be achieved without additional resources in housing capital allocations made by central government to local authorities and housing associations. According to him the government needs to adopt a longer-term programme for the homeless, rather than persist with the crisis management philosophy of the 1980s. He proposes that:

- temporary accommodation should be provided exclusively by local authorities and housing associations;
- vacant dwellings and the flow of supply should be maximized;
- there should be a greater recognition by housing authorities of the needs of single persons;
- greater legislative protection should be given to persons in the private rented sector with regard to insecurity of tenure;
- the needs of people coming out of institutional settings should also be included in this programme;
- there should be much greater consultation and liaisons between agencies;
- there should be comprehensive monitoring of local authority and housing association policy implementation, particularly the ways in which policies and practices affect different groups;

- staff training should be reviewed and enhanced in relation to housing, social security and 'race' legislation;
- increased liaison and adequately resourced links should be set up between local authorities and homeless groups and voluntary organizations;
- appeal procedures should be granted to homeless people;
- *homeless households should be treated on equal terms with other applicants for housing*
  (Murie, 1988, pp.154–63—[my emphasis]).

Pressure groups argue that more should also be done to find solutions amongst those whose perceptions have been excluded up until now — *the homeless themselves.* Their powerlessness — most homeless people are not eligible to vote — has meant that their voice has seldom been heard above the homeless debate. *The Big Issue,* if the American success of producing newspapers by homeless people for the homeless is anything to go by, is a step in the right direction since it will not only keep homelessness on the political agenda, it will also raise resources for the homeless themselves. In the spring of 1992, CHAR, the Housing Campaign for Single People, launched a different kind of charter to those published by the Major government. CHAR's charter for the homeless was based on the principle that everyone should have the right to a decent place to live and access to community care. CHAR's list of rights was headed by the right to vote and the abolition of the 1824 Vagrancy Act which increasingly is being used to criminalize homeless people (*The Independent,* 4 April 1992).

However, there seems little hope of such a sea change in intervention strategy in either the manifesto on which the Conservative Party won a fourth term of office in 1992, or the subsequent Queen's Speech to Parliament. The Queen's Speech promised new 'rights to buy' for both council tenants in a major new housing and land bill, along with the creation of an urban regeneration agency, but there was no reference to the homeless or unemployment, or to building affordable homes. The government's autumn statement of 1992 did not give permission for local authorities to release any of the estimated £5 billion of receipts already accumulated from the sales of council houses. It did, however, permit local authorities to spend receipts from council house sales in 1993 only. Local authorities were also invited to compete for a share of a £600 million allocation encouraging them to make the best use of their freedom to spend receipts from council house sales. However, the recession may mean that relatively few resources will be earned from this one-year concession on sale receipts. Between 1989 and 1991, sales fell from 141,000 a year to 66,000. Will Tuckley, housing officer of the Association of London Authorities told *The Independent*, 'people have simply not got the money to buy their council house' (14 November 1992).

It may be true, as certain government spokespersons would argue, that the rise in homelessness is related to changes in the way people are behaving, within and outside the family, but it is appropriate that state policy should respond with flexible and affordable housing provision to the significant changes that have occurred in family life in Britain in recent years. The annual divorce rate, for example, has risen six times in Britain since 1960 and the nuclear family has fundamentally changed; yet we still fail to construct the kinds of housing appropriate to the needs of family structures which have emerged as 'the family' has become disestablished by change and social behaviour. In addition, critics of present policies will continue to argue for a properly resourced and integrated government strategy to combat social inequalities on a broad front, including policies on housing finance, taxation, the distribution of income, social security and employment and other policies which have an impact on demand for and access to housing. Cutting investment in those areas where need is greatest will merely create new generations of homeless.

REFERENCES

Audit Commission, The (1986) *Managing the crisis in council housing*, London, HMSO.

Audit Commission, The (1992) *Developing Local Authority Housing Strategies*, London, HMSO.

Austerberry, H. and Watson, S. (1983) *Women on the Margins: a Study of Single Women's Housing Problems*, London, City University.

Booth, A. (1989a) 'Backdoor orthodoxies and heresies', *Roof*, September–October, pp.42–3.

Booth, A. (1989b) *Raising the Roof on Housing Myths*, London, Shelter, 1989.

Booth, C. (1902) *Life and Labour of the People in London*, Basingstoke, Macmillan.

Bramley, G. (1988) 'The definition and measurement of homelessness' in Bramley, G. et al. (eds) *Homeless and the London Housing Market*, Bristol, School for Advanced Urban Studies.

Brimacombe, M. (1987) 'Missing presumed alive', *Roof*, March–April, pp.28–33.

BBC (1966) *Cathy Come Home*, television play by Jeremy Sandford.

BBC (1991) Panorama, *Has Cathy Come Back?* December.

BBC (1992) *You and Yours*, Radio 4, 28 January.

Canter, D. (1990) *The Faces of Homelessness in London*, Interim Report to the Salvation Army, London, The Salvation Army.

Commission for Racial Equality (1988) *Homelessness and Discrimination*, London, CRE.

Concern (1992) *Mental Health and Homelessness*, London, Concern.

Crane, H. (1990) *Speaking from Experience*, London, Bayswater Hotel Homelessness Project.

Cullingworth Report (1968) *Council Housing: Purposes, Procedures and Priorities*, London, HMSO.

De La Rue, J. (1991) 'The dangers of safe sex', *The Big Issue*, September, pp.18–19.

Department of the Environment (1986) *An Inquiry into the Condition of Local Authority Housing Stock in England*, London, HMSO.

Department of the Environment (1990) *Housing and Construction Statistics*, London, HMSO.

Department of the Environment (1991a) *Homelessness Statistics*, London, HMSO.

Department of the Environment (1991b) *Discussion Paper on Homelessness*, London, HMSO.

Department of Health and Social Security (1976) Report of the Working Party on Homeless Young People, London, HMSO.

Department of Housing (1966) *Minister of Housing Circular 20:66*.

Department of Social Security (1989) *Abstract of statistics for index of retail prices: social security benefit and contributions*, Table 5, London, HMSO.

Department of Social Security (1991) *Social Security Committee, First Report*, London, HMSO.

Doogan, K. (1988) 'Falling off the treadmill: the causes of youth homelessness', in Bramley et al., (eds) *Homelessness and the London Housing Market*, Occasional Paper 32, Bristol, School for Advanced Urban Studies, pp.87–118.

Drake, M. (1989) 'Breakfast crime', *New Statesman and Society*, 3 November, p.20.

Frayman, H. (1991) *Breadline Britain in the 1990s*, London, Harper Collins.

Ginsburg, N. (1992) 'Racism and housing: concepts and reality', in Braham, P., Rattansi, A. and Skellington, R. (eds) *Racism and Antiracism: Inequalities, Opportunities and Policies*, London, Sage.

Gordon, P. (1990) *Racial Violence and Harassment*, London, Runnymede Trust.

Gosling, J. (1991) 'Street credibility?', *Roof*, September–October, pp.19–20.

Greve, J. (1964) *London's Homeless*, London, Bell and Sons/Codicote Press.

Hamnett, C. (1992) 'Running housing: housing policy and the British housing system', D212 *Running the Country*, Unit 9, Milton Keynes, The Open University.

Hardwick, N. (1991) 'But why don't the homeless just go home?', *The Big Issue*, September, pp.10–11.

HMSO, (1953) *Houses: the Next Step*, London, HMSO.

HMSO, (1965) Labour Party White Paper on Housing, London, HMSO.

HMSO, (1971) *Fair Deal for Housing*, London, HMSO.

Home Office (1991), *Consultation Paper on Squatting*, London, HMSO.

Ingham, B. (1991) *Westminster City Council: a Presentational Strategy for the 1990s*, London, Westminster City Council, October.

Johnson, N. (1990) *Reconstructing the Welfare State: a Decade of Change, 1980–1990*, London, Harvester Wheatsheaf.

Joint Charities Group on Homelessness (1989) *Who Says there's No housing Problem? Facts and Figures on Housing and the Homeless*, London, Shelter.

Mama, A. (1989) *The Hidden Struggle,* London, London Race and Housing Research Unit.

Merrett, S. (1979) *State Housing in Britain,* London, Routledge and Kegan Paul.

Ministry of Health (1948) Circular 87:48.

Morris, J. and Winn, M. (1990) *Housing and Social Inequality*, London, Hilary Shipman.

Murie, A. (1988a) 'The new homeless in Britain' in Bramley, G. et al. (eds).

Murie, A. (1988b) 'Homelessness in London: recommendations' in Bramley, G. et al. (eds).

National Association of Citizens' Advice Bureaux (1988) *Homelessness: a National Survey of CAB Clients*, London, NCAB.

New Statesman and Society (1989) Special Issue on Homelessness: 'No Place Like Home', 3 November.

Niner, P. (1989) *Homelessness in Nine Local Authorities*, London, HMSO.

Oppenheim, C. (1990) *Poverty: the Facts,* London, Child Poverty Action Group.

Platt, S. (1988) 'Life in Cardboard City', *The Observer*, pp.46–53.

Platt, S. (1989) 'The Forgotten Army', *New Statesman and Society*, 3 November, pp.12–15.

Population Trends, 64 (1990), London, HMSO.

Randall, G. (1988) *No Way Home,* London, Centrepoint Soho.

Randall, G. (1989) *Homeless and Hungry: a Sign of the Times*, London, Centrepoint Soho.

Raynsford, N. (1986) 'The Housing (Homeless Persons) Act, 1977', in Deakin, N. (ed.) *Policy Change in Government*, London, RIPA.

Richards, J. (1981) *The Housing (Homeless Persons) Act, 1977: a Study in Policy Making,* Bristol, School for Advanced Urban Studies, Working Paper No.22.

Richards, J. (1991) 'A new sense of duty', *Roof*, September/October, pp.34–7.

Roof, (1990) Editorial, January–February.

Roof, May 1991; January–February, 1992.

Rural Development Commission (1992), *Homelessness in Rural Areas,* Wiltshire, Rural Development Commission.

Seebohm Report (1968) *Report of the Committee on Local Authority and Allied Personal Social Services*, Cmnd. 3703, London, HMSO.

Sexty, C. (1990) *Women Losing Out,* London, Shelter.

Shelter (1988) *Prescription for Poor Health,* London, Shelter.

Shelter (1991) *Urgent Need for Homes*, London, Shelter.

Single Homeless in London (1989) *Local Authority Policy and Practice on Single Homelessness among Black and Other Ethnic Minority People,* London, London Housing Unit.

Social Trends 21, (1991) London, HMSO.

Social Trends 22, (1992) London, HMSO.

The Big Issue (1991), 1, 9 September.

Thompson, L. (1988) *An Act of Compromise: an Appraisal of the Effects of the Housing (Homeless Persons) Act 1977,* London, SHAC/Shelter.

Tristan, F. (1880) *London Journal* (privately published).

Unemployment Unit (1991) *Unemployment Bulletin*, December, London, Unemployment Unit.

Watson, S. with Austerberry, H. (1986) *Housing and Homelessness: a Feminist Perspective,* London, Routledge and Kegan Paul.

Widgery, D. (1991) 'Ripe bananas and stolen bicycles', in *Marketa Lukacova*, London, Whitechapel Press.

Wolmuth, P. (1989) 'Living on the margins', *Roof*, September–October, pp.40–2.

Wood, P. (1991) *Poverty and the Workhouse in Victorian Britain*, Oxford, Alan Sutton.

INDEX